FLIGHTLESS

FLIGHTLESS

Incredible Journeys
Without Leaving the Ground

LONELY PLANET PUBLICATIONS

MELBOURNE | OAKLAND | LONDON

Flightless: Incredible Journeys Without Leaving the Ground

Published by Lonely Planet Publications

Head Office:
90 Maribyrnong Street, Footscray, Vic 3011, Australia
Locked Bag 1, Footscray, Vic 3011, Australia

Branches:
150 Linden Street, Oakland CA 94607, USA
2nd Floor, 186 City Road, London, EC1V 2NT, UK

Published 2008
Printed through The Bookmaker International Ltd.
Printed in China

ISBN 1 74104 519 3

CONTENTS

INTRODUCTION

Tony Wheeler

'Getting there is half the fun', it's been regularly suggested. And these days it can be not only half the fun, but altogether environmentally responsible and totally good for your conscience as well – which is probably not the prime reason most of these writers set out on their journeys; fun was undoubtedly far closer to the top of their agenda.

Flightless, I must confess, is not something to which I can lay claim. My frequent flyer statements would prove me a liar if I did. I also enjoy the view from 30,000ft (I am distinctly edgy if I don't get a window seat) and I have said that my favourite place is the departure lounge, because it means I'm on my way somewhere – hopefully somewhere interesting. That doesn't alter the fact that the very best trips are often the flightless ones, and over the years I've been lucky enough to rack up quite a few of them.

Way back in the '70s, it was from England to Afghanistan by car and then on to Australia by every means of transport possible. Yeah, there was one flight, but only one, from Calcutta to Bangkok – and only because there was no alternative. That 'overland' journey led to the creation of Lonely Planet Publications and our very first guidebook. A year later Maureen and I were off on a year-long motorcycle trip around Southeast Asia. Starting from Sydney, it took us down to the southern end of New Zealand and then all the way to the northern end of Thailand. Our motorcycle was stolen right at the end of the trip in Chiang Mai.

There have been many more 'flightless' travel experiences in the years since those first two excursions, including the little jaunt from Plymouth (in England) to Banjul (in the West African nation of Gambia), an account of which is my own contribution to this collection. My annual New Year's resolution – to spend at least a week of the year to come on foot, travelling from somewhere to somewhere else – means that I've also managed to trek up to the Everest Base Camp, walk across England from coast to coast, climb Mt Kilimanjaro and even walk a circuit of Tibet's holy Mt Kailash. A useful little ramble, that last one: Tibetans assure you that completing the *kora* wipes out all the sins of your lifetime – the current lifetime, at least.

So in this book there's plenty I can identify with and, even more importantly, lots of inspiration for future flightless forays. The authors include some serious walkers, people who put my own little treks way into the shade, whether it's making a complete circuit of the world (a stroll that's still a work in progress), a casual little jaunt across Pakistan, some interesting walking in Oman, following the Silk Route or a trek from London to Istanbul. Other human-powered land and waterborne travel possibilities also get some attention – cycling, canoeing, pedal boating – and we've even got a story of an intrepid 13-year-long trip around the world entirely by self-powered means.

For those who are more interested in motors than muscles, there are accounts of epic train journeys. They don't come more epic than the iconic Trans-Siberian Express, a trip that's still sitting on my personal 'must-do' list. The train trip might not be as long, but taking the rails from Baghdad to Basra, in that brief window of opportunity after the overthrow of Saddam Hussein, certainly qualifies as intrepid.

Flightless includes travel by old routes, with an account of a modern retracing of Mark Twain's Middle East travels documented in *An Innocent Abroad*, and some classic travels with the author's own wheels, including Jon 'Into Thin Air' Krakauer's coast-to-coast blast across the USA on a Harley-Davidson. Perhaps a big Harley doesn't qualify as all that environmentally sensitive but, hey, is there a more appropriately American vehicle for crossing the lower 48? Coaxing an elderly Vespa around Italy also qualifies in the right-vehicle, right-place category, but I'm not so sure about setting out from London to Helsinki on a scooter. Sometimes a good slice of that getting-there fun is attained by doing it in something totally inappropriate, like a circuit of South America on a motorcycle more suitable for delivering pizzas. Or travelling from Bangkok to Brighton on a tuk-tuk. For most of us, the distance from one Bangkok traffic jam to the next is quite far enough to travel in one of those infernal Thai contraptions.

Of course, the urge to travel appropriately can be equally interesting, whether it's by ancient methods – saddling up the camel to head across the Sahara or hauling up the sail to tack a leaky dhow towards the magical island of Zanzibar – or by thumb around the Australian outback (yes, there had to be a hitchhiking story). Or let's simply endeavour to get there while sticking strictly to surface-level transport, whether that's from San Francisco to Bristol or Chengdu to Lhasa. I had a go at exactly that sort of trip from Singapore to Shanghai two years ago. When I eventually sailed up the river into Shanghai on a rickety old passenger vessel bearing the reassuring name *Jin Ping*, I'd travelled almost 7000 kilometres by bus, train, boat and a host of less comfortable (the back of a truck in Cambodia) and rather riskier (riding pillion on motorcycles in Cambodia, Vietnam and China) forms of transport.

The constant theme through all these tales is that less is more. Less speed equals more understanding, more fun, more satisfaction. The equation is easy to prove: if we're going slowly, we have more time to interact with our fellow travellers, and they're more likely to be those local characters we all hope to bump into. My own flightless travels have often been uncomfortable, they've sometimes been a little scary, they've regularly tested my endurance and my patience, but equally often they've left me thinking, 'Wow, what a trip.' That's exactly the conclusion of all our *Flightless* contributors.

THE 40-YEAR-OLD (VESPA) VIRGIN

Peter Moore

Milan

I've just handed over €1200 for a 40-year-old Vespa that may or may not work. I'm sitting at a pavement café having lunch with the man I've bought it from. His name is Gianni and he looks like Derek Jacobi in *Gladiator*.

I'm in Italy following a boyhood dream. As a teenager with lank hair and a wardrobe full of flannel shirts, I swore that one day I'd go to Italy, buy a Vespa and be as cool as Marcello Mastroianni in *La Dolce Vita*. This summer I turn 40 and I'm finally doing it.

I found the Vespa advertised on eBay. It is a coffee-coloured 1961 model with saddle seats and a little too much chrome. It was exactly what I was looking for: a Vespa as old as I am and in the same condition – a little rough around the edges but going OK.

As motor scooters buzz past in manic packs, Gianni is teaching me everything I need to know to ride this one from Milan to Rome. Petrol stations are closed between noon and 3pm. Old Vespas are

11

restricted to B-roads. The Italian word for a slice of Parma ham is *fetta*. I can ignore metropolitan police but never the *carabinieri*. Most importantly, my safe passage on this quest depends entirely on mastering a simple hand signal and the pronunciation of the word *vaffanculo*.

I point to a cluster of Vespas parked on the pavement and ask if it is legal to park like that. Gianni finishes a mouthful of carpaccio and looks me directly in the eyes.

'There is the law,' he says sagely, 'and there is *intelligence*.'

I've bought a Vespa from the Italian Yoda.

Lake Como

One week down and I still haven't seen any sign of the intelligence Gianni spoke of. I've seen Vespa riders going the wrong way up one-way streets. I've witnessed them bearing down on people crossing streets as if intent on hitting them. And I've watched them mount the pavement to get around a momentary traffic jam, scattering pedestrians and dogs in the process.

Just this morning I saw a scooter-rider lying on his back on the street after being knocked off his bike. He continued talking on his mobile phone as the paramedics attached a brace to his back.

Gianni's idea that I ride north to Lake Como before heading south to Rome was a good one, though. He hasn't ridden this Vespa for over four years. A quick jaunt around the lake will reveal any problems while I'm still close enough to Milan for him to fix them.

I have learnt two things up here on the lake: riding a Vespa is the perfect way to get around Italy (nippy, exhilarating and small enough to wheel onto a ferry), and I need a new intake valve on the carburettor.

Broni

I am 70 kilometres south of Milan and drinking spumante in the restaurant attached to a modest hotel. Broni, it seems, is the heart of one of Italy's premier spumante-producing regions.

The manager's wife is astounded that I am Australian – even more so when I tell her my plan to ride to Rome. When she discovers my journey is inspired by old black-and-white Italian movies she insists I name my Vespa after Sophia Loren. I am on my third glass of spumante and readily agree.

Sophia the Vespa already shows many of the same characteristics as her celluloid namesake. When I try to start her in the morning, she complies with the reluctance of a movie star happily dozing in bed. She will only stir after I give her a little choke, the motor-scooter equivalent of a shot of espresso. And when she finally emerges into the light, she looks drop-dead gorgeous. No matter what angle you look at her from.

Ponte dell'Olio

When Sophia breaks down, good things happen. I am spending the night in a luxurious hunting lodge atop the rolling hills behind Ponte dell'Olio because Sophia has decided she doesn't want to go any further.

The manager of the Locanda Cacciatori is a romantic at heart. He has decided that a quest as foolhardy – and so obviously *Italian* – as riding a 40-year-old Vespa to Rome needs encouraging. For only €40 he has given me a room with views over patchwork fields and carte blanche to eat whatever I want from the lodge's highly regarded restaurant.

His friend, a mechanic, will replace Sophia's points in the morning.

Bobbio

I am high in the Apennines, the mountain range that separates the regions of Emilia-Romagna and Tuscany. Sophia has spluttered to a stop again. I am surrounded by empty mountains and enveloped in silence. There are no houses, only wildflowers; no passing vehicles, only birds. Sure, it is lovely. But I haven't seen the upside yet.

I take Sophia's cowl off and start tinkering with her engine. I pretend I know what I am doing. I go through a series of mechanical gestures like removing the spark plug and cleaning it. They are more talismanic than useful.

I look up and see an old man with a walking cane and a flat cap hobbling towards me. The nearest town, Bobbio, is 12 kilometres back. His demeanour suggests he is on his morning constitutional. He stops beside Sophia and silently hands me his cap and his cane. He siphons petrol from the tank and pours it directly into the carburettor. He kicks the starter pedal with his gammy leg and Sophia springs immediately to life.

He takes back his cap and cane and hobbles on.

Cinque Terre

I walk into the historical centre of Vernazza and feel like I have stepped onto an Italian film set in the 1950s. A single path runs from the top of the town to the sea. It is lined by four-storey houses painted in faded shades of yellow, terracotta and salmon. Colourful wooden fishing boats jostle in a small harbour, which is crowned on one side by the remains of a castle and by a 14th-century church on the other.

It is Sophia's kind of town, a labyrinth of tiny lanes and cobbled alleyways. But she is chained to a light pole in a car park at the top of the town. On this stretch of the Ligurian coast, in the five villages that give it its name, *all* motor vehicles are banned.

Without Sophia I am a tourist again. I eat *trenette al pesto*, a local speciality, and the waiter short-changes me. I drink a beer in the bar overlooking the crystal sea and I am charged the half-litre price even though I am drinking from a 300ml glass. I catch shopkeepers resting their thumbs on scales as I buy slices of Parma ham and fresh tomatoes for a picnic lunch.

With Sophia I am given extra portions and generous discounts. I hadn't realised how much she has been saving me.

Livorno

Livorno is a port town surrounded by unlovely warehouses and chimney stacks. I decide it is my favourite place in Italy so far.

Livorno is home to Filippo and Marco. Filippo is known on the internet as the Waspmaster. He was the one who pointed me towards Sophia's listing on eBay, when I emailed him for advice. His friend Marco restores Vespas and has the cleanest workshop on the planet.

Filippo and Marco are showing me around Livorno. I have eaten squid-ink risotto. I have drunk *ponce*, a local drink made from rough rum, at Bar Civili. I have puttered around the ancient canals in a motorboat at midnight watching the *tarponi*, giant rats, swimming back to their sewers after feasting on the market litter.

Did I tell you I have drunk *ponce*, a local drink made from rough rum, at Bar Civili?

Maybe that's why I keep waking up on the sofa in Marco's workshop rather than the hotel room that I've paid for but never end up using.

Marina di Pisa

Tonight is the Sagra del Pinolo, the Feast of the Pine Nut. I am buzzing along the Art Deco boulevards of Tirrenia with Marco, Filippo and a local artist called Francesco. We are all riding Vespas or Lambrettas. It feels like I am living in an episode of *The Many Loves of Dobie Gillis*.

We leave the coast and ride along a road lined by heavily scented pine trees until we reach San Piero a Grado, one of the oldest churches in Italy. The fields that surround it have been transformed into a crowded carnival celebrating everything pine nut.

Over a meal of *spaghetti al pinolo* and steak barbecued over pine cones, I learn that people from Lucca call the shapely cowls of a Vespa *polmoni* (lungs). In Livorno they call them *puppe*, slang for breasts. In Rome they call them *chiappe,* buttocks. The term the Romans use makes most sense to me.

I also discover that I have chosen the wrong saint to watch over Sophia. Before I left Sydney, I bought a Mary, mother of God, fridge magnet to do the job.

'Mary is too tired', says Marco. 'She has been worn out by *centuries* of requests.'

'You need a new saint,' says Filippo, 'someone fresh off the bench with energy to burn.'

'Like Padre Pio', says Francesco. 'He was only just canonised. He still has *much* strength.'

I buy a freshly minted Padre Pio fridge magnet from a stall at the carnival. I ride back to Livorno with the smell of the sea in my nostrils and the undeniable feeling that Sophia is riding much, much more smoothly.

San Gimignano

I have decided that the patchworked hills in this part of Tuscany were created by God for the sole purpose of riding a Vespa through them. I can smell the freshly cut hay. I can feel the warm sun on my skin. The tiny 125cc engine sounds like a wasp floating on a summer breeze.

On the road back to the medieval hilltop towers of San Gimignano, I pass a group of red-faced English people on a cycle tour of Tuscany. They are slugging back water and summoning the energy for one last hill. At the gates I spot a pair of Dutch bikers on Ducatis, peeling off gluggy sweat-soaked leathers. I understand why both have chosen to see Tuscany the way they have. Cycling offers intimacy with the landscape, motorcycling the thrills of traversing winding and dipping roads.

Sophia offers me the benefits of both.

Siena

The golden stone walls of Siena are surrounded by car parks. It is summer and they are packed with mobile homes and cars with English, Dutch and German number plates.

The hotels are full too. I ride to a kiosk near the Stadio Comunale just outside the walls, where the local tourist board offers a room-finding service. I park Sophia next to a group of other Vespas and join the long queue. The young guy serving beckons me to the front.

'That is my Vespa there', he says, pointing to the PX parked next to Sophia. He asks me why I am riding an old Vespa and I tell him.

'You are the kind of tourist we want', he says, quickly finding me a room. 'If I didn't have to serve *these* people, we could ride together.'

As the sun sets I ride Sophia into the heart of old Siena. Cars are banned from this part of the town but on Sophia I can go anywhere I please. I bounce along the cobbled streets, weaving through tourists and around baskets of pasta and bottles of olive oil. I park Sophia with a clump of other Vespas on Il Campo, the famous central square.

I sit in front of the square's *palazzi* to soak up the atmosphere. The tour groups are gone and the day-trippers are returning to their vehicles before they're impounded. Soon there's only me, a band playing to a few restaurant patrons and some feral travellers playing bongos and washing in the 19th-century replica of the medieval Gaia fountain.

It strikes me that the ferals have the freedom to go wherever they want, too. It's just that my way doesn't involving getting chased out of town by angry shopkeepers and pissed-off *carabinieri*.

Massa Marittima

I discover early in my trip that the drop between the hook under Sophia's front seat and the running boards where I rest my feet is the exact same length as a plastic carrier bag. The discovery transforms my trip. I start every day buying provisions for a picnic somewhere suitably picturesque en route.

This morning I am in Massa Marittima, an ancient mining town that sits high in the Colline Metallifere, looking out across the bleak plains of southern Tuscany. The metal-bearing hills provided the town with much of its wealth during the 12th century, funding the building of the cathedral, Palazzo Comunale and other impressive buildings surrounding Piazza Garibaldi.

I visit Casa della Frutta to buy fruit and salad. The woman who serves me gives me an impromptu Italian lesson, slowly pronouncing the name of each item as she puts it on the scale.

At Panificio Romano the baker recommends the *panine frustini Geovesi*, a Genovese-style bread he sells at €3.62 a kilo. At Il Salumeria I dodge the different coloured and shaped pastas hanging in clear cellophane bags to pick up some *bocconcini* cheese, olives and local wild-boar ham. I finish with a cappuccino and a *bombolone* (doughnut) overlooking the square.

As I leave Massa Marittima, cutting across the piazza with my provisions dangling beneath the seat, a hearse pulls up in front of the cathedral. The church bells toll three sad notes – up, up, down – and two nuns scurry down the stone stairs to comfort the mourners as they emerge.

I ride past, an Australian on a 40-year-old Vespa. A photographer, attending a conference in town that's sponsored by Kodak, takes a photo. I am just another element in his carefully constructed scene.

Sutri

It is only 50 kilometres until I reach Rome. I've just taken a stiff shot of espresso in a café with a marble bar and a coffee machine with more chrome than a '57 Chevy. I return to Sophia and find an old lady standing beside her and weeping.

Her daughter translates, 'She says it is the Vespa of her youth.'

In Menaggio Sophia reminded the local librarian of the time he courted his wife with hands covered in Vespa engine oil. In Castell'Arquato a barman reminisced about his childhood, when his whole family rode on a Vespa to the nearest village every Sunday. Upon reaching it they had to decide whether to buy pizza or petrol. If they chose pizza, his dad had to push the Vespa home.

In Italy, everyone has a Vespa story.

Sophia has her own tale too. Her first owner bought her especially to woo a girl. He had an extra saddle seat fitted so she would be comfortable throughout their long courtship. And he had fitted her with all the available accessories to prove to his prospective father-in-law that he was a man of means. When the couple finally wed, Sophia was draped in ribbons and used as the wedding vehicle.

Back in Sutri the old lady brushes away her tears and waves as I ride off. And she smiles. For a moment she is young again, her lustrous hair under a headscarf as she rattles along on her Vespa, flirting with the boys and bursting with *brio* for what lies ahead.

Rome

I have a favourite 'circuit' in Rome. I sweep around the Vittorio Emmanuel monument and buzz up Via dei Fori Imperiali like Charlton Heston on a chariot in *Ben-Hur*. Trajan's Market is on my left, the Forum on my right; ahead, the Colosseum. I slingshot around it, rattle back along the cobbled back streets and start all over again.

It is three months since I set out from Milan and I am finally in Rome. A plane would have taken an hour to do the journey; a train, maybe eight; a car, a little longer. But it wouldn't have been anywhere *near* as much fun.

My girlfriend Sally has joined me. We rattle around the city pretending we are in *Roman Holiday* (she is the perfect Audrey

Hepburn; I am a decidedly low-rent Gregory Peck). We weave our way through the throngs to the Trevi Fountain. She tosses a coin in but refuses to tell me what she wishes for.

Sally says I've changed in three months. Now I can see the intelligence in driving up a one-way street to cut three minutes off a journey. I'll ride on the inside, outside and anywhere between cars to get where I want to go. And I love jockeying at the lights with other scooter riders and buzzing off just before the light turns green.

We spend Sally's last night in Rome's liveliest quarter, Trastevere. Its tightly knit lanes overflow with pavement cafés and restaurants. It is the closest thing to the lively nightspots featured in *La Dolce Vita*. I park Sophia with a flock of other Vespas beside the Santa Maria church and we plunge in, holding hands, to be washed along by the quarter's crackling *brio*.

We return to our hotel along Via Nazionale. I buzz around the roundabout at Piazza della Repubblica and into a restricted traffic zone. A policewoman standing on the corner spots me and blows her whistle. I notice from her uniform that she works for the metropolitan police. It is the branch of the police force that Gianni told me I could ignore. I wave and keep going. She shrugs her shoulders and allows me to pass.

I can't help but grin. I'm not a Vespa virgin any more.

PETER MOORE

Peter Moore has a long history of avoiding planes. He travelled overland from London to Sydney to write *The Wrong Way Home* and from Cape Town to Cairo for *Swahili for the Broken-Hearted*. He has made two trips through Italy on a Vespa and recounted his adventures in *Vroom with a View* and *Vroom by the Sea*. For more information about Peter and his travels visit his website: www.petermoore.net.

FALLEN WARRIORS

Olivia Pozzan

The sun is blistering, the hill steep and the ground uneven. Panting to a stop, I guzzle the water in my CamelBak. I don't care that it's lukewarm: it's wet. Wet is good. I drink some more. Wanting to drag out our rest stop, I study the map.

The paper does not reflect what I see. Sharp grey ridges, their serrated tops the skeletal spine of some long-forgotten creature, fade to hazy outlines on the horizon. Far below, the mountain's vast shadow stains the earth like a smudged thumbprint, its ridges and whorls formed by the wadis, the dry riverbeds and rocky outcrops at its base. As a legacy of its violent ocean birth, the rock strata of Oman's Hajar mountain range are tilted and skewed and folded into crazy angles.

'Looks like the slag heaps of Mordor', Dorian says under his breath.

In this surreal desert landscape the jagged limestone spires of the Jebel Akhdar climb 3000 metres into the sky. I know that somewhere in their midst is a green and fertile plateau. An oppressive silence settles over the jebel's rocky flanks. A peculiar vibration buzzes in my ears and I realise the air is thrumming in the heat.

The Jebel Akhdar is a harsh land, a desolate battlefield. History records only three successful raids on the Saiq Plateau: in 892 by the Caliph of Baghdad, in 1265 by a 20,000-strong Persian army, and in 1959 by the British SAS.

I am tracing the SAS soldiers' night raid up Wadi Kamah. Under Sultan Said, Oman's draconian ruler of the mid-20th century, the gates to the capital, Muscat, were religiously closed and barred three hours after sunset. The sultan was a man not given to progress. One hospital, three schools and only four kilometres of tarmac covered the land. What better breeding ground for revolutionaries, freedom fighters and rebel imams? Although years later the British changed tack and ousted the sultan, in 1959 the SAS helped the Sultan of Oman's Armed Forces (SAF) conquer the mountain and defeat the last stronghold of the Oman Revolutionary Movement.

As I follow the soldiers' footsteps up the ancient stone staircase, I listen for echoes. Little is left as a reminder of the skirmishes. Little, it seems, can touch the austerity of the mountains. But it is not the warring history of the Jebel Akhdar that has drawn me back to the Hajar Mountains. With my hiking buddies, Dorian and Pat, I am on a quest for echoes of a different sort.

Unlike the palm tree and desert dune oases of Hollywood, the real thing is far less romantic – and in the mountains, far more dramatic. Shurayah is a hornet's nest of mud-brick dwellings on the edge of the 2000 metre Saiq Plateau, where terraced gardens cling defiantly to sheer vertical canyon walls. We wander through narrow alleyways, under vaulted archways, down sturdy stone steps polished by the constant passage of sandaled feet, past a group of laughing street urchins dressed in their festive best. It is Eid al-Fitr, a religious holiday in this Muslim country, and families gather to pray, to feast and to exchange gifts.

Ramadan is the Holy Month. For Muslims it is a time of fasting and prayer. In the hours between sunrise and sunset not even water can pass their lips but after dark the feasting starts. At the first sighting of the crescent moon, the cannon booms, Ramadan ends and the Eid festival begins.

At the promise of presents and a party, the children are as excited as any kid would be. A boy runs down the lane dragging his pet calf behind him but the sweet picture of innocence takes a macabre twist when a group of swarthy men, dressed in turbans and long white robes, smile at us and raise a bloodied hand in greeting. A glimpse is all it takes – an Egyptian vulture waiting impatiently on a rooftop, a frenzied swarm of black flies – and suddenly the air reeks with the smell of blood. Eid celebrations demand a feast. There are no butcher shops. The fatted calves are slaughtered in the streets.

Ahmed, an air-traffic controller at the air-force base at Thumrait, has travelled 500 kilometres to visit his family. After offering to show us the terraces, he fixes me with a hard look and warns, 'it is a little dangerous.'

I smile a trifle patronisingly. In the Arab world, a woman just isn't tough enough. But in the past few days, lugging packs burdened with a punishing weight of drinking water, we have trekked poorly marked goat trails, scrambled down scree slopes, climbed crumbling mountain faces and braved desert heat and spiky thorn bushes. A stroll through the gardens will be a pleasant interlude.

Although Ahmed wears a *dishdasha* (the traditional long white ankle-length robe) and open-toed sandals, he sets off at a brisk pace along the concrete edge of the *falaj*. According to legend, Solomon constructed these water channels from the comfort of his magic carpet, ordering his legion of genies to build 10,000 *falaj* in 10 days. In fact, the Persians introduced this system of channelled water irrigation to Oman thousands of years ago, taking far longer than 10 days to furrow the hard earth. The once mud-brick channels have been replaced with concrete but are still as practical and efficient as they have been for the past millennia.

Clear water originating deep within the mountains runs down the winding canal as we work our way upstream. The concrete edges of the *falaj* are less than a hand's-breadth wide. Like tightrope walkers we inch past women washing clothes and cooking pots and children splashing in the cool water.

'*Salamalaykum.*' An old man flashes a gummy smile. The hem of his *dishdasha* is tucked into a belt sporting an enormous J-curved silver dagger. Above the overly decorated scabbard the camel-bone handle is polished a translucent butter yellow from frequent handling. As a traditional symbol of manhood the *khanjar* is damned impressive.

'*Alaykumasalam*. Peace be upon you.'

He cackles, his heavily kohled eyes collapsing into glittering black slits, the desiccated bones in his stick-thin shoulders clacking like a baby's rattle. Our rudimentary Arabic delights him but I worry he'll shake himself to bits. Luck favours the both of us. His paper-dry skin keeps everything intact. As his chuckles fade to a contented sigh, he returns to scrubbing the blood of the fatted calf off his hands and feet.

Ahmed leads us beneath a deciduous canopy of yellow leaves. The ground drops away in precipitous steps, the cliff face a terraced garden with date palms, citrus groves, apricots, pomegranates, figs, bananas, and cultivated fields of garlic and alfalfa. In the convoluted topography of grey mountain peaks and dusty ravines, the lush green foliage shines like a neon light. In spring, Ahmed tells us, the gardens are filled with hollyhocks, marigolds and roses. My nose wrinkles tentatively, searching for the fragrance of spring. 'Our rosewater is prized throughout Oman.' He smiles politely. I squirm. After days without a wash we sure don't smell like roses.

The *falaj* curves and climbs and suddenly above the water channel is a narrow staircase suspended in midair, a waterfall on one side and a 300 metre drop on the other. Ahmed scampers up the stairway like a mountain goat. Pat clutches the steep stone steps in panic, refusing to look down. But there's only one way out: up.

I pivot very carefully and for a moment my backpack hangs over the precipice. It's a long way down and Solomon's magic carpet and legion of genies are long gone. Dorian pauses a couple of metres below me. Behind him blue sky spears into the gorge. The adrenaline charge, plain as day on his face, mirrors mine in his sunglasses. It's the perfect Kodak moment but, of course, my camera battery decides to die. I give it the appropriate eulogy.

'Is not too difficult?' Ahmed's concerned face reappears from on high.

I feel a twinge of guilt. Did he overhear my choice words? I am suddenly conscious of my bare arms and legs. I'm half-naked, an infidel, and now a blasphemer. Have I offended his religious sensibilities?

'Come', he urges. 'It gets a little dangerous now.'

Hiking in Oman is no stroll in the park. Summer temperatures exceed 60°C, shade is nonexistent and water is scarce.

> The heat…is so intense that it burned the marrow in the bones, the sword in its scabbard melted into wax and the gems which adorned the handle of the dagger were reduced to coal. In the plains the chase became

a matter of perfect ease for the desert was strewn with
roasted gazelles.

Abdul Razak, the 14th-century Arab geographer, might have waxed
a tad lyrical, but hiking in the summer is nothing short of suicidal.
However, the mild winter carries its own dangers. Without warning, sudden rainstorms can turn a dry wadi into a raging torrent of
destruction, tumbling boulders like ice cubes in a long fizzy drink. In
one of nature's quirky paradoxes, people drown in the desert.

But for thousands of years these same dry watercourses were
the only passes through the range from the eastern coastline to
the western deserts. Camel caravans laden with silks, cloths, spices
and frankincense wound through the passes, trading goods with
the farmers, Bedouin and townsfolk of the plains. Occasionally,
the Bani Riyam would venture down from their mountain perch
trading fresh fruit, vegetables and rosewater before disappearing back
to their eyries on the Saiq Plateau. No wonder rumours of a secret
paradise attracted the attention of early travellers and explorers. But
the inhospitable mountain architecture and the xenophobia of the
mountain people kept the paradise hidden. Over time, the rumours
became legend. Today, the tribal villagers welcome the few visitors
they receive, especially those arriving on foot.

On the second night of our trek we camp in the deserted village of
Bani Habeeb, rolling out our sleeping bags on the floor of a mud-brick
hut. At this altitude the wadi that gives the village its name is wide,
shallow and dry. As it drops, in a series of boulder-strewn cascades, the
walls of the canyon rise steeply on either side. Perennial water gushes
out of the cliff face 2000 metres below filling deep pools in a canyon
barely four camel's breadths wide. In a land where water is scarce, the
volume, clarity and beauty of the wadi pools is a rare treasure.

Like Shurayah, Bani Habeeb is a hornet's nest of mud-brick
dwellings, the architects seemingly having tacked on rooms
whenever need or fancy dictated. Like explorers of a lost city we
weave through the warren of deserted dwellings, through walled
courtyards, terraced rooftops, and carved wooden doors little
more than a metre high. Finally, we light a small fire on a balcony
overlooking a garden of pomegranate trees beneath a night sky
awash with stars and listen to the soothing sigh of water in the *falaj*.
The night is cold and crisp. We huddle together, sensing in the
shadows fragments of those who also once sat on this terraced roof,

warmed their hands around the flames and listened to the tinkle of water in the gardens below.

Sometime during the fog of sleep a cannon booms a welcome to the crescent moon. I toss restlessly. In that limbo land of half-wakefulness where time blurs and all things are possible, I revisit the dream that has brought me back here.

A year ago, deep inside the boulder-choke of Wadi Bani Habeeb, I had a vision. After a day spent squeezing through keyhole clefts between massive boulders, sliding down dangerously smooth rock faces and negotiating the jumble of tossed rocks in the far depths of the canyon, Pat and I had finally succumbed to exhaustion. We made camp on a miniscule carpet of sand beside a sapphire necklace of deep blue pools. In the final flush of twilight the full moon shone round and ivory-white in the water. A magical swim in the moonlight washed us clean and the warmth and light of a small campfire lulled us to sleep.

He came out of the night, a tall muscular figure clad in skins and carrying a spear. He walked like a man who has travelled a great distance and has yet a greater distance to travel. Women and children, similarly dressed, plodded single-file along the same invisible path. As the caveman warrior passed our campsite I woke and he saw me. For a moment nothing existed but his eyes. He saw deep into my soul and an understanding beyond words or thought, a knowing that transcended time, linked us together. Without breaking pace he continued his bleak journey.

Sunrise did not destroy the magic nor the disquiet caused by the dream. Breaking camp, Pat and I continued down the river of jumbled rocks and a little while later we came across a large cave. The charcoal of untold fires stained the roof but clearly visible, white against the blackened rock, was the rudimentary outline of a figure wearing a pack and holding two walking sticks.

My scalp prickled. 'It was real! My sticks. My pack.' Logic fled my mind. I *had* stepped through a door between the worlds.

'He saw me, Pat.'

'Too much whisky last night', Pat offered sagely.

'I only had one finger.'

'Not enough whisky, then.'

Pat enjoyed my metaphysical leanings. As a devout sceptic he was wonderfully entertained and amused by my reaction to a mere dream. The echo of that dream – that otherworldly encounter – has stayed with me throughout the year. Its echo has drawn me back.

'Eid Mubarak!'

The young girls trailing our progress smile shyly. Garishly dressed in bold oranges, greens and reds, they bunch together like a colourful sprig of wild flowers. I'm thinking colour must be as precious as water. The oldest – no more than nine or 10 – steps forward and solemnly returns my greeting. She has large, black, doe-like eyes fringed with thick lashes. Under our scrutiny her childish dignity crumbles in a sudden burst of giggles. Like startled gazelles the girls scatter down the town's only paved road.

'The government built the new village of Bani Habeeb 20 years ago', explains Fahoud.

We are sitting cross-legged on a carpet in an unadorned sitting room, the *majlis* of his father's house, drinking spicy Arabic coffee from tiny thimble cups. A plastic thermos replaces the brass *dalla* as a more practical, though less aesthetic, coffee pot.

'Of course my father still tends his gardens in the old village.' He breaks off, offering us home-grown peaches.

He tells us he works in Nizwa, a large town at the foot of the Jebel Akhdar. I know it as the one-time medieval capital of the Interior and former home to the rebel imam of the 1950s. When the famous British explorer Sir Wilfred Thesiger travelled through Oman, he was – as all foreigners were – refused entry to Nizwa on threat of death. A lot has changed in 50 years. Camera-wielding tour groups overrun the once impregnable fort and the Ben-Hur–style livestock market, where cattle, goats and sheep are auctioned to the highest bidder.

Not far from Nizwa the remnants of the magnificent fortress and walled city of Bahla, another one-time capital of Oman, dominate the gravel plains. Built in the third century BC, the city's five kilometre fortified wall encloses a vast date-palm oasis. Although its ramparts are eroded and its grandeur has faded, Bahla's reputation for pottery and witchcraft has not. The wall-eyed gaze of stooped old men and veiled women reinforce the rumours of djinn and black magic. The trachoma virus might explain the sightless white opacity afflicting much of the population but not everyone accepts the logic of Western science. Officially, the practice of witchcraft is outlawed but superstitious beliefs die hard.

'Does your father miss living in the old village?' Dorian asks.

Fahoud smiles, as at a child. 'Here he has running water, electricity, television. What is there to miss?'

Kneeling on the carpet, his father silently follows our conversation. He does not understand English, we cannot speak Arabic, but his gaze is unnerving. One eye is rheumy with age, the other is milky and white. Like the Mona Lisa smile, it appears to stare unwaveringly into every corner of the room.

Fahoud is an army officer but he deftly deflects my questions about the Jebel War and subtly resists drawing his father into the discussion. My curiosity is piqued. Surely his father remembers the 1959 assault by the British SAS. Suddenly, understanding dawns. The rebels sought sanctuary with the villagers on the plateau. Fahoud's father might not have welcomed the SAS or the Sultan of Oman's Armed Forces with open – or empty – arms.

Our conversation is interrupted as a young boy of about six bursts excitedly into the room. He is jumping out of his skin, begging permission to help the men butcher the fatted calf, the sacrificial lamb, the unlucky goat. Fahoud laughs, pinching him affectionately.

'This is my brother Ali. My father's youngest son.'

I nearly choke on my thimble of coffee. Fahoud's father is as ancient as the mountains. He can barely walk.

As if reading our thoughts Fahoud explains without embarrassment, 'My father's wife is a young Indian girl.'

In typical Arab fashion, a man isn't a man unless he sires a horde of sons. This grey-haired geriatric has proven his mettle but what about his poor wife? His poor young wife. I don't know whether to be impressed or repulsed. He stares at me. I stare back. His wizened face, as wrinkled and nutty brown as a walnut shell, falls into creased folds developed from a lifetime lived beneath the desert sun. Little can be read in those deeply etched grooves yet his beaming smile says it all.

Abandoned watchtowers stand silent sentinel over the passes. Their sightless black eyes follow a pair of eagles riding the thermal uplifts.

The silence, the landscape, is timeless. Prehistoric. Instead of eagles I imagine pterodactyls soaring in the sky. Down below, rocky outcrops spread in isolated patches towards the pale blue ridges on the horizon. Like patterns in the clouds the jagged foothills form patterns of their own. I see the profile of a grim face and trace the dip and rise of an armoured chest-plate. Here and there, a helmet, a sword, a severed limb. I imagine mighty Titans battling across the sky for many days and nights. The rocky outcrops below are the legacy of that war, the fallen warriors that trembled the earth when they crashed to the ground.

The echoes of war have permeated our hike up the Jebel Akhdar, from the warring armies of Baghdad and Persia to the SAS assault, from the air-traffic controller at Thumrait to the rebel veteran of the Jebel War and, finally, to the caveman warrior of my dreams.

The wars are over, the camel trains are gone, but the magic of the mountains is as potent as ever. After an exhausting day negotiating the boulder-strewn Wadi Bani Habeeb, we camp at the mouth of the gorge. The warm afterglow of sunset softens the cliff face, but high overhead the black mouth of a cave hints at hidden secrets. Caves honeycomb the range. Close by, on the other side of the mountain, lies the second largest cave chamber in the world. Although its mouth is just another hole in the ground, the 4-million-cubic-metre underground chamber can comfortably swallow the largest Egyptian pyramid. It is delightfully named the Majlis Al Djinn – Meeting Place of the Spirits.

The car is a welcome sight, the cool box even more so. It isn't long before our bellies are bulging with pasta, hot buttered damper and an overdose of chocolates. In a pleasant carbohydrate stupor we settle in front of the campfire and pass the whisky bottle around. The flames weave their mesmerising spell. As I take a swig, I imagine jebel spirits swirling through the darkness towards the Majlis Al Djinn.

During the night a sudden and violent wind – the *shamal* – rushes down the wadi, waking us from a sound sleep, covering us in a thick layer of dust and sand. The guttural cry of a wildcat echoes in the gorge. My arms turn to gooseflesh. Caracals and leopards are rare in the Hajar Range but not extinct. Maybe the bloodied remains of the Eid feasts have lured them into the open. Just as suddenly as it started, the wind drops. I try to stay awake to catch a glimpse of the elusive Arabian leopard, but I cannot. I doze fitfully, disturbed by the sound of soft footpads in the sand. The *shamal*, the feral cry and the furtive night noises feed my half-awake brain. We are close to the town of Bahla and I'm not thinking of its reputation for pottery.

In the surreal world of neither dreams nor waking life, I see twisted limestone spires hanging from an indigo sky and a round moon floating in a deep pool. Crouching on a boulder far below the weathered turrets is my caveman warrior, as still and silent as a stone statue. He stares fixedly down the wadi. Without sound or movement, he cries out to me.

Whether it be the witches of Bahla or the magic of the mountains, his call stirs something deep inside me and I know that even when I leave this mystical land his echo will stay with me forever.

OLIVIA POZZAN

Adventure writer Olivia Pozzan has led caving expeditions in the Middle East, ridden camels in outback Australia, competed in adventure races in northern Africa, and trekked extensively around the globe. For her, hiking is an immersion in the landscape, culture and atmosphere of a place. Olivia writes for various publications, including Lonely Planet books, and lives on Queensland's glorious Sunshine Coast.

THE GREAT AMERICAN RIDE

Jon Krakauer

It is the 19th of June, and the eastern seaboard should be smoulder-ing in the first embrace of summer, but rain drums down from a sky the colour of dirty aluminium as you jockey with the truckers and grim-faced commuters fighting their way out of Manhattan. You have never liked wet weather, but at the moment it is even less welcome than usual because you happen to be riding a motorcycle, and you're headed for San Francisco, and if the rain doesn't quit soon – it's not supposed to, according to an unaccountably cheer-ful woman on the Weather Channel – the next 4000 miles on the Harley are going to seem really, really long.

Approaching the Pennsylvania border, you move into the passing lane to get around a Winnebago just as a beer truck going the other direction splashes through a gigantic puddle, nailing you from across the median with a thick brown slap of rainwater, much of which finds its way inside your collar, trickles down your chest and pools icily at your crotch. As the highway climbs over the Pocono Mountains, the temperature drops abruptly and the rain slants down harder still. By now you are soaked to the skin through your expensive rain suit. Water flows in rivulets down your shins, filling your boots, and the visor on your helmet is fogging so badly that it's difficult to see the road.

At least, you remind yourself, you are not suffering alone. Stretching into the mist ahead and behind – mostly, if the truth be told, ahead – are 13 companions also bound for the Golden Gate, all of them astride chrome-encrusted Harley-Davidsons. They are a disparate bunch: some the tightest of friends, others barely acquainted. They all have one thing in common, however: a potentially deadly affliction, highly contagious, that has stricken millions of American males since its first major outbreak in the 1920s. Its distinguishing characteristic is a mule-headed infatuation with loud, fast motorcycles.

You, too, are among the afflicted. You caught the bug in 1969, after taking a seat in a crowded theater and watching Peter Fonda cruise across the screen and into history on a gleaming Panhead Harley. You were 15 when you first saw *Easy Rider*, not even old enough to get into the R-rated movie without a forged note from your parents, but you experienced a searing epiphany there in the dark. Something wondrous was revealed to you. You wangled a job pumping gas at the corner service station, banked your paychecks and, as soon as you received a driver's license, bought yourself a bike.

A 70cc Japanese machine, it was a far cry from the brawny 1200cc choppers that were the real stars of *Easy Rider*. You were merely a pimply-faced, small-town kid with a stupid haircut, putt-putting down residential streets on a pint-size Honda. You wore a star-spangled helmet as you rode, though, just like the one in the movie, and in your mind's eye you were Captain America – roaring down the highway to the rasp of a Steppenwolf guitar riff, roaring across the landscape with the wind in your face, roaring toward adventure, toward a sense of unlimited possibility, toward the intoxicating promise of manhood.

By the time you turned 17, you'd sold that first Honda after a harrowing encounter with a Buick. But now, 23 years later, the fantasy planted by Fonda and Dennis Hopper has borne more fruit. An honest-to-God Harley is thundering in your grip, and you intend to take it from one edge of the continent to the other. You've embarked on the Great American Ride.

As you remember it, Fonda and Hopper never got rained on. In real life, the soggy weather continues to dog you across eastern Pennsylvania. By lunch you've covered 200 miles; only 3800 more to go. Already, your hands are numb from the vibration of the handlebars, and your butt feels like it's been used as a punching bag. The chill has penetrated to the very core of your bones.

Then, near a town called Bloomsburg, the rain suddenly quits. You leave the interstate and point your bikes down a series of back roads lined with trees and farmhouses and children playing on porch swings. Thunderheads still tower in the distance, and wisps of fog hang on the hilltops, but the pavement is dry now, and the sun actually peeks between the clouds now and then. Your clothing dries. The shivering stops. Moving through the Appalachians on the snaking, two-lane blacktop, you lean easily into sweeping turns and hold the throttle open down long straightaways. The bike begins to feel like a seamless extension of your arms and legs and reflexes, responding to your wishes without effort or conscious thought.

As evening approaches, your scruffy caravan pulls into a tunnel at the edge of Pittsburgh. The low-throated rumble of 14 Harley-Davidsons is amplified by the tunnel walls into a booming vibration that threatens to bring the roof down. Convinced you are drooling hounds of doom and that the apocalypse is at hand, motorists peer at you from their sensible Fords and Toyotas with expressions ranging from disgust to abject terror. You steal a glance at your cohorts and see that Pitman, Kennan, Hill and Wenner are all grinning like errant school boys.

There is a lone female rider in your posse, Rosie Davenport, a mature, impeccably mannered woman from Wichita, Kansas. You expect Rosie to give you all a thorough scolding, Jiminy Cricket–like, for taking such delight in terrorizing innocent citizens. Instead she smiles broadly and tells you, 'Ever since I was little, I suspected boys got to have more fun than girls. I was right, of course, which is why I've been playing with boys ever since.'

In the first reel of *Easy Rider*, after a long day on the road, Fonda and Hopper arrive at a dumpy motel in the middle of the night and rev their engines until the manager appears. 'Hey man, you got a room?' demands Fonda. Without bothering to answer, the proprietor slams the door, locks it and switches on the 'No Vacancy' light.

The crew you're riding with, attired in torn denim and greasy leather, looks as menacing as you'd expect a biker gang to look. They smell bad. Most are in need of a shave. Unlike Fonda and Hopper, however, they never seem to have trouble obtaining lodging. This has something to do with the fact they pay for their rooms not with rolls of drug money stashed in their gas tanks but with American Express cards. When they're not out raising hell on motorcycles, most of your compadres sit behind desks, wearing suits and ties.

The fellow in the skull-and-crossbones head scarf, for instance, is Bob Millard, who holds a physics degree from MIT and a Harvard MBA and presently toils lucratively on Wall Street. Woody Johnson, dressed head to toe in gnarly black cowhide, is heir to one of the largest family fortunes in the US. The leaders of the pack, the trio known as the Bad Boys, are Sheldon Coleman, Bob Pittman and Jann Wenner. Until 1989, when it was bought out from under him in a hostile takeover, Coleman oversaw the Coleman sporting-goods empire; Pittman, the man who introduced the world to MTV, was president and CEO of Time Warner Enterprises; Wenner is editor in chief of various magazines.

All the men you're riding with are fathers; at least one of them is raising as many as four children. Two or three times a year, however, these corporate stalwarts and devoted parents don ratty-looking leathers, jump on their Hogs and rumble off together on white-knuckled weekend rides. Because this trip began by crossing New York's George Washington Bridge and is supposed to end at San Francisco's Golden Gate, Sheldon has taken to calling the gang the Bridge Club. In the summer of 1991, the club was on a three-day run through the Adirondacks, 'when road fever struck,' Pittman recalls. 'Someone said, "You know, it's high time we did the ultimate bike trip. Next year let's ride across the whole damn country." And the rest of us said, "Right on! Let's do it."'

A departure date was set. To persuade as many of their buddies as possible to brave the wrath of wives, children and business associates and actually go on the ride, Pittman and Wenner composed an impassioned letter of invitation, promising 'a vain attempt to regain our misspent youth.'

'Since most of us are in the throes of a midlife crisis, we need a major trip to prove that we can do anything an 18-year-old can… The rules are simple. No wives and no dentures. No whining, no slow-pokes… What to tell colleagues at work? "Doing market research on consumer attitudes across the country for next 10 days.'" Fourteen of the 30 people who received the letter took the bait and committed.

There are literally thousands of potential routes across the country. It was clear that the trip's success would depend in large part on choosing a good one. 'I wanted to stay off freeways as much as possible,' explains Coleman, who volunteered to devise an itinerary. 'I also wanted to steer clear of big cities and get from New York to San Francisco on the prettiest, most kick-ass roads that existed.' He spent weeks poring over maps and consulting with veteran bike tourers across the country. The route he eventually concocted turned out to be a masterpiece.

It's no trick to find spectacular roads across the western third of the nation, where mouth-watering scenery and wide-open spaces are as common as dirt. The real test of a route's quality will be found in the East and Midwest, and that's where the genius of Sheldon's itinerary first came to the fore.

Take Ohio. You are no stranger to Ohio, having driven across it something like 20 times. On each of those trips, you viewed the Buckeye State as an onerous obstacle between you and some other, better place – a stretch of flat, boring real estate to be dispatched as quickly and painlessly as possible. But that's because you always traveled in a 'cage' – the derisive term bikers reserve for cars – and never strayed from the teeming swath of Interstate 80. The line Sheldon has plotted across Ohio avoids freeways altogether and passes through no community bigger than a small burg. Near the town of Cadiz, the route veers off on the winding pavement of US Highway 36, introducing you to the forested hills of the Tappan Lake region, a sylvan paradise of heart-wrenching beauty. Astonished, you are struck by how overwhelmingly rural and unspoiled much of the nation remains, even east of the Mississippi, even as the 20th century draws to a tumultuous close. You see Ohio in a whole new light.

More often than not, people driving automobiles regard tight curves and narrow two-lane roads as annoyances. They flock instead to the numbing monotony of the interstate, where they can travel in an effortless, rolling trance. On a motorcycle, though, you can't afford to drive on autopilot. Whenever you're on two wheels, your continued health – your very life – hinges on paying close and constant attention, hence the appeal of challenging back roads that hone your concentration to a fine edge. Curves and rolls that would be hell in an automobile are unadulterated bliss on a bike. Indeed, as you glide down a serpentine stretch of Ohio asphalt, you are reminded that one rides a motorcycle not primarily to get from point A to point B but simply to ride.

A motorcycle is a passport to a world of stirring sensation, of intense kinesthetic pleasure. But there is a price to be paid; the hazards of biking are very real. All of you know people who have been killed or severely injured. When he was young, Woody Johnson lost a brother in a motorcycle accident. Midway across Indiana on your trip, you are graphically reminded of the danger when Lanier Hurdle – a cousin of Pittman's – goes into a sneaky off-camber turn carrying a little too much speed and comes out of it flying ass over teakettle down a sod embankment.

Arriving at the accident scene a few seconds later, the first thing you see is the tyres of a big Harley upended in the weeds. Cousin Lanier is lying motionless just beyond, flat on his back with blood on his face. Just when you think he's either dead or paralysed, Lanier – a lawyer from Mississippi – sits bolt upright and shouts in a husky Southern twang, 'How's the bike? How's the bike? Did I damage it bad?'

It takes four people to right the 800lb behemoth, but after you pull the last clumps of turf from the cylinder heads, it turns out to have suffered no discernible damage whatsoever, not even a scratch. Cousin Lanier fares slightly worse – his chin is bleeding, he's gone into shock, and he's torn some ligaments in one ankle – but he is remarkably unscathed, considering. Indeed, when you tell Lanier you're sorry his injuries are going to prevent him from continuing the ride, he shoots you a look of utter incredulity and snaps, 'Quit riding? What the hell are you talkin' about, son?' After letting his nerves settle for 20 minutes or so, Lanier climbs gingerly onto his Hog, starts it up, and the Bridge Clubbers roll on down the road as if nothing untoward had happened.

Although Cousin Lanier reins in his speed after this brush with disaster, the rest of you soon resume your reckless ways, surrendering to velocity's delicious call. Only a day after Lanier's tumble, an entrepreneur named Rocky Hill – a solid Reagan-Bush Republican in his other life – suddenly cracks open his throttle and pulls away from the pack, and a few of you try to stay with him.

The speedometer climbs to 85, 90, 95, and you lean into turns so hard that the footrests scrape the pavement. You hold this pace for 20 minutes, then 30 minutes, then 40, until a church steeple heralds the approach of a town. You relax your grip on the throttle with a long exhalation of relief, slow to a crawl and coast down a sleepy tree-lined Main Street out of Norman Rockwell (or David Lynch, depending on your state of mind). At the only gas station, you top off the tank, then seek refreshment in the mom-and-pop grocery next door. A few of the Bridge Clubbers are disappointed by the absence of Evian or Perrier or some reasonable facsimile, but you are more than satisfied by a pint of Strawberry Quik, a heavenly pink nectar you haven't tasted since you were 12.

Fifteen minutes later you hear somebody say, 'Let's rock,' and you climb back on the bikes. At the far edge of town, the highway stretches into the distance through fields of corn and hay, shimmering hypnotically in the heat, undulating across the soul of summer. You grab the handlebars firmly, settle into the saddle and start kicking through the gears: Braaaap! Braaaaaaap! Braaaaaaaap! Before you know it, the needle's brushing 90 again.

You travel this fast only when the road is empty and its surface smooth as 50-year-old cognac, but a high-speed run never fails to leave your clothes soiled with the stink of fear. A blown tire or stray dog on the road would have dire consequences. As Lanier mused one evening, 'Can you imagine what would happen if y'all came over a hill going 95, and there was a Mack truck in your lane, barrelin' right at you? Why, you'd look just like one of those big ol' bugs splattered across my windshield.'

Despite the vividness of Cousin Lanier's imagery, most of the Clubbers 'crack 100' – break the 100mph barrier – more than once during the trip, no mean feat on a stock Harley. Although an unmodified Harley-Davidson has a remarkable amount of low- and midrange torque, it isn't really meant for high speed. It will get to 90 in a hurry, but you have to run it wide-open for a disconcertingly long time to coax it past 100mph. 'It's pretty exciting,' Rocky says. 'I forget to breathe, though. And I can only stand it for a little while before that 100mph wobble begins to wear on my nerves.'

One hundred miles per hour on a Harley is in many ways a less than pleasant experience. The rush of the wind is literally deafening, drowning out even the thunder of the engine. When a bumblebee meets your shoulder – and there are many, many bumblebees between New York and San Francisco – it feels like you've taken a slug from a .38. Furthermore, on the machine you're riding, a popular model known as the Heritage Softail, the 1340cc Harley engine is bolted directly to the frame without benefit of rubber motor mounts to dampen the vibration. Above 85mph, the bike begins to shake like a paint mixer; at 100 the shudder of the huge twin cylinders feels like it's rattling the fillings from your teeth. It's irresponsible to go that fast in the first place, of course; it makes no sense whatsoever. Adrenalin is a powerful and alluring drug, however, and neither responsible behavior nor making sense has ever been a hallmark of biker culture.

As the least experienced rider in the group, you don't muster the poise to make a run at 100 until the fourth day of the ride. West of Dubuque, on a ribbon of flawless asphalt, you finally decide to do it. The needle creeps up to 96, 97, 98. Between the shudder of the engine and the fire-hose blast of the wind, your head shakes so badly that your vision blurs. The noise is almost unbearable, the tension even more so, but you force yourself to keep twisting back the throttle: 99, 100, 101, 102. At 103 you've had enough and back down to 85. Suddenly it feels as if you're barely moving. Perspiration soaks your shirt. You're panting hard, and every nerve in your body is buzzing. Part of you is aghast at what you have just experienced, but a different, more insistent part already craves another taste.

You worry about crashing when you're going that fast, of course, but you worry nearly as much about encountering the police. Fortunately, one of the good things about back roads is that the constables tend to be few and far between; cops prefer to haunt the freeways, where the traffic is heavier and ticket-writing quotas are easier to meet. Which is not to suggest that you and your colleagues have had no contact with the law. On four occasions the Bridge Club was pulled over en masse for speeding, only to be let off with nothing more than a stern verbal warning. Only one rider, slapped with two citations in Knox County, Ohio, actually received a ticket. This streak of good fortune remains a mystery to you, although it's no doubt less a function of good karma than the presence of a smooth-talking Southern attorney, name of Cousin Lanier.

One hardly needs to be rich to ride a motorcycle across the land. Bikers have been roaming the nation's roads in great numbers for decades, and, historically, many have come from the lower end of the economic spectrum. But having a little money does have its advantages. The Bridge Clubbers, for instance, have hired an ace Harley-Davidson mechanic named Gary Wagner to follow close behind the pack in a Ryder truck. Not only does the truck carry a full complement of special tools and spare parts, but it holds three extra bikes as well, gassed up and ready to ride. The reason for securing the services of what amounts to a mobile motorcycle shop is that a Harley is, well, a Harley.

Harley-Davidsons inspire either fanatical devotion or bitter scorn. In all fairness, it should be emphasized that Harleys have become considerably more reliable since 1984, when the company introduced the relatively sophisticated Evolution engine that now powers all its bikes. Nowadays a Hog is unlikely to blow oil all over your leg. But nuts, bolts and sundry other parts can still rattle off Harleys with astonishing frequency, necessitating a regular bolt-tightening session at the conclusion of each day's ride. Despite such preventative measures, over the space of four days your bike sheds a taillight, an exhaust pipe, a footpad and enough random bolts to stock a hardware store.

When compared with top-of-the-line German, Italian and Japanese bikes, the bald truth is that Harleys are less agile in tight turns and don't go as fast and are probably less reliable. They also cost more, in some instances nearly twice as much. Yet, in the eyes of most American riders, a Harley is the only real motorcycle still in production. Nearly 70% of big bikes – over 850cc displacement – sold in this country each year are Harleys. As the British motorcycle authority Graham Scott has pointed out, nobody but Harley-Davidson has 'yet made a bike that so perfectly suits the sheer size of the American land mass.' You can feel every twitch of a Harley's muscular heart as you ride, a visceral throb that no Yamaha or Suzuki can match.

Riders of sleek Japanese crotch rockets and Italian café racers sneer at the Harley's clunky engineering, garish American styling and avoirdupois. When a Hog cruises past, they laugh at the feet-forward, Barcalounger riding posture. But the very things that riders of other motorcycles see as shortcomings are viewed as attributes by Harley devotees. The machine's tawdry chrome trappings and squat, hulking lines make the faithful swoon. One of the most popular Harley-Davidsons has been a model actually called the Fat Boy; it's what

Schwarzenegger rode in Terminator II, and the company can't build them fast enough to keep up with buyer demand

Even the notorious Harley vibration is cherished by Hog aficionados. The company makes several models with rubber-mounted engines – the Low Rider, the Tour Glide, the Dyna Glide – but continues to bolt the motor directly to the frames of Softails and Fat Boys because that's what many riders prefer. Having your bones rattled by the V-twin's enormous pistons is considered an essential part of the Harley experience.

When you come right down to it, a Harley is much more than a motorcycle; it's a religion. Call it the Church of Our Loud Chrome Savior. What other machine, after all, inspires men and women to tattoo the most intimate corners of their bodies with a corporate logo? What other vehicle elicits solemn oaths of allegiance and undying love? Throughout most of your ride cross-country, John Pannone, a motorcycle-safety instructor from Connecticut, wears a T-shirt that captures the essence of the mystique. 'Harley-Davidson,' proclaims the slogan across Pannone's chest, 'if I have to explain, you wouldn't understand.

Riding out of Yankton, South Dakota, in the chill of first light, you cover 124 miles before breakfast. When the growling of your stomach gets the better of you, you park the bikes on the unpaved main drag of Burke, South Dakota, population 743, and enter a whitewashed building identified as the Burke Bowl and Café. The bowling lanes are closed, but the eggs turn out to be fresh and the coffee strong.

The Bowl and Café, you discover, is the social nexus of greater Burke. Inside, a dozen folk in bib overalls and flannel shirts, their median age about 65 or thereabouts, are passing time over steaming cups of joe. Woody, wearing a green John Deere cap he bought yesterday in Iowa, immediately strikes up a conversation with a good-natured South Dakotan, whose own cap reads 'The metallic age: silver hair, gold teeth, lead butt.'

'So you're a John Deere man, I see,' the old-timer remarks. 'Yessir, now there's an outfit knows how to build a tractor, you betcha.' Woody gives a knowing nod, then quickly segues into a different subject without letting on that he's never been any closer to a farm implement than the produce isle at Safeway. You dawdle in the Bowl and Café for more than an hour, chatting happily with its denizens about motorcycles and wheat futures and Bill Clinton's run for the presidency. When you go to pay your check, the bill for your breakfast – which was huge and magnificently unhealthful – sets you back $2.49.

The further west you travel, the better the riding gets. The sky feels bigger with each passing mile, the landscape more immense. Hour after hour, the sun washes the plains in clean, sparkling light and the pavement beneath your wheels splits a blond sea of prairie grass, heaving in the wind like ocean surf. Late in the afternoon the road climbs into a craggy brown fist of mountains redolent of sage and cool pine forests. You understand immediately why, in the cosmology of the Sioux people who live here, the Black Hills are the most sacred place in the universe.

'You thought about work much since we left?' Millard asks Jann while the latter stretches a kink from his back at a rest stop.

'I tried once,' Jann replies solemnly, 'but my brain refused to cooperate. I just couldn't get it onto the screen.'

It is the fifth day of your odyssey. You got on your bike at seven this morning and won't park it until after eight tonight. A Harley that's being ridden hard will run out of gas in as few as 120 miles, so you stop often to take on fuel, but even with four or five stops a day you end up spending a lot of hours in the saddle. Although it's exhausting and occasionally frightening, it's rarely dull. 'I haven't been bored yet,' insists Millard, whose face has turned the colour of boot leather from the sun and incessant wind. 'To ride well you have to concentrate intensely, which keeps you alert and makes the time pass pretty fast. Concentrating that hard occupies a certain part of your brain completely, but it leaves other parts free to reflect on the scenery and ponder Big Questions. It's a little like Transcendental Meditation – you enter this altered state. It's kind of addictive, if you want to know the truth.'

The days are so long and all-consuming that come sunset there's little time or energy for anything except tending to the bikes, a hot shower and five or six hours of sleep. A couple of stiff drinks with dinner is as much revelry as anybody seems to manage, betraying the party-hearty biker image. This trip is about riding hard and little else.

Despite the acute shortage of leisure time, most of the Clubbers spend an hour every evening hand-buffing their Hogs until the chrome and lacquer take on a blinding shine. 'A clean bike goes faster,' Sheldon insists with a straight face. You don't really feel a great need to go any faster, however, and you're actually proud of the mashed insects and road grime plastered thickly onto your machine – you wear this gnarly crust as a badge of biker verisimilitude – so you forgo the nightly cleaning ritual, as does Millard, until your brethren harass you into compliance.

Rocky, in a fit of anal-compulsive overload, eventually washes Millard's Low Rider for him. Your case is touchier, in that 'your' Softail has actually been borrowed from your editor in chief who badgers you relentlessly about its filthy state, insisting that your bike is an embarrassment to your associates. When that tactic fails, he tries to make you feel guilty, arguing unconvincingly that you're mistreating his beloved Harley. In Cody, Wyoming, six days into the trip, he finally pulls rank and tells you that, if you don't wash the damn bike, he's going to put it in the truck and let you walk. The next morning, as you work through the gearbox on your now-gleaming steed, the bike does seem to go a little faster, although you're careful not to mention that to the boss.

Cruising towards Yellowstone beside the fast waters of the Shoshone River, you head toward a wall of cumulonimbus clouds towering 30,000ft above the Absaroka Range. Every minute or two a flash of lightning forks from the cloud base, followed many seconds later by a muffled crash of thunder. Forty miles down the road, you ride into a dark curtain of rain, accompanied by hail the size of peanuts. Frozen pellets blanket the ground a half-inch deep, creating a bizarre winter landscape at the end of June.

On the ninth morning, you wake up in Boise, Idaho. Your odometer says you've covered about 3300 miles; less than 700 to go now. The country you ran through yesterday – out of Wyoming over Teton Pass, up the broad, dreamy valley of the Big Lost River, past the granite ramparts of the Sawtooth Range – was so pretty it made your soul ache. It was the best ride of the trip, without question the best of your life. Like a child facing the end of a day at Disneyland, you grow morose and agitated at the prospect of journey's end.

You leave Idaho before dawn, hoping to get a jump on the sun; the next 400 miles through Oregon and Nevada traverse a blistering expanse of desert. Feeling your oats on the empty Nevada blacktop, you pull away from the pack outside McDermitt and soon have the speedometer inching up towards 100. Just as you're congratulating yourself for breaking into three digits, you notice a headlight in your left-hand mirror. A moment later a red-and-white blur rockets past as if you're standing still. It turns out to be your editor in chief on a Yamaha FZR1000 at a speed he wouldn't disclose. You don't catch sight of Jann again until a gas stop in Winnemucca, where he let's you know that he's been waiting 20 minutes for you to arrive.

The Yamaha has traveled across most of the country in the back of Gary Wagner's truck, with the other spare machines, but every now and then Jann rolls it out and takes it for a run. It's a very hot bike, one of the fastest street-legal motorcycles on the market. With its radically aerodynamic lines, quiet purr and streamlined engineering, it's also most emphatically not a Harley.

Not surprisingly, the bike has prompted an ongoing barrage of snide commentary from the other Bridge Clubbers, who are all devout worshippers at the holy altar of Harley-Davidson, and, thus, view the Yamaha's presence as an unpardonable act of backsliding on Jann's part. Before we left New York, Sheldon expressed his disapproval by 'accidentally' dropping the Yamaha five vertical feet, upside down, from the truck's tailgate. The only damage he managed to inflict was a broken mirror and a slightly bent handlebar, which were easily fixed.

The final night of the trip in a Lake Tahoe hotel, Michael Cinque – who's been riding a painstakingly restored 1969 Shovelhead Harley – stands up during dinner to make an announcement. 'You know,' he begins, 'they pound a Japanese bike into scrap every year at those big Harley rallies in Sturgis and Daytona. In that same spirit, when we get to San Francisco, I propose that we throw Jann's Yamaha off the Golden Gate Bridge.'

'Great idea!' yells Sheldon over Jann's yelps of protest. 'All those in favor say "Aye."' Although the motion carries by a resounding majority, Jann negotiates a stay of execution by agreeing to put the FZR back in the truck for good; he will ride the remainder of the way into the Bay Area, like the rest of you, on a big shiny Hog.

At the California border, Rocky warns the group, 'From now on every road will be crawling with police, so keep the helmets on and stick to the speed limit. If we ride like we've been riding, we'll all wind up in jail.' Heeding Rocky's words, you roll down from the Sierra crest in slow, tight formation, and keep riding that way all the way to Sausalito, where you exit Highway 101 and break out some champagne for a final ceremonial run across the Golden Gate. In a couple of hours, you'll be sitting on a jet bound for home.

Gazing up at the huge orange span, you experience a surge of roiling emotions. After 10 days on the road, your borrowed Harley feels like a fifth limb; you can't imagine spending a whole day, let alone weeks or months, away from it. On the other hand, you've just ridden 4000 miles, and many of those miles passed in a state of undiluted terror. Both mentally and physically, you're completely whipped. To your great surprise, you made it coast to coast without anybody's getting killed or locked up – considerably better than Fonda and Hopper made out in *Easy Rider* – and for that you feel deep gratitude and a heady sense of accomplishment. But the fun is over. Ahead you see only the plodding march of real life, the prospect of which does not cheer you.

'I think we're making a big mistake,' Bob Millard suddenly tells the gang, apparently sharing your melancholy sentiments. 'Look, if all of you were to cancel your appointments for the next 10 days, do you really think you'd regret it, five years from now? Let's turn the bikes around right here, and just keep on going. Seriously, how about it? Who's with me? The roads in New Mexico are supposed to be awesome...'

JON KRAKAUER

Jon Krakauer is the author of *Into The Wild*, *Into Thin Air*, and *Under the Banner of Heaven*. His new book, *The Hero*, will be published by Doubleday in October, 2008.

REAL LIVE RUSSIANS

Robert Reid

I'm old enough to remember looking into menacing tornados over the Oklahoma plains and wondering whether they hid Russian bombs. For a kid in Cold War–era mid-America, war with the Soviets seemed certain – that is, if bad movies, local news or Sting's horrible song 'Russians' were to be believed. But amid the fear, a forbidden fascination was born: visions of another huge land, with fur hats and frowning faces, dill-dotted soups and onion-domed churches, Lenin statues and USSR athletes. By the time I got to college I was learning Cyrillic, reading Dostoevsky and contemplating a goatee. But I still hadn't met a Russian.

Finally in 1991 – a few months after the Soviet Union's epic collapse – I took an all-inclusive, ultrainsulated study-work program to St Petersburg, where I mostly just goofed off with students from Arizona, Alabama and Massachusetts. We'd sit around my hotel room sipping terrible 10¢ bottles of 'street beer' and watching Pete the foul-mouthed minor-league baseball player throw cucumbers out of the window at passing trams. My connections with real live Russians were pretty much limited to an insane parachute lesson at a WWII airbase ('You will pull this for parachute, if not work you will pull this…let's go') and the little old key lady on our floor who robbed $500 from my roommate then kindly returned his empty wallet. If I wanted to understand Russians, clearly I needed to go back.

A couple of years ago, a job sent me briefly to Vladivostok. Daily flights connect Russia's port city of the Far East with Beijing in a couple of hours, but I had other plans. I pulled out an old Soviet Union map from a 1970s *National Geographic* to plot out the most time-consuming way to get there. I'd start in Moscow, seven full time zones (and seven days minimum by train) west, and hop my way on and off Russia's continent-spanning trains on the world's greatest overland journey – on board the Trans-Siberian Railway and detouring a bit north on the lesser-known BAM (Baikal-Amur Mainline). Surely I'd meet some Russians out there.

Day 1: Moscow

I've long troubled my travels with the idea that actual enjoyable attractions – eg a Kremlin tour, a night at the Bolshoi – mean a lot less than more fruitless endeavors like shopping for oboes, buying stationery in junior-high bookshops or touring closed socialist insti-tute halls. So, back again in Moscow, I skipped art museums and the Arbat shops, with the singular goal of getting a library card at the ex–Lenin Library, a few hundred meters from Red Square. Now known as the Rossiiskaya Gosudarstvennaya Biblioteka (Russian State Library), the grey building's sign still reads 'Lenin Library', and is supposedly one of the world's largest. Inside, a cranberry-haired middle-aged woman and her lazy eyelids wouldn't let me in. 'Why do you want visit library?' she asked. '*Chitat*?' (to read), I suggested hopefully. She pointed her fleshy arm outward, then to the left, and I followed it, wandering back outside and next door where a sign read '*administratsi*'. Here I managed, through dumb smiles and insistent ignorance of rejection, to be led through a form, a line, a digital head shot, and a laminated card for a couple of dollars. I was in. Triumphantly re-entering the library's racks of some 20-

million volumes, I wandered to the upstairs reading room, noting old socialist murals of Lenin teaching eager youth. I tried to look local, politely sitting a minute or two with a book I couldn't read – *Tomsk Economic Goals for 1998*, or something – and slipped out when my cranberry-haired friend wasn't looking.

Days 2 & 3: to Novosibirsk

For my first leg across Russia – a mere 50-hour ride to Novosibirsk, about a third of the way to Vladivostok – I got on the famed Trans-Siberian Railway. It was surprisingly nice. Four bunks in a cabin, with cleaned blankets and pillows. Each carriage has a *provodnitsa* (attendant) who brings in little meals and vacuums the little carpet once daily. Most of the time, I watched forests and factories zoom by, or read Chekhov stories written after his whoring trip across Russia a century ago.

About 10 hours east, a thin, grey-haired man entered my empty cabin and politely said 'hello' in English as he stored his briefcase under the bed across from mine. We ended up talking most of the next 20 hours. Mr V—, a 68-year-old dean at a Novosibirsk institute, enjoyed the rare opportunity to exercise his deep, warm voice in English. As a boy, he and his family were 'captured by German troops and made slaves – somewhere near Hamburg', he told me. 'I feel bad that I can't remember how to speak German any more.' After the war, Stalin tended to reward returning POWs with a one-way trip to a Gulag camp, and his family ended up in Magadan, one of the most notorious Gulag-built towns, in the frosty Far East on the Sea of Okhotsk. Mr V— retold all this with the same cheerful disposition with which he told me about his favorite movies (*Pretty Woman*, *Terminator* and *Emmanuelle* – 'parts one, two and three', he noted). Shortly before we pulled into Novosibirsk, he put on a dress shirt and combed his hair for the arrival. After 20 hours of talk, he was off – one of the last sober Russians I'd meet on a train.

Day 4: Novosibirsk

Russia is not a country big on historic destinations, and Novosibirsk, 3300 kilometers east of Moscow, certainly isn't one of the few standouts. It's a grey, socialist-made city of 1.7 million people, famous for Akademgorodok, a community of elite institutes in a patch of nearby woods that are home to a tick that can kill you. The grey Hotel Novosibirsk across from the train station scared me – its 23 stories looking like a wall of foggy windows guarding jail-box rooms and tragic curtain choices. I wheeled my little suitcases to a smaller hotel a few blocks away, where I was immediately offered 'some kind of woman', something I'd learn would be an everyday occurrence in the backwaters of Russia.

Instead I called up Sasha, a young Novosibirskian man I happened to meet back in Moscow, and he and his brother Oleg, a waiter, came by in a borrowed car to show me a few sights. We crossed the Ob River to the War Memorial Park, where soldiers guard the eternal flame at the tomb of a Siberian unknown soldier and kids climb on WWII planes, tanks and rockets. Twisting the ends of the bleached spikes on his flop-top mullet hairdo, Oleg explained his dream of opening a Japanese-Italian-Chinese restaurant – 'all macaroni', he explained. Heading back to drop me off at my hotel, Sasha pointed out a fading slogan on a grey housing block that read, 'Long live the working people'. 'Ha, very funny', Oleg said. Under it I saw a freshly painted rendering of a six-fingered hand with one of its two middle fingers raised below the words '*Pank is not dead*'. That got less laughs.

Days 5 & 6: on the BAM

Anyone compiling a list of spectacular failures must include the USSR's 'Hero Project of the Century': the BAM (Baikal-Amur Mainline) – a failure that's up there with Napoleon in Russia or Beckham in the USA. The Soviets sank more roubles into this 4300 kilometer train route to nowhere than they spent on their space program (something akin to $20 billion). The BAM clanks past little other than 'drunken forests' (where blackened trees lean over severed roots in the permafrost) and purpose-built mining towns every 500 kilometers. Finding a seat's never a problem. As a business, the BAM loses $70 million a year.

Eighteen hours east of Novosibirsk, the train turned off the Trans-Siberian's sturdier tracks – which take the bulk of cross-country travelers to Beijing – and onto BAM's wayward route towards the

Tatar Strait, further east than all of China. Life on the BAM had its differences, I noticed: no carpet vacuuming, and a wheel rattle loud enough to wake you in the night. My carriage mates included a Ukrainian grandmother who looked like Boris Yeltsin, a Siberian grandmother who looked like Joe Pesci, and a bitter 30-something gymnast who'd swing into his overhead bunk as if on the parallel bars. 'The South Koreans have talent,' he complained of the recent Olympic winners at one point, 'but they show no passion, no heart.' Later Yeltsin handed out tiny Ukrainian chocolates and Pesci pulled me to the hallway. 'You must see this,' she said, in deep awe, 'Bratsk dam… beautiful.' We stood silently shoulder to shoulder as dusk descended over one of the world's most powerful hydroelectric dams – easily one of the most unattractive scenes I've seen in many years of travel.

Day 7: Severobaikalsk

Severobaikalsk is a grubby town of grey housing blocks and 35,000 folk on the north lip of the world's largest body of fresh water, the stunning Lake Baikal. In summer, visitors come to take boat tours to islands – but it was only June. Once my train putt-putted away, I could plainly hear the horrific screeching sounds of the thick ice cracking on the lake's ocean-sized surface. Still I wanted to experience something of Baikal. I looked up an English-speaking guide mentioned in my guidebook, and asked if there was anything to see at this time of year. I soon discovered that Rashit, a 60-something stroke survivor and local guide, held the same sway over town that Max does over his fellow students (and their parents) in the film *Rushmore*. Soon a crew showed up, including a Nordic-looking fireman and his 11-year-old son who, like me, had no idea what was coming next. Rashit ordered us into the fireman's SUV and we drove to Baikalskoe, 45 kilometers south, to climb a cliff overlooking the snow-capped mountains and an endless frozen lake looming way below. Afterwards we met the beefy middle-aged Andrei at the lake back in Severobaikalsk. He shook my hand while eagerly inflating a kayak. 'It is possible to find some water with no ice', he said. We went for a short ride (my kayaking debut), each of my paddle swipes dumping icy water onto Andrei's lap. Next came the hot part. We drove to Andrei's house. In his grassy backyard was a tiny birch-covered shack, which he ushered me into: a *banya* (Russian steam bath). 'Everyone has one here', Andrei said, eyes widening at the delight of taking a turn with an American. Soon, he – naked, but so plump no private parts could be seen – followed the custom of pounding birch leaves across my bare chest as volcanic steam sunk into my skin. I was scared.

After an intoxicating dunk in a tub of cold water, we sat with Rashit in Andrei's kitchen and talked about trains. Rashit lamented that, after years of work on the BAM, no one celebrated its finish in the 1980s. Gorbachev even blamed the USSR's 'stagnation' on money used to build towns like Severobaikalsk. 'It saddens us that no-one sees the achievement of BAM,' Rashit said, sipping on a glass of compote fruit juice. 'It's not something that could ever be built these days.'

Day 8: to Tynda

My three cabin mates on the 26-hour ride to Tynda were pretty much the three I wanted to avoid all trip: drunken brothers with tattooed knuckles. Russia doesn't always have the best reputation for joyful acceptance of outsiders and, though that reputation is greatly exaggerated, these guys seemed like classic xenophobes. Every cheerful attempt at a '*dobri den*' or '*privet*' was met with a glare or turned head. So I read a lot or just stared at passing snow-capped mountains that would have been dotted with tacky resorts if they were in Western Europe or North America.

Day 9: Tynda

Everyone gets 15 minutes of fame, or a lost town that loves them unconditionally. I found the latter in 'BAM's capital' of Tynda, a compact Hong Kong–dense strip of grey housing blocks and nothing for hundreds of kilometers around. My cheerful Azerbaijani taxi driver lingered long after dropping me off at a sick-ugly guesthouse where I learned it was necessary to 'pay double if you don't want construction workers in your room'. Later, while I was trying to locate the BAM museum in town, a couple of smoking teens (fresh from a fight, it appeared) volunteered to walk me to it. A graceful Kazakh woman led me through the museum's 10 halls, patiently explaining detailed ethnographical concepts to a foreigner who missed those vocab lessons.

On my walk back to the guesthouse, an SUV suddenly slammed on its breaks as it passed me, and Alexei, a computer-tech spaz, jumped out. 'Where are you from? Let's go to the river!' Before I could answer, he held open the door and I got in. We zoomed off to pick up a few things – his friend Kolya, his 8½-month pregnant wife, some vodka and dried fish. 'This will be great!' Down a muddy path from town, however, the SUV's wheels sunk in a small lake of mud. Kolya got out to direct, but Alexei could not wait – and slammed the gas pedal down, splashing Kolya's flannel suit and cowgirl tie with mud.

We drank at the river for a while, talking about Russia and rock climbing, until the mosquito swarms blocked our view of the sunset, then continued a vodka rally at Alexei's apartment. I barely remember him walking me back to the guesthouse, where I vomited in the hotel hall's trash can and fell asleep on the floor in my construction worker–free room. The next day I found a parting gift Alexei, presumably, had stuffed into my pocket: hangover tablets.

Days 10 & 11: to Komsomolsk

My next trip would be my last on the BAM, a wee 37-hour ride to Komsomolsk. I was still hurting from the night out in Tynda. My wagon mates were two truck drivers (Vladimir and Aleksandr) heading to Khabarovsk to pick up a 'job'. Aleksandr hadn't been on a train for more than 15 years and I had to show him how to lift up the seat to store his bag. Within minutes they had filled the small table by the window with a bottle of vodka, *three* shot glasses, cans of beer, pulled-apart pieces of brown bread and a tomato or two. 'I had much vodka yesterday. Can't drink', I said slowly, hopefully, but they weren't having that. After a few refusals, I diplomatically succumbed to a couple of shots – they, many, many more. Before long, red-faced Aleksandr pointed into my face laughing; Vladimir – also in tears of laughter – managed to say 'I'm sorry – this is so wrong.' Wee hours came and went quick. They were up by 9am, immediately sipping half-drunk cans of beer. Soon, a 40-year-old Kenny G lookalike, a speed-metal guitarist from Birobidzhan (and part-time artist), dropped by to draw a 'souvenir' sketch of us three amigos – in return for a 'donation'. Vladimir asked for an extra copy for his own memories of the ride. Once we pulled into Komsomolsk, the truck drivers carried my bag to the platform and offered near-hug, handshake embraces. I tried to say something nice as a departing gesture. Aleksandr said, 'You speak Russian badly, like a Slovenian.'

Day 12: Komsomolsk

After Novosibirsk, Severobaikalsk and Tynda's dreary greys, sunny Komsomolsk's pretty pastel self came as quite a shock. Its history has always been a bit upbeat. Strident young communists, mostly male, volunteered in the 1930s to build it in a heady fervor, then begged the party for a campaign to get a few women out here. These days, trams clank along tree-lined streets with brick sidewalks and European-style buildings – something like a country cousin of St Petersburg. Another positive change was the temperature, which was warm enough for Russians to swim and windsurf off a small beach on the wide Amur River.

I checked into the 'Krushchev dacha', an uninspired house surrounded by trees off a main street. Built for the Soviet leader Nikita Krushchev in the 1950s, it has since housed Brezhnev and Gorbachev – but is a bit lonely these days. The woman running it happily showed me all the rooms, including the meeting room, where you can practically hear the shaking *kopecks* in nervous lowly dignitaries' pockets as the big guy came down the stairs.

At a hotel restaurant I bumped into my first foreigner since before Novosibirsk: a stockbroker from Tokyo with a dark tan and wild hair, named Hirosama Ando. I was proud of my cross-country trip, but it was nothing compared to Ando's. He'd just finished a six-month winter bike ride across Russia's Far East – from Sakhalin Island north of Japan, across the frozen Tatar Strait, up to Yakutsk and to Anadyr, in Russia's forbidding northeastern corner, way above the Arctic Circle. And back again. 'No trucks or trains or planes. I basically go with my bike anywhere a guidebook doesn't cover', he said in English. A couple of years before he had ridden from Murmansk (near Finland) to Magadan (up Alaska way). He showed me photos he took of nomads who had never seen a foreigner, much less a Japanese guy, on a bike, in winter. He said the wind was worse than the cold but, 'there were no problems. People are very nice. If someone was passing in a truck, they'd stop me to offer some help, usually some reindeer meat', he said, 'I drank a lot of vodka too.' He added, 'If you go, take bear spray.'

Ando was with a local bike group, who invited me to a 'bikers-only garden party'. We met up with a handful of 20-year-olds in bike garb and Vladimir – mustached, maybe 55 – who took us to his country *dacha* outside town where we feasted on potatoes, cucumbers, and tomatoes from his garden. Russian men are not generally short on machismo, and it was endearing to see these bike-club members, with their many medals, panting in awe of this Japanese rider. I was there, I think, just to maintain their sense of superiority (a *train* traveler.) Afterwards they all saw me off on my final leg, heading eight hours south to rejoin the Trans-Siberian at Khabarovsk, then 13 hours east to Vladivostok. At the Komsomolsk train station a teen biker who had been silent the whole afternoon finally stepped up to talk, surprising me with a bit of English. 'One question,' he asked, wearing a heavy-metal shirt depicting a skeleton that seemed to have gotten enraged over something, 'do you like hockey?'

I stumbled to answer, then didn't ever get his name. Clearly I need to go back. Maybe with a bike.

ROBERT REID

Robert Reid (www.reidontravel.com) blogged about mustache-counts on his last trip across Russia. He returns to Russian railroads in 2008 to update Lonely Planet's *Russia* and *Trans-Siberian Railway* guides. He has worked and lived in far-flung places – San Francisco, London, Ho Chi Minh City, Melbourne, Tulsa – but is now semi-permanently based in Brooklyn, New York.

A VIEW FROM THE EDGE

Karl Bushby

On 1 November 1998, at Punta Arenas in southern Chile, Karl Bushby took the first steps on a 36,000-mile path that will lead him home. At that moment the dream became reality and Karl began a journey that will be the longest continuous walk ever. It is possible to journey by foot from the southernmost point of South America back to England and leave behind you an unbroken trail of footsteps. This incredible journey will cross four continents, 25 countries, a frozen sea, six deserts and seven mountain ranges and will take an estimated 12 to 14 years.

The morning of Sunday, 14 January 2001, sees Karl walk nervously northwards from Medellin, Columbia, taking the road that leads to Turbo on the coast of the Gulf of Uraba. He'd spent two months in Medellin awaiting the arrival of the dry season and planning his attempt at crossing the infamous 'Darien Gap' into Panama. Traversing this narrow isthmus between northern Colombia and the Darien region of Panama means not only crossing a large river delta but also dense jungle and mountains. No-one, save a few friends, gives him a cat in hell's chance of getting through. Now it is time to go. Not far north of Medellin he will enter territory that falls under the control of the two major guerrilla groups, the left wing FARC (Revolutionary Armed Forces of Colombia) and the right wing AUC (United Self-Defence Force). An open war rages through this part of the country, not only between the Colombian Army and the FARC, but also between the two guerrilla groups. Westerners are a prime target for kidnapping and, quite often, murder. The whole Darien area and that part of northern Colombia has now become known as the most dangerous place on earth.

The first phase of the crossing is a road journey of approximately 150 miles to the village of El Tigre, where Karl will leave the road and head westward into the jungle. To keep unwanted attention to a minimum on this phase, he has disguised himself as one of South America's many vagrants. He carries dehydrated food for his time in the jungle and intends to buy food for the first phase while on the road.

Wednesday, 17 January 2001

Having slept slightly better than usual, I'm up and at it for an early start. I'm extremely hungry and stop for breakfast at a small roadside café around 07:30. Sitting nearby is an old man with a young girl. When they ask where I'm going, I tell them 'northwards'. The young girl then spurts out, 'You are the man walking around the world and crossing the Darien!' Oh, just bloody marvellous! No, for Pete's sake, I'm just a penniless pauper. Somehow all the effort I've taken with my disguise seems worthless. Anyway, I have some rice, *arapea*, and then a fish, which I eat with a litre of milk. I plan to do the same thing at around midday.

The heat picks up again and I struggle from the word go. I cross the Rio Couca and into Antioquia in a shit state. It's uphill all the way now as I hit the second mountain range. I'd been convinced there would be somewhere along this road where I could pick up another meal before the end of the day, but how wrong I am! It had been too early to eat when I reached Antioquia and, besides, I have to be careful with the money as always. The landscape has now changed, taking on an almost desertlike appearance – very dry rock and sand with sparse tree cover – an enormous change from around

Medellin some 40 miles back and, to tell you the truth, a bit of a surprise. Feeling as I do, I am a little worried about just how I'm going to cope. I am destroyed after the first few hundred metres, then forced to take breaks every 500 yards or less. Once again the pace seems really slow. I tire quickly, but have to push on as best I can, realising now that I could be in for a long haul without food or even water. There's little water going spare and my urine has been like Guinness since yesterday. Before the end of the day I'm a sick man and feel rotten.

I find a spot just after 16:00. My distance today has been pathetic, but I'm done for. I have to scale a bank, which is only about 30ft high, to reach the two trees I can use for my hammock, but even this seemingly easy task proves a nightmare. Time and time again I try and fail. Long dry grass covers rocks and stones, in among which are thorny vines. They seem to form an impenetrable barrier, and at one point I end up face down in the dirt at the bottom, after being cut to ribbons on the thorns. I almost give in, too tired to even lift myself off the ground. I just have to slap myself back into life and battle my way up to the top. Once I'm in place and the hammock is finally sorted, I open one of my ration bags for the jungle phase. I have little choice, I'm not going much further without food. Not having enough water, I just eat the nuts and lie like a zombie in my sack. I am so tired, yet sleep just won't come. I don't know why – maybe it's something in the nuts – but I lay awake, going out of my mind and being savaged by the infuriating midges which, given their very small size, can easily pass through my mosquito net.

At around 22:00 soldiers begin to pass by on the road. Snakes of troops pass periodically over the following four hours in platoon-sized groups. I can hear them talking loudly before actually seeing them, but now and then catch silhouetted outlines of men in staggered file in the lights of passing cars. I presume it's the army, as it's unlikely to be the FARC this far south.

Thursday, 18 January 2001

Now extremely hungry, I set off uphill once more. I am only about halfway up the hill, if that, when I begin to feel much the same as I did when the day ended yesterday, ie lousy. At about 13:30 I finally find what appears to be the top and also come across a small store.

However, it only sells Coke, not a particularly good start. The people in the shop tell me that their friends had told them they'd seen a gringo walking up the hill. So, even in this get-up I'm news. I push on once more, still climbing but now not so steeply. Not much later I find a place to eat and am given a really good meal. Night draws in and I find what is becoming my normal squat: a steep ravine, thick with trees and undergrowth with a rocky stream running down the centre. The land is far greener and wetter over on this side of the mountains. Earlier today I threw away my sleeping bag to lessen the weight, hoping that I'd be dropping to a lower altitude. However, I'm still very high and so am going to have to suffer a cold night. By 20:00 I am shaking like a leaf and freezing my nuts off. I put up with this for about four hours before I've had enough. I leave the hammock and sit on a thin ledge above the stream and, after locating as much dead wood as I can find within reach, build a fire to warm my frozen bones. I'm well enclosed, so I feel I can get away with it, as I've climbed a fair way above the road and so am safe. For three hours I sit by the fire and sew up the rips in the mosquito net. After that I go back to the hammock and just wait for dawn. Yet another long night.

Friday, 19 January 2001

I'm on the move early, as I can't wait to get moving. Still having lots of problems with my disguise/camouflage, and it's getting very hard to keep up this pretence as everyone still treats me the same, referring to me as '*mono*' or 'gringo'. I'm beginning to wonder if it's worth the effort. Today things are looking up, I move well and cover more distance, and on top of that I eat well. However, my feet are in bad nick and getting worse. It comes to the point where I lose my temper with my ill-fitting, cut-down old boots and change them for the new ones, throwing the old pair over the side into the valley, then wonder whether I've done the right thing.

I reach Canasgordas, a town that's the start of what I refer to as a 'hot spot', a scene of regular fighting. From this place on, up the road to Mutata, is basically the front line of conflict. I manage to avoid the centre and take a road that loops around it but, unfortunately, on the northern end of the town the roads join again to cross a bridge over the River Sucio. On the northern bank are just half a dozen more buildings before the end of the town itself. As I cross the bridge I see a group of men rise from their seats outside one of the buildings, obviously taking an interest in me. They give the appearance that they are ready to intercept me on the road and I begin to feel very uneasy. Making a snap decision, I leave the road and head into a small store-café, where I order a Coke from the barman then sit down. They aren't going to go away, but at least this gives me a few more seconds to think. I see the barman glance at me and then the street, then back at me. Something is going to happen and it isn't good. Sure enough, within moments, the men appear in the doorway. The first two in are a touch on the fat side but solid with it and mean-as-hell-looking, one of them with a badly scarred face. They both walk over to my table and stand staring at me without saying a word. Five younger guys, in their late teens, come in behind them then go round pulling down the metal shutters in the store. I am trapped. This is looking very ugly, and I begin thinking I'm about to get it, big style. My mind is racing, there is nothing I can do. I sit back in my chair and smile. These guys are one of three options:

1. FARC
2. AUC
3. Bandits.

I really think I am about to lose everything I own, possibly more.

'Give me your papers', says one of the big guys.

'Yeah, sure, but why do you want to see my passport?' I smile, as I give them what they want. I ask straight out, 'Who are you?'

You've got to play it cool, you can't show your fear; these people will feed on that. Forget any idea about getting upset and shouting about your rights or how you're going to contact the police; don't even say 'no'. These two hard men are intent on maintaining their gangster-style image and want respect and fear. Keep it friendly, cool, but do as they say.

'We're United Self Defence.' (AUC)

I quickly flick my eyes around the group, attempting to read each face in turn. Is this a bluff, are these people FARC testing my reaction? There is nothing in their eyes that leads me to believe they are anybody but who they say they are, no anticipation of my possible answer on the faces of the teenagers. Given the area we're in, they probably are AUC and I have to go with that.

'Well, thank God for that, fellas. For a moment I though you might have been the FARC and I really don't want to meet them. But you fellas, that's cool with me. Rather you than them. The guerrillas are a big problem for you, and for me – in fact, for everyone – and if you are here, then they are not! So I'm pleased to meet you.'

'My name's Karl', I continue, offering my hand. They still refrain from smiling but take my hand and shake it (there you go, now we're getting somewhere). Then there's a series of questions. From where? And why? Also, why am I dressed like that? I give it to them as it is and quickly show them the newspaper cuttings to back up my claim. One of them sits down with me to look over the papers and the teenagers gather around. The other mobster is keen to show his revolver tucked between his belt and the rolls of fat (bet I could get to you before you got that out!). The atmosphere changes, it is working. They are impressed and the conversation changes from an interrogation to aspects of the expedition. However, I think I'm still about to lose when they insist on seeing what money I have. I drag out all I have in my pockets with a great flourish, and place it on the table. Naturally the majority is hidden elsewhere.

'That all you have?'

'Yep! Why would I need more? All I need is enough for food for (I glance down at what I have on the table), oh, say four days more, and after that I'll be in the jungle; you see, I have food for that in my rucksack. Once in Panama I'll be able pick up some more money.'

'Only four days?'

'Yeah, sure. Look, it's taken me only four days from Medellin to get to here; four more and I'll be off the road at this point.' It looks right on the map and these country bumpkins buy it. The young apprentices are very interested in the newspaper clippings. A few more jokes and the two big men begin to drop their gangster act, starting to smile and nod their heads in agreement. They open up the shutters (Christ, that feels good) and I'm allowed to keep everything. We talk briefly about the towns ahead and who runs what. It's at this point that the owner brings my Coke over – he obviously didn't see any point in opening the bottle before now. My companions don't seem to want to answer too many questions so I let it be. I drink up, wish them well with the fight ('Keep up the good work!') and set off out of the store. Almost forgetting to pay for the Coke, I turn.

'No! No problem, it's on us.'

'Awww, you guys!' (Pigeons!)

I set off at a fair pace. I have to find somewhere to sleep pretty quickly as it's getting late. Well, I guess that last incident confirms it: I'm inside the hot spot.

———

Five years and 9,500 miles later, Karl makes his way around the coast of Alaska towards the point where he will make his attempt on the Bering Straits, Cape Prince of Wales. There are three 'gaps' on the footpath home, all of which will have to be crossed in their own special way. These are the Darien Gap, the Bering Straits and the English Channel Tunnel. Without doubt, the most dangerous of these is the Bering Straits. Ice from the Arctic Ocean flowing south towards the Bering Sea is forced through the shallow 56-mile wide gap between the USA and Russia, turning it into a churning mass that can pile broken ice 20ft high or grind it to the consistency of a semifrozen soup. Leads of open water constantly open and close as the ice moves south and then northwards again, sometimes faster than a person can walk. It is never still, never fully frozen and a straight route is never possible. You don't walk across the Bering Straits, you crawl, climb, walk and swim. Many try, most fail. For Karl there is no choice. He must make it across to be able to continue the expedition and his walk home.

———

Monday, 2 January 2006

This morning things don't look much better, but at least the wind has slowed a little. It's a cloudy, dull day and there are no signs of a trail, just flat, bleak, windswept Arctic tundra. I decide to give up the search for any snowmobile trails and bite the bullet. I am going to have to break a trail to Koyuk, north across Norton Bay. No big deal to navigate, just a bitch to do in this snow. I left Shaktoolik with only three days' worth of food and fuel so I'm in no mood for time-wasting and need to get on the move. Standing still I'm just burning up calories. I turn north and go for it. As I can travel in a straight line to Koyuk this route could save me some time. I'm not sure just what the condition of the ice is, though, and have had varying reports.

Going is slow, hard work, the snow inconsistent, soft in one spot, hard in another, with frozen bars of spindrift making the surface uneven. The light creates a shadowless, featureless image so that it's hard to see texture on the ground, making it easy to miscalculate your step. The way ahead looks like a flat white sheet of paper but in fact is nothing like it. I become frustrated by my pace, yet as the sun disappears the surface beneath my feet suddenly changes; it's smoother and easier to travel on. I'm walking using my head lamp again and can now make out the lights of Koyuk some 20 miles north. Before seeing this light I had been navigating by the bars of spindrift snow that formed solid strips across my path, like clock hands at one o'clock. But now I'm walking not on snow but on smooth ice. Wow! It has never been this good. I'm overjoyed, singing along to my MP3 tunes, which I can just hear over the roaring winds. Somewhere though, in the back of my mind, alarm bells ring. If it's too good to be true, it probably is! I become somewhat nervous as the ice becomes reflective. The sky has cleared and the new moon is up. Looking back I can see its reflection, as though on water, beautiful, yet menacing. But ahead are the lights of Koyuk, ever beckoning the moth to the flame. I'm hoping that the surface continues like this but I cannot see that far ahead of me, the limited beam from my head lamp giving me just a few feet of visibility. The light from the moon is not strong enough to aid me. The surface feels solid beneath my feet so on I go.

I suddenly feel the ice flex beneath me. I step back, but it is already too late. I'm going through. I manage half a turn to my left then crash into the water to the top of my legs. I scramble back towards the sled but the ice gives way again and this time I'm in up to my chest. I don't know how but, like a cat out of hot oil, I just seem to leap out of the hole. As I rise to my feet my right leg punches through the ice again and by now cold water is hitting my skin. It has taken a number of seconds for the water to get through the layers of clothing. I crawl a short distance then pull the sled back about 50ft. Quickly, without even really thinking about it, I begin unpacking the tent, my hands already painfully cold as the wind bites hard. Luckily there are no delays in erecting the tent and I rapidly get my stuff inside. I fix the stove together and try to light it, but something is wrong: the flame is not what it should be. I give the fuel bottle a few more pumps but there's nothing more, yet I can smell its strong odour. A quick examination detects fuel jetting out of a broken seal and forming a pool on the bottom of my tent. I look at the flame now, wide eyed, expecting an all-consuming fireball in the next breath – nothing! I blow on the small flame to extinguish it, but it remains lit. I blow again with this same result, a sense of panic gripping me as I realise that this potential disaster could ignite at any second. The flame goes out! I'm shaking, but I don't know whether it's from the cold or the fear. I quickly mop up the spilt fuel and switch over the bottles, my hands fumbling as I struggle for any sensation. Finally a flame roars as the stove comes alive. I whip off my wet and freezing clothing, dry off, don my dry clothes and get into the sleeping bag. However, the night is far from over. I now have to dry what I can – certainly my jacket, gloves and outer wind-proof jacket. I have spare socks, trousers and base layers. I had been wearing my ski boots so they are out of the picture but I have my bunny boots.

Once the immediate problems are sorted out I begin to think about the next couple of days. Should I call someone? What numbers do I have? Looking through my long list of contact numbers, I realise to my disbelief that I do not have one emergency number. How could I have overlooked this point? I set up the sat phone with the intention of calling Ramey, a friend in Fairbanks, and requesting the numbers of emergency services for this area, but I get the engaged signal. I ring back in half an hour, same deal. Same problem an hour later. Unfortunately, this is something I must sort out here and now. I contact Catty in Colombia, who then sends an email to Ramey, spurring him into action, and at last I have the vital numbers.

Now fully armed with these, I decide to relax if I can and get some sleep. Wondering how thin the ice I'm sleeping on is makes me extremely nervous. There's an image in my head of all those Alaskan crabs down in the inky black sea right below my sleeping bag. If my tent goes through the ice, I've had it. It would be a miracle if I even had a chance to get out of my sleeping bag, never mind the tent. Needless to say, I sleep little, sitting bolt upright when I hear something or feel the ice move below me. Every now and then it moves in a wavelike motion under the tent, as though I'm on a waterbed.

Tuesday, 3 January 2006

As soon as there's some light I open up the tent and look around. Mother of God! I climb out and tiptoe around like you would on glass. This ice is thin, new ice that's recently formed. Sea ice is different from its freshwater counterpart in that it's very flexible and spongy. It initially forms in small platelets that freeze together then form large plates and then pans. Where I'm standing, the platelets that form this pan are clearly in view. In some places I can see the sea below me. This is really quite freaky! I pack and slowly start moving south, back the way I came. I'd woken to find the tent was only 10ft from open water. As I tentatively walk, waves on the sea ripple the ice under my feet, stopping me in my tracks, not daring to breathe. After about 100ft I can see that the route I took onto the ice is now just open water. There's also open water to my rear and left. To my right is the open sea – just how the fuck did I manage to get out here? As I look at these open areas in disbelief, two seals pop their heads out and stare at me. Oh, you've got to be joking, this is just too much! The pan that I'm on seems to be connected to the main pack ice in three places and between them is open water. I very carefully try to make my way off the pan using one of the 'bridges' but none of these areas can take my weight and I have to leap back when I feel the ice give. There's no doubt about it, I'm marooned, trapped for the time being. I stand for a while, thinking. Koyuk is still 18 miles away across the bay, while the nearest patch of coastline is nine miles. My options seem somewhat limited. If I make a mistake now, I'm straight into a whole world of crap.

Where's all the dry suits and specialist equipment now, then? The Kokatat suits have gone back for repair and my original dry suits have been sent on to Cape Prince of Wales. I'd intended to do this leg of the journey travelling light and fast, emulating those endurance racers who followed the Iditerod Race trail last winter. They crossed over this bay, but that was in February or March. I guess the ice must have been a lot thicker then.

The wind continues to blow strong and cold. The seals pop up again at another point. Loath as I am to do it, I will have to call time on this one. I don't know where this ice is going to wind up. I set up the sat phone and speak to the lady controller in Nome. She says that there are no troopers available and could I call back in 15 minutes. So I do; still no troopers. Half an hour later another call gets me an answering machine. I now try contacting a different station and have better luck, getting passed straight to a state trooper. I explain the situation, stressing the fact that it's not an emergency but I'm definitely in a pickle and someone should know about it. The trooper seems to agree, then asks if I feel I need assistance. I take a deep breath, hating to do this, but then say, 'Yes'. Let's get this over with. The trooper then has to go through the correct channels to more officers in Nome and I can phone back periodically to see how things are shaping up. It's all taking a bit of time but I have stressed that I'm OK and there is no immediate emergency. An hour or so later a light aircraft flies in from the Koyuk direction, does a couple of low circles around me, then leaves. I contact the Nome station but they don't know who this was. Apparently they are sending a helicopter. I just stand around now, very frustrated, more than a little cold, cursing at the seals.

Suddenly I hear loud pops then a rhythmic hissing coming from the southeastern corner of my pan. I move slowly in that direction and see that the pan I'm on is being forced into, then under, the main ice pack. The new ice in that area is being forced into the air in huge wet slabs, folding over then breaking off in large sections. I'm watching a pressure ridge form right in front of me. This is absolutely awesome to see and the noise is nothing short of crazy. Sometimes it howls like a pack of dogs, then it's a high-pitch scream. It hisses like a boiling kettle to the accompaniment of grinding giant gears. I become even more interested when it rapidly occurs to me that the colliding ice is creating a possible escape route. I can see my pan moving under the new ice like a large white sheet and not far beyond that there's more stable-looking stuff – if things just keep moving! I put a call into the state troopers explaining that Mother Nature herself may have got me out of the situation, but he says that the helicopter has been tasked and will have left Nome already to be with me within the hour. There will also be snow machines coming out from Koyuk and Shaktoolik. Bugger. My luck holds and for the next 15 minutes I slowly inch my way over the binding ice, then ease myself on to the main pack ice. Eventually I manoeuvre onto safer ice and into a field of massive pressure ridges. I now move as quickly as I can to the south and then east towards the shoreline. Before too long a plane appears overhead and begins circling again. By now I'm out of the pressure ridge field, onto old snow-covered ice and can see the lights of the snow machines racing towards me. The locals seem happy that I've made it out and I explain what has happened, before apologising for dragging their arses out there. However, they appear none too perturbed, light up some cigarettes and chatter on about the ice. From out of the west comes a chopper, which puts down next to our group. Again I explain to the crew what happened but, like the others, they seem quite happy, saying they don't see what else I could do. One says, 'Hey, that's why we carry sat phones, to make sure we can pull ourselves out of situations like this.' They then head off home.

I now follow the snowmobile trails northeast towards Koyuk and it's quite late when I finally manage to find the main trail, which runs north–south. Hell, it's a real good one and I'm over the moon. On this trail I move well and put some distance in. It had been a real pain pushing through deep snow in just my bunny boots for a number of hours to get to this point, so I push on as quickly as possible to try and make up for lost time. I eventually get too tired to carry on and call it a night. When I check my GPS I'm surprised to find just how close I actually am to the place I had fallen in. I'm about three miles north and one mile east. During the night the wind drops and snow begins to fall. 'Christ!' I think, 'there goes the trail!'

KARL BUSHBY

Karl Bushby, a former paratrooper in his late 30s, is attempting to become the first person to complete an unbroken path from the tip of South America back to his home, Hull in the UK. At the time of publication he was roughly halfway along that path, having succeeded in crossing the Bering Straits between Alaska and Siberia. It is possible that he could complete the journey by 2012. His book, *Giant Steps*, offers further insight into this great adventure.

BANJUL OR BUST

Tony Wheeler

The wheels spin and we're going nowhere. We're stuck.

In the sand.

In the Sahara Desert.

Again.

Up in front Ian and Dan have successfully steered their pretty little Renault 4 onto harder ground and are already trudging back to us with the sand ladders. Maureen and I wearily clamber out of our increasingly sorry-looking Mitsubishi and start to dig the sand out from under the front wheels.

We've driven down through Europe, taken the ferry across to Morocco, headed south via Casablanca and inland to Marrakesh. Then we've crossed the Atlas Mountains and made our way back to the coast. We've travelled through the Western Sahara region and crossed the border into Mauritania. We're on our way to Dakar, but this is definitely not the Paris–Dakar Rally. That costs a squillion dollars, involves travelling at warp speed or beyond and tends to leave a trail of death and destruction in its wake.

The Plymouth–Banjul Rally is nothing like that. As the name indicates, it doesn't commence in Paris, but then nor does it begin in Plymouth (the English port best known as the place where Sir Francis Drake reluctantly finished his game of bowls before heading off to sink the Spanish Armada). The rules are very loose: you can pretty much choose your starting point, although it officially kicks off in London's Hyde Park.

It doesn't end in Dakar either; it continues one country further south to conclude in Banjul, the capital of Gambia. And it very definitely doesn't cost anywhere near a squillion dollars. The rules (although the rulebook admits rules are only there to be broken) stipulate the target cost for the ideal Plymouth–Banjul vehicle is £100.

Shamefacedly I have to admit I broke that very first rule. I splashed out all of £300 on our baby-blue 1988 Mitsubishi Colt. Maureen and I arrived in London on a chilly Sunday in late January. The next day we handed over the cash and drove off, discovering a few miles down the road that there were not just four but five gears! The next morning, in daylight, we also found out that there was a spare wheel. Not that it would have done us much good: there was no jack.

A few days later, with our sleeping bags, tent, a small collection of spare parts and some large rolls of duct tape stuffed in the back, we turn up at the official starting line (the Serpentine Car Park in Hyde Park) at the official starting time (11am). Nobody else does. Through south London we pass so many African hairdressers, African restaurants and African phonecard shops that it scarcely seems necessary to drive to Africa.

That night, in heavy rain on an autoroute in France, the wipers aren't working very well but, apart from such minor inconveniences, we are beginning to respect our 'trusty' little Mitsu. It starts, it stops, it cruises comfortably; who knows, it might cover 8000 more kilometres and get us to the finish. Dinner that night proves, once again, that the French can certainly do bad food when they put their minds to it. And not very good wine either.

Day two drags on and on. A couple of other cars heading towards Banjul pass us on the autoroute, going way faster than we can manage and looking far more serious, right up to the heavily loaded roof racks. We cross into Spain, climbing so high into the mountains we're above the snowline for a spell, then stumble into Vitoria and chance upon a very nice hotel with a car park, a bar, and a reasonably priced restaurant that throws in a nice bottle of red with dinner at no extra cost. This starts to look like much more fun.

More drive, drive, drive takes us via Madrid, Granada and Malaga to the Mediterranean coast. The Spanish drive fast: sitting on the speed limit means we're firmly relegated to the slow lane while everything else whistles past. Tarifa, just beyond Gibraltar, is the first meeting place and there are lots of cars around the hotel, some of them worse-looking than ours, some of them much better; the entrants are already sinking cold *cervezas*. I like the French-blue Renault 4 and the bright yellow American school bus – although the Americans are having tyre trouble and plan to depart tomorrow morning to look for fresh rubber in Fez. The Renault-4 owners deal in old clocks and barometers.

Africa is a stone's throw away across the Straits of Gibraltar, clearly visible from the hilltop near our hotel. Other entrants drift in, including 'Short & Sweet', which is down as a Lamborghini on the entry list. The reality is that this all-girl team bought their battered Alfa 33 in France on Saturday. I cannot think of a less suitable car to drive to Africa. With spraycans of black, silver and gold they've done a dramatic repaint and used that all-purpose duct tape for a major improvement: attaching their iPod to the dashboard. Two young guys are 'already on our second car': their Chevy Blazer suffered a fatal transmission haemorrhage, so they parked it by the roadside in France, bought a Renault 21 and carried on.

Then there's the VW Beetle, which has already had four breakdowns en route, all handled with amazing ease. One of them took place right outside a classic car outlet in Le Mans. A mechanic emerged, diagnosed the fault, helped them push the Beetle off the road and into the showroom amid the Ferraris and Jaguars, drove back to his home to get the parts (he had a Beetle too) and fixed it for nothing. And there are two 18-year-olds in a Volvo station wagon: their parents had planned to do the trip but couldn't come at the last minute and sent the kids instead.

Next morning the high-speed ferry whisks us across to Africa where we sit for several hours while Moroccan customs do nothing at all except extract piddling amounts of baksheesh. I'm sweating on our trusty Mitsubishi's somewhat dodgy documentation. The previous owner was German and all I seem to have from her is a photocopied form that I can't read – nor can the Moroccan customs officials, who eventually wave us on our way.

We plan to stay in Rabat at the same hotel we'd used on a previous visit to Morocco, but can we find it? Eventually we recruit a taxi driver to lead us there, which he does with great efficiency and at moderate cost. Maureen is seething at my incompetence; I seethe too when I discover I already had the hotel waymarked on my GPS, but a fine meal – the best of the whole trip, it will turn out – and a nice bottle of Moroccan Syrah (Shiraz) make things look much better.

The next couple of nights we spend in Marrakesh, where finding our hotel, a charming old traditional courtyard *riad*, is difficult, but driving to it in the convoluted streets of the medina is even more of a challenge. Still, the staff are friendly, even if the place is overrun by a caterwauling horde of stray cats. Remarkably we don't bump into any of our fellow competitors during our Marrakesh interlude, not even in the evening while we're wandering among the food stalls and snake charmers in the Djemaa el-Fna, the city's great square.

Departing Marrakesh we find ourselves on the Atlas Mountain road to the coast, rather than the fast highway. This is a good, if accidental, choice as it's a beautiful, winding, mountainous route which reaches the snowline in a couple of places. The highpoint is marked by a small café, where we find a couple of fellow contestants already dining. We join them for excellent saffron-flavoured Berber omelettes with tasty tomato salad and bread. Before we depart, more teams turn up, the first we've seen since leaving the ferry arrival area in Tangier.

Agadir provides us with our first malfunction, a flat tyre, which is repaired speedily, efficiently and cheaply in a very modern tyre dealership. Then it's south through Tiznit, an interesting-looking walled town where I kind of wish we'd stayed the previous night, and on to Tan Tan, where we briefly see a couple of other competitors. For much of the way we're running close to the coast with a steep cliff falling into the sea or down to the beach, where we see abandoned ships. Where the cliff plunges straight into the sea, there are often fishermen's shacks and guys sitting on the cliff edge with fishing poles. The final stop for the day is Tarfaya, where Antoine de Saint-Exupéry was based at one time. There's a sign at the entrance to the messy little town proclaiming the existence of an Exupéry museum, but we can't find it.

The next morning, in exiting La'youn, we're stopped for speeding before we're even out of the town. Morocco seems to have an enormous number of radar speed traps so we have been crawling cautiously along the four-lane road on the outskirts of town. Not cautiously enough, but (after boring them to death with your bad French', according to Maureen) the cops let us off with an instruction to drive *doucement*. The 'Barbados Beach Boys' in their Citroën 2CV got gonged coming in to town last night and paid up.

A kilometre down the road there's another police halt where, for the first time, we're asked for a *fiche*. This document is a sort of personal info-sheet with passport details, car details, home address, photograph and so on. Wisely we've printed off 30 copies each, as recommended by the organisers, to avoid wasting time filling in the details by hand. By the end of the day we've got through a few more *fiches* with other police stopping us for a chat and enquiries about our occupations, where we're going, where we're from or simply how we're feeling.

Dakhla is the last stop before Mauritania and the second gathering place for Plymouth–Banjul teams. We're supposed to join forces here with other competitors and, once we cross into Mauritania, recruit a local guide to steer us across the sandy stretch of the Sahara. We team up with the clockmakers in their Renault 4 (team '2 in a 4'), Alan and Graham (the 'Old Gits') in their bright yellow Nissan Sunny and two ex-RAF guys (the 'Red Barrows') in a very flashy looking Volvo station wagon. They bought that for £100? More teams roll in. The 'Short & Sweet' girls in their unsuitable Alfa are still going strong, but the Renault 21 of the 'Bedup Boys' looks even more disreputable: it now has a wooden front passenger-side window. The 'Penitent Yanks' in their big yellow school bus are towed in: the bus is dead.

From Dakhla there's a dull stretch of desert to the border and the instant we leave Morocco the road disappears. For about four kilometres we bounce along indistinct paths through the desert, passing unfenced compounds of – seized? dumped? – cars, many of them looking in great nick, before arriving at the shambolic Mauritanian border buildings. If you wanted to convince new arrivals that this was a country on its last legs, these shanty-town border offices would do the trick. We're stamped, listed, noted, visaed, paid and soon on our way into town.

'This is completely unnecessary', Maureen complains, quite accurately, an hour or two into the desert the next morning. And she's quite right, a couple of years ago the only way to get the 500 kilometres from Nouadhibou to Nouakchott (other than by the ore train) was by crossing the desert and then driving down the beach. Now there's a smooth modern road. But some of us are still going to try the old route.

'And beat the hell out of the cars, en route', Maureen continues.

Well, yes.

After a look at the shipwrecked fleet in Nouadhibou's harbour, we drive 173 kilometres down the modern road, before stopping to drop the tyre pressures by 50% and turn sharp right into the desert. Where I soon get stuck in the sand. And again. This is getting embarrassing, but fortunately the others get stuck as well and I soon master the technique of shimmying across the soft sand, foot flat to the floor and not slowing down or shifting up or down, no matter what.

'We could be getting this car to the end in as good a shape as when we got it', Maureen says. 'Look at it now.' Both front wings have bends in them where stout bottoms pushed against them as we tipped the car sideways to get more sand under the wheels.

'Gas, gas, gas', is the usual instruction from Achmed, our guide, as we approach each stretch of deep sand. That night we camp by the trail, after more stops and one point when we and the Renault boys lost sight of the other two cars and headed off in the wrong direction. 'I opened the door and the sea came in', Alan reports.

The next day we reach the beach and skitter down it for 100 kilometres or so, often driving through the incoming water. Periodically flocks of seabirds at the water's edge scatter before our approach. There's a two-hour pause at the national park entry point, waiting for the tide to change. Then, another 30 kilometres down the beach, our route is blocked by a rocky promontory running out into the sea, the waves break against it. Should we wait for the tide to go out further?

'No, this is as good as it gets. You must drive into the sea, steer tightly around the promontory and emerge onto the beach on the other side', Achmed insists.

Graham immediately drives in and strands the Nissan on a rock. Alan emerges soaking wet and we all rush in to help. The Nissan feels afloat, but amazingly the diesel engine keeps running.

Having seen how not to do it, the rest of us get through unscathed. The technique is to wait for the sea to roll back and then rush it, making a tight turn right after the promontory. We emerge from the beach back onto the road, pump up tyres and cruise into Nouakchott,

Mauritania's capital. A local park turns out to be the car-washing centre of town and two guys cheerfully attack my car with buckets of soapy water and an assortment of brushes to get rid of the sand and salt water.

Crossing the border into Senegal is one of those experiences that leaves a bad taste in the mouth about how things work in Africa, the pervasive corruption (what we encounter here is all low-level stuff, but no doubt it goes right to the top) and sense of being owed: '*cadeaux, cadeaux, cadeaux*' – 'gimme, gimme, gimme' – all the time. We have to make nine payouts in the few kilometres between one side of the border and the other and have already undergone plenty of police checks before we even get to the border. On the outskirts of Nouakchott at the first police checkpoint of the day, it's: 'passport' – check; 'local insurance' – check; 'import document' – check; 'driver's licence' – check; 'transit tax permit' – now what's that?

'Oh, you don't have that? Didn't you pay for it in Nouadhibou?'

Well hardly, since it doesn't exist.

'So you will have to pay a fine.'

No we won't.

'Well then, you will have to go back to Nouadhibou.'

More talk, more waiting and eventually perhaps the fine can become a little gift. A tin of tuna does the job.

The Zebrabar camp that night is a delight: cold beers and food arrive immediately, we set up the tent and crash. Next day the Swiss guy who owns the camp takes Dan and me into town. En route there are lots of wild and exuberant political rallies for the upcoming election; the Senegalese seem a pretty excitable bunch. The town of St Louis is connected to the mainland by a Gustav Eiffel bridge (not as well known as his signature tower in Paris).

I hang around to check emails in an internet café and, riding back to the campsite in a bush taxi, get tangled up in another demonstration. This time there are people all over the car and somebody tries to grab my cap off my head. I manage to snatch it back, but then I get the feeling my glasses are also about to be grabbed so I take them off. Demos can always turn sour and the standard advice is not to be the odd one out. Well, I'm certainly the odd one out here, the one whitey amongst the eight or 10 of us crammed into the taxi – probably the only one among thousands in the whole area – but fortunately this gathering is simply raucous, not sour.

Back at the camp 'Rattle & Hum', a Ford Sierra, is suffering from major structural collapse. This is countered by jacking the two sides of the engine compartment apart from the engine block in the middle and then bolting a bloody great steel bar across the engine compartment from one side to the other. Behind us, one of the entrants, the 'Costa Blanco Dons' in a Jeep Cherokee, have disappeared somewhere in the Sahara. The other cars in their large group have been searching for them for 36 hours.

The next evening there's a sudden rush of arrivals, with the news that the missing twosome have been found stuck in a sand dune by a spotter aircraft commandeered by two other entrants, the 'Norwegian Army' crew. A helicopter was then sent in to pluck them out, although it's said a local car was homing in on the missing vehicle as the helicopter took off. No doubt some Mauritanian will soon have salvage rights on a Jeep Cherokee.

Back on the road we make a midday stop for a quick tour of the mosque at Touba, the biggest one in Senegal and a shrine to Cheikh Amadou Bamba, a Senegalese mystic-cum-independence-fighter. Maureen doesn't come in and, while she's keeping an eye on the cars, a 'guide' comes by, chats her up and comments, 'You must have been really good when you were 20.'

'Hard to tell whether I was being insulted or complimented', Maureen says.

That night strolling down to the riverside pier at Toubakouta, our night stop, we meet a pelican waddling resolutely up the path in the opposite direction. It clacks its bill noisily at us, as if to say, 'Fish, fish? Put it here.'

Unlike the border crossing into Senegal, leaving this country and entering Gambia is easy street. Not for everybody, however: the Gambian immigration shack has a cell with a bunch of unhappy people sitting on the floor.

It's a final potholed slalom to Barra, the famously troublesome ferry crossing to Banjul and, sure enough, the Gambian 'bumsters' are there to hassle us, but they're not any real problem and eventually the lethargically slow and heavily overloaded ferry disgorges us in the centre of Banjul. Soon afterwards we're sinking cold beers at the finish line.

If this was the Paris–Dakar and not the Plymouth–Banjul, the advertising campaigns would be gearing up and the winning cars readied to be flown back to Europe to be displayed at some forthcoming car show. But our 'Banjul or bust' £100 bangers aren't going anywhere. The entry agreement is that we will leave the cars behind: all those that finish are auctioned off and the proceeds are given to local African charities. So a couple of days later we're lined up outside the national stadium to see the finishers go under the auctioneer's hammer. There's lots of interest in the little Renault. Bystanders come over to reminisce about a Renault 4 being the first car they owned, or the car they learnt to drive in. It's clearly the most loved car in the rally. When the hammer comes down, the trusty Mitsu fetches 36,000 dalasi, almost precisely twice what we paid for it back in England. The Renault gets exactly the same amount, but the New Zealand couple's diesel Mercedes, clearly destined to live out its life as an African taxi, is the day's prize, fetching 82,000.

'Thank God that's the last time we have to talk cars', Maureen announces as a taxi takes us back to the hotel. I'll second that thought.

TONY WHEELER

It was another lengthy drive in an elderly car – London to Kabul in Afghanistan – that led to the very first Lonely Planet guidebook. *Across Asia on the Cheap* told the story of that 1972 overland trip, although on that occasion Tony and Maureen kept the cash when they sold the car.

ON THE COAT-TAILS OF TWAIN: FROM CONSTANTINOPLE TO CAIRO

Amelia Thomas

'This book,' said Mark Twain in 1869 in *The Innocents Abroad*, 'is a record of a pleasure trip.' Twain had embarked on a journey from New York to the Holy Land and Egypt, taking in en route the sights, sounds and smells of the Azores, Italy, Spain, France and the Crimea by steamship. The principal part of his journey, however, was the overland route of the already long-established Victorian 'Grand Tour', between Constantinople and Cairo, which included some of the Middle East's most spectacular ancient wonders. His travels would take him through what was then the Ottoman Empire, Greater Syria and Palestine, and today comprises Turkey, Lebanon, Syria, Jordan and Israel. This, minus Twain's luxury steamship detour to Cyprus and the Greek Islands, would be our route too.

'We left a dozen passengers in Constantinople, and sailed through the beautiful Bosporus and far up into the Black Sea', he reflected on embarking for Sebastopol. 'We're not going to make it', I gasped on arriving at the vast, seething Haydarpaşa railway station with just seconds to find platform three for Syria.

The city, up to this point, had been – unlike Twain's own miserable experiences with rabid dogs, swindlers and Turkish baths – highly pleasurable: a few days exploring junk shops in dim cobbled alleyways; eating by day in neon-lit *lokantas* with moustachioed, munching men and drinking by night with the bright young things flitting through the bars around Beyoğlu; a walk beside the Sea of Marmara, watching dolphins playing in the bay; warm beer and banana splits with backpackers at the cheap bars jostling along Sultanahmet's wooden, crooked streets; a trip to the Grand Bazaar, counting the amount of appalling pitches from its salesmen. 'Please don't walk by – you break my heart!'; 'I wish I were a fish, so I could swim in your deep blue eyes'; 'Want to buy some things you don't need today?'; 'First, buy a carpet – then, come disco dancing with me for free!'

On Saturday evening, a fortune-telling rabbit beneath the soaring dome of the Aya Sofia twitched its pink nose and plucked an index card from a box of pre-prepared fortunes, to inform me that I had 'a long way to go'. What the rabbit omitted to mention was that our taxi to the Karaköy ferry terminal – whose bobbing bark would take 20 minutes to transport us across to the railway station on the opposite shore of the Marmara Sea – did not; it was stuck in an unexpected Sunday morning traffic snarl on the wrong side of the Golden Horn.

Thanking the taxi driver for his stationary efforts and plying him with a crumple of lira, we grabbed our bags and made a dash for the ferry, sprinting across the Galata Bridge, past pole-fishermen, milling couples and early morning mosque-goers. Half an hour or so later, we had crossed continents, from Europe into Asia, arrived with moments to spare at the grand neo-Renaissance pile that comprises Haydarpaşa Station, and located our cheerful, blue-painted and fortunately delayed sleeping car. A shopping frenzy followed: the once famed Toros Express comes, these days, without the velvet-and-aspidistra-decked dining car of its former years. We bought bananas, biscuits, sandwiches – and a decent number of Efes beers for recovery's sake. And then we were away, pulling out on the twice-weekly train that would whisk us from cosmopolitan, Starbucks-heavy Istanbul, across 1300 kilometres of barren hinterland to Aleppo, in Syria.

New, hurriedly built Istanbul suburbs quickly swept by, giving way to patchy Turkish countryside and the glinting Bosporus, punctuated by motionless oil tankers and the odd solitary speedboat. Our two-berth cabin was German built and suitably efficient, equipped with bunk beds, pillows, sink and coat hooks. Every half hour or so, a sprightly Syrian attendant rapped on the cabin door to ply us with hot, sweet tea; by noon, a long liquid breakfast of tea and beer had soothed us into a contented state of pleasant inertia.

The afternoon rose and waned. The train climbed through ravine and valley, all arid beige and greys with a sluggish brown river progressing along its bottom. We snacked on *pide* sandwiches filled with boiled eggs and olives; exchanged pleasantries with a middle-aged couple – Ron and Sandy from Minnesota – on their way to visit their daughter at a language school in Damascus; and shared peanuts with a blond Norwegian who was planning to travel on from Syria to Afghanistan – where, he had heard from a boy at a hostel in Zagreb, the action was really to be had these days.

By dusk, the train was chugging along a barren mountain plateau; by night, it had reached Konya. Our American next-door neighbours cracked open bottles of fiery aniseed raki and invited us to join them. We brought halva and *lokum* (Turkish delight); the Norwegian contributed long, salty fronds of sheep's cheese and a net of tangerines. Outside, the darkness rolled comfortably on.

It was late morning when the train slowed toward the border. Freshly washed at the diminutive cabin basin, we descended from the train at Islahiya, blinking in the hot, dusty daylight. Here, the border was everything a border should be: bleak, inefficient; filled with bored, displeased military men, lolling barbed wire and ragged cats. Passports were begrudgingly taken away and returned, some time later, with cryptic combinations of rubber-stamped ink and irritable handwritten scribbles. Weary from the wait, the passengers re-embarked and we rolled slowly across the frontier. Soldiers, armed with machine guns older than themselves, eyed us from their positions. Minutes later, the passport process was to be repeated at Meydan Ekbez, on Syrian soil. Officials were far friendlier, though the service was equally slow, and they grinned and waved outside the window as the train finally pulled out on its way.

Whatever railway timetables might optimistically tell you, the Toros Express will never – and never did – arrive at Aleppo on Monday afternoon at precisely 14.17. Another, hungrier afternoon came and went, with only butter biscuits dipped in the same sweet tea for sustenance. The landscape outside was a perpetual Muybridge zoopraxiscope of donkeys, olive groves and mountain scree. Hunger had given way to ravenousness by the time our train pulled into Aleppo after 8pm. A taxi driver with heavy black eyebrows was waiting outside. 'The Baron Hotel, please', I said, clambering into the back seat. He nodded curtly. *'Chokran.'*

Twain did not venture to Aleppo, taking his steamboat direct from Cyprus to Beirut and thence on to Damascus, via mountain passes and spectacular Baalbek. We would be reversing the journey – from Aleppo on to Damascus, with a side trip to Baalbek, Beirut and back. Agatha Christie and Charles Lindbergh, however, made it as far as Aleppo's Baron Hotel, as did Kemal Ataturk and Lawrence of Arabia, who spent the night in rooms 201 and 202 respectively. In room 203, Christie found the inspiration and the writing desk on which to pen *Murder on the Orient Express*. Hercule Poirot himself embarks on his journey from Aleppo's railway platform. And here we, too, would be bedding down for the night, soothed by a hearty dinner, a roaring log fire, friendly attentive staff, and the distant clanks and gurgles of century-old plumbing.

The next morning was Tuesday, giving us two full days to make a lightning-speed round trip of Aleppo, Baalbek, Beirut and then on to Damascus to catch the winsome old Hedjaz Railway service to Amman, capital of Jordan. We rose before dawn, exploring the immense Aleppo citadel, its warren of medieval and Ottoman souks and old, snoozing Christian quarter, before boarding the morning bus from the grimy Hanano Garage to Tripoli in Lebanon. Five hours later, in busy, workaday Tripoli, we negotiated an old Mercedes taxi to take us along the rim of the green Qadisha Valley, filled with waterfalls and ancient rock-cut monasteries, then up over the spectacular Mt Lebanon range.

The taxi wheezed, croaked and spluttered, but the landscape outside was silent, rising from precipice to barren mountain peak and back down to neat, pastoral plateau. Night drew in as we descended into the darkening heartland of the fertile Beqaa Valley. Once 'Rome's breadbasket', the Beqaa was now home to the Hezbollah party and surreptitious fields of cannabis, to some of the most wondrous monuments of the ancient world, and to a second of the Middle East's historic old hotel gems. 'At eleven o'clock, our eyes fell upon the walls and columns of Baalbec,' said Mark Twain, 'a noble ruin whose history is a sealed book'. We, too, reached the town at 11 but, in our case, at night.

We checked in to the deserted, redolent old Palmyra Hotel, a dim rabbit warren filled with Bakelite telephones, vintage safes and antique marble busts, all dulled by the veneer of several decades of dust. There, we slept with the ghosts of Jean Cocteau, whose fluent sketches adorned the walls, and Charles de Gaulle, who once stayed in the same high-ceilinged, chilly suite, beneath whose counterpane we rustled crisps and swigged miniature whiskies spirited up from the empty hotel bar.

Wednesday morning awoke warm and sunny. Yellow Hezbollah flags fluttered in quiet streets, though there were neither masked men nor Kalashnikovs in sight. A woman in tight jeans emerged from a lingerie shop to swab down the pavement with a mop and bucket. Another bustled past in a full burka, a narrow mesh slit shielding her eyes, dragging behind her two little girls in frothy pink dresses and bobbing ponytails.

In Twain's time, little was known about the origins of Baalbek's great ruins, known variously through history as Heliopolis and Sun City. Today, they are thought to be a combination of Phoenician, Ancient Greek and Roman engineering. The massive Temple of Jupiter dates back to around AD 60. Its columns stood graceful and stolid, as warm morning light played on carved capitals. I thumbed my copy of *The Innocents Abroad*, gazing up where Twain did, noting masonry collapsed in earthquakes since his visit. 'A race of gods or of giants must have inhabited Baalbec many a century ago', he concluded. 'Men like the men of our day could hardly rear such temples as these.' I glanced at the dreary upstart hotels lining the opposite side of the road out of town. He would be satisfied to see his point proven.

A quarter of a mile away downhill, Twain continued, was the quarry from which the stones – many bigger than London buses – had been cut and hauled to make the immense temples' foundations. I gazed at my more contemporary guidebook, trying to work out in which direction. There was a tap on my shoulder. 'Hello,' said a familiar face, 'do you need help?' In Lebanon, unlike many other places to which a traveller might venture, this question is never followed by an invitation to a gem shop, or to see a cousin's carpets. It's always sincere, heartfelt, and the person offering will usually go well out of their way to help you.

'The quarry', I explained, frowning at the map.

'I'm also a tour guide,' said the young man who had checked us into our hotel room late last night, 'I'll take you there'. 'Don't worry,' he winked, 'no charge'.

On the road to the quarry, Charbel Nikola introduced himself properly: a third-generation Baalbek tour guide, and night porter at the Palmyra since the guiding business in Lebanon was, inevitably, quite slow. 'The '90s were the best time for work', he explained, 'The civil war was over and people were curious. Today,' he sighed and shook his head, 'many are again afraid to come here'.

At the quarry's edge, a teenager in jeans and a tight vest sat reading the newspaper. Above him a large, hand-painted sign proudly announced 'The Biggest Stone in the World.' His father Abdul Nabi Al-Afi, he explained, had saved the quarry, which had been used for the last century or so as an unofficial rubbish dump. Single-handedly, the retired army sergeant had hauled away tonnes of rubbish, bit by bit, in wheelbarrows and bags, until the largest cut stone – possibly abandoned by its creators for just this reason – was visible once more. Nowadays, said his son, the immense carved cuboid was known as Hajar al-Hubla, 'stone of the pregnant lady', and women hoping to conceive often climbed to its peak. 'Go on,' he grinned, 'have a go. And take this'. He handed me a folded yellow pennant, bearing Hezbollah's characteristic image of a rifle raised triumphantly in a clenched fist. 'A souvenir.'

Leaving the quarry, we collected our bags and boarded a midmorning minibus. A brief journey followed, up through the Beqaa Valley on one of Lebanon's frantic, anarchically navigated highways, where three lanes frequently become four, six and seven, impeded only by military checkpoints. A white-knuckle 90 minutes later, we reached Beirut.

Beirut today is as much an enigma as a capital city. Pockmarked and pitted, still bearing the scars of a 16-year civil war along with successive skirmishes, attacks and invasions, it's at once cosmopolitan and closeted, a place of $3000 champagne magnums in heady nightclubs and penniless Palestinian refugees immured in outlying camps.

It was lunchtime as we strolled along Rue Hamra with the students of the American University, stopping for cheap shwarma and conveyor-belt sushi, topping it off with an apple-scented nargileh in a smoky café filled with bearded young Che Guevaras. The malls of Verdun, to the south, were full of ladies lunching, their tiny Pomeranians tucked into Valentino handbags. The ragged fishermen on the Corniche rocks were watched by old men mulling over clacking backgammon boards. The city centre, rebuilt since the civil war, was quiet and pristine, a strange open-air museum to a war that, according to its gleaming reproduction architecture, had never even happened.

We shopped for clothes and magazines, browsed in bookshops filled with coffee-table tomes depicting the horrors of death in the streets outside the window, then boarded the last bus at 8pm, back on the road to Damascus. 'Properly, with the sorry relics we bestrode,' Twain complained, 'it was a three days' journey to Damascus'. We would, border officials and maniacal drivers permitting, be there before midnight.

The Hedjaz Railway train pulled out from the ancient narrow-gauge line of Damascus's Kadem station promptly at eight o'clock on Thursday morning. Despite having tickets in hand, a six-seat berth to ourselves and a guard reassuring us the train would indeed be running, it wasn't until I heard the groan of old wheels grinding against tracks that I absolutely believed it would. The passenger carriage, built in turn-of-the-century Nuremberg, was almost entirely empty. 'No photo', shouted the guard merrily as we pulled away, 'Soldiers – big guns!' This, it seems, has always been the case on the Hedjaz line, built by the Turks in 1908, for a colossal $16 million, to link Damascus with Medina. In 1917 during the Arab Revolt, when the passenger carriage we were now perched inside was merely a few years old, the line was attacked by Lawrence of Arabia (well rested, obviously, after his stay at the Baron Hotel) and, despite valiant restoration attempts for nearly a century, the railway never fully recovered.

Picking up speed to an impressive 50km/h – 'I think I can, I think I can, I think I can' – the train shuddered through desert dotted with military encampments and snipers guarding lonely watchtowers. At Deraa, near the border, we disembarked to exchange Syrian for Jordanian carriages and show our passports. The replacement carriages were wooden and of a similar vintage to their Syrian cousins with a low, un-upholstered bench running along either side. The Jordanian station further on at Mafraq was decorated by cheerful, respectable pictures of the late King Hussein and his dashing son King Abdullah in army dress, regal dress and casual weekend wear. The station officials smiled and saluted as the train pulled out.

By early evening, the Little Train that Just About Could was chugging wearily toward the small, ivy-clad railway station at Amman and we were preparing ourselves for long baths to wash away a dusting of desert and the aches and pains of an afternoon on a bumpy wooden bench. 'The very first thing one feels like doing when he gets into camp all burning up and dusty', agreed Twain, 'is to hunt up a bath'.

For him, though, the Hedjaz would have been the height of luxury. To reach Jerusalem, Twain travelled direct from Syria on horseback along ancient caravan routes across Mt Hermon, while suffering from a mild dose of cholera. Still, he wasn't one to complain. 'I enjoyed myself very well', he said, 'Syrian travel has its interesting features, like travel in any other part of the world, and yet to break your leg or have the cholera adds a welcome variety to it'.

'Welcome variety' – broken bones and diseases aside – does not include several hours' wait at a stiflingly hot border, surrounded by teeming masses lugging their lives' possessions in the largest suitcases known to man. It doesn't involve being interrogated by border staff who weren't yet born when Wham! sang 'Wake Me Up Before You Go Go', or excruciatingly slow taxi drives through rocky scrubland, devoid of any features but the occasional Halal butcher's premises with a worried-looking goat tied up outside. But so it was to be when, the next morning, we left our comfortable hotel in Amman to negotiate the King Hussein bridge from Jordan into Israel and, after hours of pleading that we weren't patsies for the Syrian Secret Services or in the employ of the Ayatollah, we were granted passage into Israel.

It was, in contrast to the mayhem of the border, a serene and contemplative bus journey through the rocky, Bedouin-inhabited hillsides towards Jerusalem. Israel's 'Security Wall' snaked ominously off, in abortive stretches, to one side of the road. Overbearing sandstone blocks of flats, part of the encroaching Jerusalem suburbs, hung over the brow of the hill. The Old City of Jerusalem itself, as the Friday afternoon Shabbat crept in, was golden, magical and silent.

In Twain's time, Jerusalem was a town of just 14,000 people; today, its residents number about 50 times that. Walking the Old City walls, observing its ancient roofscapes, he called it the 'knobbiest town in the world'. Saturday morning was quiet as we wandered the knobby passageways with tall, ancient buildings on either side, past the Church of the Holy Sepulchre and along the Via Dolorosa, where a group of Spanish pilgrims hauled a man-sized wooden crucifix past the Fourteen Stations of the Cross. In the Arab quarter, we stopped at the cavernous Star Café for thick cardamom coffee. Old men looked up from their card games briefly, before continuing in a haze of cigarette smoke. A group of men in knitted yarmulkes strode past, machine guns slung casually over their shoulders. We ate hummus and falafel at a café, watched the bobbing heads at the Western Wall and the prostrate prayers at the adjacent Al Aqsa Mosque.

Later we boarded an afternoon bus filled with weekending teenagers and raucous extended families, which whisked us down alongside the glossy waters of the Dead Sea – depleted by industry, so that 'Beware of Flooding' signs now stood improbably in cracked mud fields – past Masada, where 1000 Jews once took their own lives rather than surrender to the Romans, and on along empty, lamp-lit desert highway, to the seaside playground of Eilat.

Eilat, though situated geographically on the north shore of the Red Sea, lies stylistically somewhere halfway between Blackpool and Reno. As we emerged from a hotel on Sunday morning as Israel's working week commenced, it appeared to consist entirely of shabby shopping malls, appalling public art mounted on traffic roundabouts, rusting casino boats, beachside souvenir vendors and flashy Disneyesque hotels with names like Queen of Sheba and Herod's Palace. We ate, drank, dipped our toes in the Red Sea waters and continued on quickly to the Egyptian border, just a couple of kilometres further down the road.

Our fourth border crossing in just less than a week proved the smoothest of all. The Israelis seemed cheerful to see us go and the Egyptians, with their neat, manicured lawns surrounding the quiet border buildings, equally happy to receive us. Twain completed the journey from Jerusalem to Cairo by boat, via Jaffa and Alexandria; we took a cramped Bedouin taxi – levered in with four Australian backpackers and an intrepid honeymooning couple from Yorkshire – west across the Sinai desert. Osama, our happy driver, was missing a lower front tooth, providing the perfect resting place for his cigarette. 'Look, friends', he turned to the back seat, screeching around a hairpin bend, 'Down there – the Fjord. Is beautiful'. The postcard-perfect bay swept past in a blur of burning rubber.

Cairo lay some six hours' drive across the desert, past numerous military checkpoints where passports had to be collected, taken away, passed around, squinted at, passed around again and then finally handed back. Halfway through the lunar-landscape journey came, to our elation, a solitary outpost containing a petrol station and a bakery. We all bought stale, crumbly biscuits, while Osama filled his tank, then headed on, beneath the Suez Canal, toward the grand and ancient capital of Egypt – as desiccated as our biscuits – where ancient history and French colonial mansions rub shoulders with neon Coca-Cola billboards and monstrous motorway flyovers.

Osama deposited us at the venerable Windsor Hotel to check in, shower and imbibe something strong and refreshing, in equal measure. 'We are stopping at Shepherd's Hotel,' said Twain, 'which is the worst on earth except the one I stopped at once in a small town in the United States'. Shepherd's burnt down in the early years of the 20th century, though its modern luxury namesake stands on the same spot. The Windsor, in contrast, was built in 1901 and has kept the same furniture, menu and staff ever since.

A warm evening breeze, heavy with the scent of cooking and diesel fumes, lilted in through our hotel window as we scrubbed and dressed for a night propping up bars in the chic, well-heeled district of Zamalek on the banks of the Nile. Tomorrow, we would see the pyramids at Giza, the Nilometer, the eternally enigmatic Sphinx and the crowded, bustling streets of Old Cairo, much the same scenes that Mark Twain saw in 1869 and that many generations of travellers have observed both before him and since. From here Twain would head back to Alexandria, and from there across the Levant and Atlantic, home to America. We, in contrast, were continuing south, by wagonslit sleeper train to the Valley of the Kings at Luxor, then on to languid Aswan and the great Lake Nasser where Africa truely began.

We sat back in the Windsor Hotel's plump armchairs, contemplating centuries and continents, and ordered another double measure from the ancient, creaking bartender. He nodded rheumily and wandered out of the bar. The temples of Baalbek, the pyramids of Giza, the Old City of Jerusalem may indeed, as Twain suggested, be wonders as old as time. But the barman at the Windsor, surely a contemporary of old Tom Sawyer himself, was tonight vying valiantly with the Windsor's mattresses, along with the Baron's wallpaper, the Palmyra's bed linen, the Hedjaz railway's upholstery and the Sinai bakery's biscuits, for the joint honour of that title.

AMELIA THOMAS

Amelia Thomas is a writer and journalist working throughout the Middle East. She has written for numerous Lonely Planet titles and has three toddlers and a baby, who all enjoy tagging along on far-flung overland voyages. Her new book, *The Zoo on the Road to Nablus,* tells the true story of the last Palestinian zoo.

INTO THE SAHARA

Anthony Ham

We leave behind the protection of city walls and cast out into the desert. Across a plateau of gently undulating sand, countless tyre tracks lead through thorn bushes and out towards the blue ramparts of the Aïr Mountains. The great caravan town of Agadez recedes behind us. Even so, it remains the dominant presence – goatherds headed for town trail straggling herds in their wake; a truck bound for the city and piled high with people and other cargo stirs up the dust away to the south. Here, in northern Niger, the truck can only have come from the remote salt mines of Bilma and the prospect of reaching Agadez prompts its occupants to burst into song. They are as excited to be reaching civilisation as I am to be leaving it.

At a string of shabby huts of no discernible beauty, the 4WD leaves us to our fate and returns to Agadez, the noise of its engine soon drowned out by the wind. Moussa, my Tuareg guide, is silent, waiting with the patience of ages – for what, I do not yet know – while a small Tuareg girl in ragged clothes and a boy with a distended belly stand alongside, also silent, watching. Beyond the nearby trees, a woman emits a low moan. Discreetly Moussa leaves some tobacco, tea and a few clothes, which he has brought from Agadez. He does it without wanting me to see, but the children's squeals of delight give him away.

Moussa introduces me to Yahhye, a good-looking man who cares for the camels that are being led towards us across the sand. Yahhye has a dark and weathered face, strong forearms, an enchanting smile and eyes that sparkle. All else is concealed beneath grubby grey robes. I like him instantly and am pleased to learn that he will accompany us. It is his wife who lies groaning under a flimsy straw cover strung between the trees. He tells me simply that she is ill. I sense that this modest, dignified man greets his family's difficult life and the arrival of strangers with the same equanimity. He regards the slow approach of the camels with a look of infinite patience.

It is difficult to fathom why anyone would live here, on so wretchedly barren a patch of ground, when the relatively abundant Aïr Mountains are within reach and tracks to Agadez pass close by. When I ask Yahhye – Moussa must interpret, as Yahhye speaks only the Tuareg language, Tamasheq – why he lives here, my question is incomprehensible to him. When he finally answers, it is with polite bewilderment. 'My family has always lived here. I have always lived here.'

In their own good time, our camels arrive. The lead camel, Moussa's, is a sturdy, dignified creature of 35 years who has been to Bilma and beyond – how jealous I am! – plying the salt-caravan route in the proud tradition of its kind. Mine arrives with his long, traipsing stride, grumbling and forbidding with his yellow teeth, hairy ears, green tongue, long luscious eyelashes and poisonous breath. His name is Egidir.

As we set out, sent on our way by the ill omen of a woman's moans of distress, we pass the burnt-out shell of a car to the west of the camp. I ask Moussa whether it is a gutted casualty of the Tuareg rebellion, which pitted well-armed rebel groups against Niger's resentful army, closing off the Aïr from the outside world and transforming the Sahara Desert of northern Niger and Mali into one of the most dangerous places in the world for much of the 1990s. Moussa says nothing for a long time. I wonder if he has heard me. Finally he answers. 'No. Bandits did this. Before, two or three years. Now they are gone.'

I leave Moussa in his impenetrable silence, or rather he leaves me and pushes on. Within minutes, or perhaps it is hours, Yahhye's home has disappeared from view and desolation hangs in the air. We are the only things moving on the arid plain. The loping, rolling gait of the camels can do little to disturb the oppressive stillness that weighs heavily upon me. The horizon, which sharply demarcates the vast hemisphere of sun-muted blue sky from parched earth, could be minutes or a lifetime away. From afar, a rock becomes a small mountain, a stunted shrub a forest, a shimmering plain an abundant lake. In the absence of anything on which to anchor my gaze, meaningless things, like the texture of the tiny pebbles that carpet the desert floor, become important. Fragments of detail – a thorn bush, a camel's two-toed foot, a pile of stones (perhaps a cairn, perhaps a grave) – appear and then wither away in the heat. A wind blows in from the north. Obeisant straw-coloured grasses bow in unison as if to Mecca and small, hissing eddies of sand bring sound and movement to the day. And then the wind continues south, leaving in its wake a terrible emptiness.

At first our camels walked nose to tail in a close party of three. Now we are strung out over perhaps half a kilometre. Moussa rides as the advance party, a smooth oneness of man and beast. In true Tuareg fashion, he has celebrated his return to the desert in silence. Yahhye walks indefatigably in the rear, just behind the slowest camel, ensuring that none stray from the path. From time to time, Moussa waits, calls a question to Yahhye, who pauses then answers with a single 'Hah!' or an 'Aiiyah!' Then we are again overtaken by silence.

The world turns black as we move amid great piles of boulders. Scoured and polished by Saharan winds, these rocks glisten with the patina of the Sahara's epic geological history. Underfoot, jagged shards of stone crack as if they were the brittle carapace of some prehistoric animal. Without warning, a brooding silence again settles upon the land like an aftershock, ringing in our ears a warning not to linger, admonishing our presence with its judgement that humankind does not belong here. A large black bird of prey circles high overhead in ever-widening and ever-higher arcs until I lose sight of it. What can it be searching for here, of all places, in this diabolical land?

Unconcerned, Moussa and Yahhye maintain a slow, almost reassuring rhythm. Both are lost in their thoughts. I envy them their comfort in this world. Yahhye walks past with a jaunty step, stick in hand, cheerful. I find it difficult to remember why I like him.

The beauty of a sand dune, the relief of an oasis, the romance of desert solitude – these are what draw me to the Sahara. But there is none of that here, where it feels like nothing more than a hot, empty place. Despite our imaginings of a beautiful desert, barely one ninth of the Sahara rises as sand dunes, and sand softens just one fifth of the desert's surface. Barren mountain ranges of granite – the Aïr, Acacus, Tassili, Adrar-n-Iforhas, the mighty ranges of Ahaggar and Tibesti – provide aesthetic relief in the deepest Sahara. But gravel plains such as these are its truest terrain. It is the planet stripped bare and reduced to its most dispiriting and hostile form.

After an eternity, we dismount at a grim fellowship of bamboo and straw huts and collapse onto the sand floor of the largest hut, which has been cleared for our arrival. We eat a simple lunch of bread and water and lie in the shade. Conversation is sparse. Scruffy children watch us through the open doorway. They smile easily when we do, but soon disappear to play with sticks in the sand. The older boys examine our camels with sage-like wisdom.

Yahhye and Moussa recline in the corner of a hut with a woman from this village with no name. They discuss the news. From under his robes, Moussa discreetly produces tobacco, some money and tea and passes them to the woman, who conceals these gifts, the conversation unbroken. Moussa and Yahhye have not passed by this way for some weeks. Everyone is pleased to see them.

Slowly the village falls silent. The second meal of the day has passed. The tea has been drunk. Everyone curls up on a mat, some to sleep, others simply to rest. Too tired to sleep, I walk outside and find myself wrapped in blankets of heat and silence. This is the time in the Sahara when nothing moves. We pass the afternoon.

We leave camp when the sun is already low and traverse loose stone and sand for more than an hour, one long rhythmic stride after another as the day eases gently towards the darkness. At first, the sand is deep and soft, then it yields to a thin layer of crusted salt atop hard-baked earth, then smooth pebbles giving birth to a single thorn bush, then smooth pebbles and sand offering up stunted scrub. The shadows begin to lengthen. Moussa scans the horizon, locates a landmark and wheels to the right in a long, slow arc. The camels keep close together, labouring forward with unhurried steps that leave small craters in the sand.

Close to sunset, we climb to a small plateau of boulder upon black boulder. Encircled by these sombre monoliths, there is neither wind nor noise of any kind. An involuntary shiver runs down my spine and a spell of muteness falls upon us all. For the briefest of moments, there is a sense of the unutterable. The desert comes alive or dies – which, I cannot say – and the world is held in abeyance. The terrible silence is a presence, at once claustrophobic and immense, so close, so heavy and so sudden in this primal, venerable cathedral of stones. In the profound stillness, there lurks an ancient dread, from before human beings walked the earth, marking our insignificance with the uneasy awareness that time, unfathomable and deep, has passed. I feel immeasurably older.

We ascend a gentle rise which could be the very rim of the world. Our pace slows from the exertion on strong camel legs, or perhaps it is because the camels, too, have noticed the suspension of time. Nothing is visible save for the azure sky. I hold my breath. A crater comes into view, at once expansive and made intimate by the long, low hills that have encircled it since the volcano wrought its terrible fury upon the land. And then, from this peak of no great significance, I find the village for which I have longed all of my life.

Small gatherings of flaxen huts in fenced compounds, ten or more, inhabit the valley floor. Above them hangs a scarcely perceptible layer of smoke, an incantation cast by a benevolent spirit. The long, hot day has passed into distant memory and the setting sun summons up eternity in its spell, capturing a moment in which all of the world's beauty finds confluence on one small patch of earth. I know this place without ever having been here, I have visited it many times in a lifetime of longing.

The camels falter. A child runs towards us, still far away, and then stops. Yahhye lets out an impatient *'Aiiyah!'* to which Moussa responds *'Agh!'* We drive the camels down into the valley. Moussa rides tall and erect across the plain. He shouts a greeting. The women of Tchin-Taborak shout back.

Alongside a well under the palm trees there is a garden. Paradise, according to the Qur'an, is a garden, and for the first time I understand. Only a religion born in the desert can truly imagine the paradisiacal lure of the oasis standing on the edge of desolation. The neatly planted rows of vegetables are, even at sunset, an incandescent green, a green that I never dreamed I would find in the desert.

A she-camel draws up water from beneath the ground as if ploughing the land. She waits. Water flows from the goat-skin bag into small, mud-walled irrigation channels. She turns around and walks back to the well to allow the bag to be lowered once again into the water. The monotony of the camel's movements, the patience of its carer and the miracle of fresh, clean water coming up from the earth are like a spell of music with the setting of the now-sallow sun.

Small children watch, curious and shy. They remain so until their mothers call to them from across the village. Old Tuareg men come to greet us and our party. They are friendly, softly spoken and gentle. Their greetings are elaborate and deeply ritualised, warming the chill that has descended upon the village. There are as many consecutive handshakes – slipping apart then reuniting – as there are questions. How are you? Are you well? And your wife? And your children? The baby? The camels? The rains? The harvest? And you? How are you? The greetings are drawn out, enacted with understated but obvious affection. From where have you come? And to where do you travel? What news do you bring?

The day darkens and enormous stars shimmer in myriad green-blue constellations. Moonlight bathes the village in the predawn light. A plane hurries high over the Sahara, heading south. In 1989 a French UTA airliner, flying from N'Djaména to Paris, exploded over the Sahara and rained down upon the Ténéré Desert in a phosphorescent shower of fire and bodies. It was a violation of many things, among them the sanctity of a desert night such as this. I search for shooting stars. The fire crackles and spits and a camel groans from behind the trees.

There is so much that is beyond words on this night, here under this tamarisk tree by the fire in a place called Tchin-Taborak – a name with the resonance of rebellion and remote hearths. There are children on the periphery of the firelight. An elder wanders in and out from the darkness. Moussa prepares the tea. He boils it for an eternity, allowing it to ripen over the charcoal. The teapot sits atop a simple wire bracket. Its position is changed from time to time, always with the utmost seriousness. As the tea nears readiness, it is poured from a great height into small glasses, sturdy and well-loved. From teapot to glass, from glass to teapot, from a flick of the wrist to long, slow arcs of scalding liquid, nine or 10 times, I lose count.

The first tea, aided by a third of a cup of sugar, is strong enough to fortify a camel. It is functional, a medicinal tonic for fatigue and designed to awaken, reinvigorate and sharpen the wits. The Tuareg love this first taste, especially early in the morning and during the hot afternoon hours. It is bitter, almost unbearably so.

Across from me sits Yahhye. He is a man who laughs infectiously – 'Ha, HUH!' – at the many things in life that amuse him. Tonight he makes rope. The straw is dipped in water; four or five strands are stretched then woven together in an action as swift as lighting a match. Throughout, the straw is stretched tight around his big toe. He works absent-mindedly, scarcely glancing at the product of his labour until he has finished.

The second tea is a tea of sweetness, an antidote to the necessary fortifications of the first. Where the first tea is utilitarian, the second is primarily for pleasure. The sugar dose is raised to almost half a cup.

A day has passed. Another will follow it, marked not in hours but by sunrise, the midday heat, the golden hour of sunset, the evening chill, then night. An old man joins us from the darkness and slips into place alongside the fire, serene in his silence.

The third tea is eminently drinkable, sweet and lightly laced with mint. In times of plenty, small dried flowers from Morocco and Algeria can be found in the markets of Agadez and added to the tea as a reward to the senses for having endured the day. This final glass, although more will be offered, is an accompaniment to conversation, a prelude to evenings of storytelling and news brought by travellers.

Yahhye and Moussa talk in Tamasheq, raw and guttural and as elusive to the untrained ear as the desert wind. I find myself lost in a preponderance of *ts* and *ns* and *tchs* and *ghs*.

Yahhye says a word.

No-one speaks for some time.

Then Moussa replies.

Another long pause.

Then both men fall easily into laughter and resume a conversation that I suspect began long ago, as if they share a history which has lasted longer than their own lifetimes.

At times, lost in my own world, I become aware of silence and wonder if I have slept. And then Moussa speaks and Yahhye smiles in recognition. I hear mention of gazelles, of villages with indecipherable names, of salt caravans that became part of the fabric of legend. Fearful of breaking the spell of this desert evening, I sit in quiet awe, listening to the crackling fire and the scarcely perceptible wind.

I watch spellbound as the moon casts a spectral glow over the patient, resting land in this remote place. The stars fall as soft footfalls upon the earth.

I curl up on the sand and dream of desert spirits in enchanted, forbidden kingdoms.

ANTHONY HAM

Anthony is a Madrid-based author and photographer who writes for Lonely Planet and for magazines and newspapers around the world. He travels to the Sahara whenever he can and is writing a book about the Saharan cheetah and the Tuareg of Niger.

IN A BORDER PICKLE

Ethan Gelber

For 281 days – from September 25, 1997, to June 30, 1998 – a team of dedicated volunteers circumnavigated the Mediterranean Sea from Morocco to Spain, mostly by bicycle. In the middle, between the Egypt–Israel border and Turkey, they dealt with a series of dispiriting visa and border mishaps. Such complications are still common to overland travelers today, especially in the Middle East, a region mired in the same (or worse) animosities and challenges as it was 10 and even 50 years ago. This is the tale of one team's dogged pursuit of principle – and their qualified successes.

Incredulous. That's the best word for it. He's confused, a little overwhelmed. There are too many of us. We should be passing through one at a time, respecting border decorum. Even the normally languid Egyptian security officers are not sure what to make of us. They stir. We're all speaking at the same time, a united but confused front, trying to convince our man that bending the rules – actually breaking the law – is a good thing, somehow a constructive thing; even beneficial to regional stability – which is, of course, patently absurd. A boat-rocker he's not; he sets his jaw and disappears behind his dark, prominent eyebrows and pouting moustache. Utterly incredulous.

We discussed strategy for days before reaching this border. Planning to complete a counterclockwise circumnavigation of the Mediterranean Sea by bicycle, we knew the Middle East would be a particular trial. Between Egypt and Turkey we must find our way across the Gaza Strip, Israel, Jordan, Syria and Lebanon, in that order. Unfortunately, though, Syria and Lebanon won't extend welcomes to anyone known to have traveled in Israel. Somehow we have to hide evidence of that passage. We aren't overly uneasy about convincing the Israelis of the need for entry and exit stamps on a removable page rather than in our passports; they're known to comply if asked politely. However, just as damning is an Egyptian exit stamp from Rafah, on the border with Israel. Pretty incontrovertible proof, that. Imagine the impassioned defense at the Syrian frontier: 'Um, well, yes, we exited Egypt on the Israeli border, but we didn't go to Israel. Really. See? We have no proof of entering.' Which is why our efforts at persuasion had to begin in Egypt.

Without looking at us the immigration officer opens our passports one by one and, with that full-fisted staccato whack, pounds an exit stamp into each. Our hopes of an easy road are savagely pulped in five strokes of humiliating, authoritative denial.

'Well, now we're going to have to come up with a whole new plan,' I mumble, despondent.

'But we should at least be happy we're through,' remarks Anthony, often one to seek a silver lining.

The truth is we are excited. Forty-eight hours earlier we crossed the Suez Canal and put Africa, our first continent, behind us. After more than 2000 kilometers of tough cycling, we have just sped with minimal ruffle through immigration and customs at a notorious border. We had even tried to complicate things with our (denied) request for exit stamps on separate sheets of paper. Perhaps that's why the truculent staff are happy to see us expedited out the gate and gone.

'I can't actually believe we've failed before we even got started,' gloom-and-dooms Padraic, affectionately called Sunshine by Anthony. The three of us have been together all day, every day for more than two months; with another seven to go our sensitivities have grown calluses from the mutually supportive chiding.

'Let's just do our best not to get stamped in by the Israelis,' I naively suggest.

If our 'best' is to achieve Israeli non-compliance with our wishes, despite our smiling and gracious model politeness, then we should have aimed for much, much better. (Of course, our smiles are in large part inspired by the sight of the young female staff, practically the first women we've seen since entering the Maghreb.)

'Is it the way I look?' wonders Anthony, who, standing nearly 2 meters tall, can be imposing, especially when leering concupiscently.

'Probably your smell,' says Padraic.

What's certainly true – perhaps a big red flag to the overcautious border teams – is that we have just pedaled 40 dusty kilometers, and unpacked and repacked our bags and bikes several times for security, customs checks and X-rays. But waving like a pennant even more crimson and colossal is our commitment to spend several days and nights in the Gaza Strip.

Our pedal along the Mediterranean littoral isn't purely for pleasure. Who in their right minds would spend nine months just for fun in tough, close and sweaty quarters with anyone other than spouses, lovers or family? No, our journey is an educational happening called BikeAbout – The Mediterranean. BikeAbout is a fusion of personal passions – cycling (environment-friendly and health-conscious travel), cross-cultural communication and direct community engagement (people-friendly travel), and international education using simple, classroom-ready technology. In short, it's responsible travel in the days before that ethical catchphrase would become common currency. It's also early blogging; we're maintaining a daily web-based account of our travels, updated manually and enlivened by digital pictures and streaming videos, sound files and interactive kids' games. This is part of the core instructional component of the journey: the progress of our adventure is being followed on the web by tens of thousands of schoolchildren yearning for contemporary and relevant information about lifestyles in the Mediterranean.

This commitment also means we're on the clock, with a set of fixed touch points and a rough calendar of visits that need to be respected. The little Palestinian jag, therefore, isn't just self-indulgence. As in many of the communities we've visited thus far in Morocco, Tunisia, Sicily and Egypt (civil war made Algeria unsafe, politics made Libya inaccessible), we are awaited in Gaza City by a local host organization, a youth center eager to share with us – and our audience – the reality of life in the Gaza Strip.

Unfortunately, even during this relatively peaceful period between the two *intifadas*, the Israelis are suspicious of international travelers overnighting in uncustomary destinations. In concrete terms, this means we have the problem of their entry stamp inked indelibly in our passports right next to the Egyptian exit imprint. Double whammy!

The 'Important Information' page of US passports pulls no punches: 'This passport must not be altered or mutilated in any way. Alteration may make it invalid, and, if willful, may subject you to persecution.' Damn. That rules out an indelicate obliteration of our tattle-tale stamps.

'Maybe we should accidentally put them through the laundry and hope for the best – or worst,' I suggest.

'We could rile up a wild dog and feed them to him,' says Anthony.

'And lose an arm in the process. Not worth it,' says Padraic, 'or the wrath of Uncle Sam.'

Fortunately, our month-long winter break (from pedaling and from one another) is soon upon us. And with time to research alternatives, unexpected options are found. Almost unbelievably, the US passport agency, anticipating situations like ours, will issue a limited-validity duplicate passport to travelers in a dilemma. Yes, with a valid excuse, you can legally possess two distinct genuine US passports. So, during the break Anthony, Padraic and I acquire our smacks-of-spyland duplicate documents. With his new travel pass, Anthony, who's holidaying in Egypt, also succeeds in scoring a Syrian visa, whereas Padraic and I, in the US over the break where we are faced with less cooperative Syrian representatives, aren't so lucky.

Reunited in Jerusalem, we discuss the road ahead. Only Anthony can travel as planned: from Israel to Jordan on his old passport and then, on his new one, through Syria, Lebanon and back to Syria. Padraic and I will also go to Jordan, where the three of us will tackle Amman's halls of power to try to get our bright-purple 'J Valley Crossing Point' Jordanian entry visas transferred to our new passports without mention of the Israeli–Jordanian crossing. Then Padraic and

I will apply for Syrian visas. We envision entering the land of Assad together, a triumphant trio.

Setting: Amman, the lobby of the Jordanian Department of Residence and Borders. The signs: pretty much all in Arabic, not an alphabet we know. The crush of people: two atmospheres of pressures, at least.

'This is going to be as fruitful as crossing the Rafah border,' says Padraic.

Despite Mr Sunshine's naysaying, transferring our visas and omitting a Jordanian port of entry is no trouble at all. With the aid of friendly and obliging officials, we're out of the labyrinth, untouched by the Minotaur, in about an hour.

The following morning, we're first in line at the Syrian embassy and cockily optimistic. At the hushed reception window we present our new Israel-evidence–free passports. We have time for only a few breaths before they're returned. No visas for us.

'What? Why?' I blubber.

Simple: there's no port of entry on the Jordanian stamp.

'But that's not our problem, not our fault,' I lie.

The staffer is utterly unmoved. The Syrians know all the tricks.

I suggest we go back to the Jordanians and ask if they'll bend the rules, add a false entry point. It's worth a try. And try we do, both at the helpful but hands-tied Department of Residence and Borders and then even at the nearby Ministry of the Interior. Hopeless. Stuck.

The next day, Anthony has succeeded in making a quick call from Syria to one of our new Jordanian friends. His cryptic 'No visa, no visa, no visa!' is confirmation that, armed with his visa, he's safely across, but nothing's available at the border for me and Padraic. Having set an if-all-else-fails rendezvous with Anthony two-and-a-half weeks hence in Adana, in southeast Turkey, we'll have to find another way through. Or around.

Or over. All of our land avenues are literally blocked: Jordan's other Arab neighbors – Saudi Arabia and Iraq – are no-go zones; Israel offers no new outlets but the sea, which we already know from earlier research promises no traffic to the Lebanese coast. Our time window is severely restricted as well. Eid al-Fitr, the traditional multiday celebration of the end of Ramadan, is due to begin at any moment and will shut everything down when it does. Since we're also working against our own ticking clock, if we're going to go, we have to go right away – by any means possible, even plane (anathema to a land-bound bicycle journey).

In the evening of the next day, my 32nd birthday, we descend toward the Lebanese capital fearing expulsion. It has rained torrentially, leaving treacherously deep-seeming ponds on the runway. The dark, war-savaged urban landscape doesn't seem any less ominous.

'Look natural,' I say to Padraic as we near immigration.

'As what?' he wonders, 'A person with no visa and a long stay in Israel?'

I consider it my birthday surprise when the border beef – including scowling leather-clad Syrian overseers – barely glance at our documents and just stamp us in.

Meanwhile, Anthony has his own challenges. In Damascus he must wade shoulder-deep into Syrian red tape. At the Immigration Office he's in search of authorization to re-enter Syria after his own visit to Lebanon. His primary discovery is that 'next door' is rarely just next door. From the Registry Office he is directed next door (through a series of rooms) to the Section of Residence, then next door (down two floors) to Archive 1, then Archive 2, then back next door (up two flights) to the Registry Office, next door (2nd floor) to the Chief of Travel Documents and Residence, again next door (back up a flight) to the Section of Residence, once more next door to the Chief of Travel Documents and a final stop in the next-door (4th floor!) Office of Telegrams.

'After two hours, feeling a little dazed, confused, dizzy and even nurturing the earliest pangs of a headache, I stumbled outside, successful,' reports Anthony, semi-miraculously reunited with me and Padraic in Beirut. It's been only six days but we feel like we've vaulted mountains. Despite ourselves we're glad to be back together.

Our time is split between the dazzling distractions of Beirut, pedaling north along the Lebanese coast (the south was said to be too dangerous) and endlessly charting our travel options.

When we can delay no longer, we go for broke at the coastal Lebanon–Syria border station. In a drenching downpour (a possible sympathy factor?), we leave Lebanon and cross the narrow no-man's-land to the Syrian frontier. Anthony, with his re-entry authorization, goes first. But all is not as it should be. He's only allowed to return the way he entered, on the Damascus road. Maybe at the Immigration Office he forgot to visit that one additional office just next door where this question would have been asked and he could have provided a clear response. Instead he cajoles, pleads, somehow succeeds.

Padraic and I follow. The confusion on the well-meaning immigration agent's face is instantly obvious.

'Where are your visas?'

'We don't have any,' I say. 'We'd like to get them here.'

Obviously no American has ever proposed such a thing to this agent at this location. He's not sure, which we see as an opportunity.

'We'll pay whatever the fee is and you can just stamp our passports and wave us through,' I urge, incompetently hinting at a readiness to go off the books. The well-trained, rule-respecting guard doesn't get it and I'm not savvy enough to know how to press my point. He politely and regretfully says no. Like Anthony we question and implore; unlike Anthony we fail to convince.

For the second time in 11 days, Padraic and I arrange to meet Anthony a week later, in Adana, Turkey, then watch him disappear into the wilds of Syria. For the first time, though, we retreat back across an international border into a country from which we have just officially been farewelled, passport stamps and all. Sheepishly, we make our way to the same friendly Lebanese guards who had bid us a warm and wet adieu. Boy, are they surprised to see us. We explain.

'Your friend is no friend,' sympathizes one guard, referring to Anthony, as another cancels our exit stamps.

We jealously express agreement and then turn south, now into the teeth of the unrelenting southerly that had hastened us north.

Plan B involves us making for another border station, less than 25 kilometers away. This time, wise to the exit-stamp confusion, we explain to the Lebanese that today we're visiting the Syrian authorities to arrange a crossing tomorrow. We want to ask the ranking officer to send a telegram to Damascus with our visa applications and a request for next-day processing, which someone had suggested is a possibility. The Lebanese watch us disappear into the Syrian administrative complex.

President Hafez al-Assad grins from prominent framed pictures in every drab room, much as the American President does in every state facility in the US. A young, engaging officer in crisp uniform, seated behind a surprisingly small desk, models a classic Middle Eastern moustache. We explain our intentions and, refreshingly, he seems to consider it feasible. We're thrilled. However, he needs to call Damascus first and ask for instructions.

Uh oh.

For form's sake we wait and drink the offered tea. But we know what Damascus will say: denied. Completely and utterly. Foiled.

Crestfallen we make our way back to the Lebanese officials. The obliging guy to whom we had explained our situation is no longer on duty, so we have to make excuses to a mystified newcomer. Why do we have one cancelled exit stamp from the same day at another border and no exit stamp for this one? So much for avoiding confusion. But we're allowed to pass.

'Imagine being denied,' I ponder aloud, 'stuck between Lebanon and Syria because of visa irregularities.'

Padraic doesn't have time for consternation. He's already spied a taxi with a trunk big enough for two bikes. We speed back to Tripoli by motorized transport and from there by bus to Beirut, where, at the station, I revisit an office I'd earlier consulted about travel to Damascus. I'm told to return at 9am, when arrangements can be made.

Bright and early back at the office, we haggle. We hit on an inflated but acceptable price for a private minivan with an 'experienced driver' (wink, wink) to take us to the border, help us get our visas (nudge, nudge) and then deliver us all the way to Damascus. Say no more.

Padraic is in charge of this attempt. He disappears with the driver at the Lebanese passport processing point, but leaving Lebanon has never been the problem. A few kilometers further along, we pull into a major parking lot and Padraic wanders off to face the Syrian music. I wait…and wait…and wait some more, increasingly encouraged by hopes that the long delay is a sign of good things to come – until the duo re-emerges and Padraic shakes his head. Third failure. Game over.

'The driver was hopeless,' he grumbles. 'He didn't know any more than we did. Maybe even less.'

'So we resorted to alternative measures. Again,' I tell Anthony, after fortuitously finding him in Adana, Turkey, a day earlier than expected. 'We winged to Istanbul and then took a 14-hour bus ride to get back down here.'

'Was there any other way?' he responds.

'Well, yes: the pickle guy.'

Padraic and I had stopped for a snack in the warmth of the Beqaa Valley on the way from the Syrian border back to Beirut. There we had met a chipper and communicative gherkin merchant who nodded knowingly at our tale of travel woe. Pulling his chair conspiratorially close, he had confided, with the smarmy sass of a salesman: 'I can get you to Damascus. It's easy. In the back of a Syrian army truck.'

'Maybe we should have given it a shot,' I muse.

'I think it's fair to say we exhausted every legal avenue,' Padraic avers, rolling his eyes.

'And at least you didn't miss much, only things like the absolutely awe-inspiring Crac des Chevaliers,' grins Anthony, failing to salve our disappointment, rubbing our noses in having missed one of Syria's greatest wonders.

'Yeah,' I say, ignoring Anthony, 'we were in enough of a pickle already.'

ETHAN GELBER

At 16, Ethan Gelber embarked on his first bicycle expedition: a 30-day solo pedal through New England, USA. Since then, he's cycled extensively all over the world, part of his growing commitment to sustainable travel, about which he writes as a professional freelancer. In 1996 he founded BikeAbout (www.bikeabout.org), a non-profit organization whose inaugural project was an educational, 'wired', two-wheeled circumnavigation of the Mediterranean Sea. The journey's Middle Eastern challenges are recounted here.

TOHOKU DREAMING

Simon Sellars

The last job they gave me was book-ended by madness.

It began somewhere in the labyrinthine insanity of Tokyo. I was trying to sleep in a tiny apartment, sweat pouring off me in great sheets. I was on assignment for one of the major guidebook publishers and I'd gone barmy from information overload. From reviewing 20 hotels a day. From the language barrier. From asking the same inane questions of hotel flunkies in an insane feedback loop. There was a heat wave and my skin was itchy and damp, mould growing on my pyjamas from the humidity.

I passed out, a slab of meat on a tatami mat.

I felt rough hands under my armpits. Two figures swam before me, hazy in the interpolation of waking life. Faces, the telltale syntax of body language – the shapes took on familiar tones, and I knew.

It was the Company! They'd tracked me down! Would I never be set free?

My commissioning editor, known to me by the code name 'Jackie', knelt down beside me. 'Sellars, wake up. C'mon, soldier', she whispered, calm and businesslike. 'You've got *work* to do. Real work!'

Jackie's boss, Rachel, stood at the doorway. 'Yeah. Real *work*', she hissed, barely containing her revulsion.

They dragged me to the bathroom, forced my head under the shower, turned on the cold water. Rachel shook her head. 'We've got kids on file who'd sell their grandmother to do your job.'

'Yeah. Your *job*.'

I began to scream and they took it in turns to slap my face.

'Wake up, soldier!'

I forced my eyes open…

…and this time I was awake for real. And I really was in a tiny Tokyo apartment sweating on a tatami mat in mouldy pyjamas, but everything else – just a nightmare. Shaking, I went to the kitchen and poured red cordial into a glass. Two women were in the living room. My blood froze. Not the Company! But I recovered, pushing through the pea soup of half-sleep and out the other side: *living in Japan…from Australia…expat friends…Nancy and Clare!* I was staying at Nancy and Clare's place.

They were watching the *Super Terrific Happy Hour* on TV. I excused my dishevelled, lunatic appearance. 'Bad dream…'

And then the room began to shake. The red cordial leapt organically from the glass like sentient alien blood in *The Thing*.

'Earthquake!' Nancy yelled, bolting for the door. But all I could think of was those moronic public-service announcements from the '50s, instructing schoolchildren to 'duck and cover' in the event of nuclear attack.

I scrambled under the kitchen table, gesticulating like a jelly-wrestling octopus. 'No, under *here! Duck and cover!*'

The others came and we stared wildly at each other, breathless, on all fours under the table. Scared numb out of our wits. The floor gently rippled every few seconds. Then it buckled crazily.

Clare took control. 'Everybody *out!*'

We ran outside to the balcony, which was swaying like a flimsy hammock. What to do? Wait for it to snap like a twig? Run for the street and risk death by falling concrete? Or get back under the table? The building was shaking so much my vision was blurred, like in sci-fi films when stars smudge in hyperspace. Everything was distended, the balcony like sponge under my feet.

Panic set in: we were out of commission, couldn't speak or move. And then it was all over, with no structural damage to the building or us. I tried to light a cigarette but my hands shook so much I dropped it. I couldn't even *see* my hands – my vision was still in hyperspace. Slowly, ever so slowly, we found our minds and went back in. The quake's epicentre was in the ocean and tsunami warnings were on every TV channel.

Clare translated. 'Big tidal-wave warning in Tohoku. That's where you're off to, isn't it?'

It was. I had an assignment to write about Tohoku, known as the 'Japanese deep south' (even though it's up north), an agricultural, mystical 'back country' tarred with fear and disdain by city slickers. The guidebooks painted a grim picture, caricatures of stultifying industrial towns and unwelcome foreigners provoking barely controlled hostility in the locals. But I took the job because Tohoku reminded me of my childhood. As a kid I was fascinated by the Australian island state of Tasmania. Back then, Tassie was considered fit only for sheep-shaggers and inbred mental defectives. These days it's as hip as the bony projection of a femur. But I loved the old Tasmania – remoteness was very romantic to a boy as painfully shy as I was. Tohoku is like Tassie from the '70s: unloved, forgotten, ignored, ridiculed by stand-up comics.

Another bonus: it wouldn't involve flying, which as a travel writer I've increasingly come to hate. Everyone thinks travel writing's a glamorous life. Not when you're waiting in a queue at Heathrow for four hours to have your underwear swabbed for explosives, dodging security, surveillance, crowds – the sheer grind of mainstream travel. In any case, is there anywhere left to go? It seems like the entire planet has been commodified and quantified, buried beneath a spider's web of budget flight paths. Except for Tohoku. It's untouristed. No-one rates it.

Plus, I like ghost stories. And Tohoku has plenty of those. It's as spooky as Botox.

The next day I had to leave as my schedule was tighter than Madonna's forehead. I hugged my friends.

'You must learn the proper earthquake procedure', I told them. 'For all I know, you need to fashion tinfoil hats to protect against harmful gamma rays erupting from the Earth's crust. Make sure you find out: Japan can trick the unwary.'

And with that I caught the bullet train north on my way to Aizu-Wakamatsu, a small town with a reconstructed samurai castle in Tohoku's Fukushima prefecture. On the train I sat next to a very tiny lady who told me she was from Akita prefecture.

'Our skin so soft, Akita girls', she told me. 'Softest in Japan…'

I didn't dare touch her to find out. She seemed not of this world, her skin not so much soft as translucent.

I arrived late at night and I was lost. I had no idea where Aizu's youth hostel was. The streets were empty save for a gang of scrawny kids, their modishly long hair spiked to the heavens like deep-space telemetry. They seemed to live in the train station.

'*Sumimasen*,' I whispered. 'Youth hostel?'

Baring his teeth, the gang's leader stared at me with obvious contempt. I thought he was going to bite me. Then he snapped his fingers and the entire mob, en masse, reached for black hoods to pull over their faces, blocking out their exposed flesh. Moving towards the station, they merged seamlessly with the shadows – and maybe the afterlife. I never saw them again.

An elderly fishmonger walked by. He wore rubber boots and a white smock and smelt like he'd been kissing carp all day long. 'Youth hostel?' he said, pointing at his Toyota van.

'*Hai*!' I exclaimed. 'Youth hostel! *Arigato gozaimasu*.'

He patted my head and threw my bags in the back of the van. We drove in silence for 20 minutes and I couldn't be sure he was awake, so still and quiet was he. Actually, I thought the van was guided remotely and he was plugged into it telepathically, but it was just a super-advanced GPS doing all the guesswork. Then suddenly the van stopped.

The fishmonger's mouth moved. 'Youth hostel.'

I clambered out and was greeted by the hostel's manager, another old guy, as leathery as a samurai's undershirt. He spoke a few words to the fishmonger and received a wrapped fish in return. Aizu was desolate, bleak, as silent as a tomb. I even saw a tumbleweed rolling down the hill (or the Japanese equivalent: a cherry-blossom branch?).

The fishmonger drove off and the manager snaked his arms around my shoulders. 'Sake.'

'Yes, sake.' I was tired and grumpy. Getting drunk was the only way forward.

We tossed back Japanese rice wine in the dining room. The manager said he loved his town, was proud of its fighting qualities. 'Aizu is samurai spirit.'

He told me about the Byakkotai, Aizu's famous samurai who committed ritual suicide during the Boshin Civil War. 'Aizu-Wakamatsu, authentic samurai tradition! Mussolini!'

'Mussolini was a samurai?'

'Mussolini love Byakkotai! Aizu bear his name!'

He told me that Il Duce, smitten with the story of the Byakkotai, had commissioned an ostentatious monument to their memory that commands the summit of Aizu's Iimori Mountain. I wasn't impressed. I'd been trained to despise fascist dictators, but before I could argue the toss the old man had passed out, snoring on the floor. I went to bed.

The wind that night was insane. It screamed and whistled and battered the wooden A-frame of the hostel, the windows and the doors, invading my dreams so that I imagined I was being chased by a huge, hissing, mutant kitten with lantern-green eyes and really nasty, sharp claws.

I was a mess the next morning. 'Bad dream', I told the manager. 'The wind…big cat…claws…sharp!'

He laughed, telling me that Japan had been hit by 'Typhoon Number 10', leaving 34 dead on the coast. 'Don't cry like a girl!' he scoffed. 'Japan hit by *ten* typhoons this year. Only your first!'

A 'girl', eh? And yet I could see myself hanging tough with this Japanese Hemingway for weeks on end, trading good-natured insults about each other's masculinity, but I had to push on. Guidebook writing is relentless. There's no time to be a tourist or to make friends and your only companion is the quick and brutal clock.

From Aizu I took more trains, aiming for my next stop, Tono, a town in a rustic valley with a strong animist culture that forms the heartland of Tohoku lore. Inch by inch, I penetrated deeper north; the bullet trains only go so far and then you must take the country service. To get to Tono, I had to wait four hours in a town I never knew the name of. I had no provisions and no money, and there was no ATM. My minimal Japanese was not good enough to ask for schedules or to gather any shred of information that would confirm I had landed on the right planet. I still didn't know where I would end up. The only way to know for sure was to wait for the train and see where it took me. But I had no idea when it would even arrive. It could be that night or the next day, the next week, so I was forced to pass the time by pretending the kanji characters on the train station's signage were Space Invaders lasering my eyes out.

I passed out on a bench, dreaming about aliens trying to read my mind. Arnold Schwarzenegger was in the dream, and he told me to wrap something moist around my head to block the aliens' superpowerful telepathic tractor beams that would wrench the thoughts from my skull like ripe fruit…

When the train came, it was midnight, and 50 Japanese raced onto the platform from out of nowhere. Their noise woke me from my deep slumber, and I was most surprised to find a wet towel wrapped around my head. I tried to act natural, casually tossing it aside, and followed the throng on board.

Eventually I arrived in Tono, in the dead of night. Eerie mountains ring Tono and at night its still, inky black atmosphere can give a person the fear. I checked into a small hotel and slept like a dog. In the morning, the manager sat all the guests down.

'Tono is *kappa* territory', he told us.

'I know about *kappa*', I piped up. 'They're water spirits. Sandy from the TV show *Monkey* was a *kappa*. They're really dumb and they can be easily fooled.'

The manager glared at me. His burning gaze was a red-hot poker giving me a frontal lobotomy free of charge. 'You're the fool. Never go near one. They'll pull your intestines through your anus. Just for fun. Then you can't shit and you die.'

A bespectacled Japanese geek in red motorbike leathers turned to me, peering over his glasses. 'You know Osira-sama? That's the best Tono legend.' He looked to the manager for approval. The manager nodded sagely.

'Osira was once simple Tono farm girl,' the motor geek explained. 'She had horse she loved so much, they get married. But father is disgusted, hangs horse from tree. Sad girl clings to lover, but father beheads horse. Then girl and horse fly to heavens to become gods. She becomes Osira: Japanese symbol of fertility.'

I was confused, unsure how bestiality begets fertility. But I didn't want to lose face. Instead, I was the one nodding sagely. 'Ah yes. I once saw the *Jerry Springer Show:* he had a guest that married a horse.'

The biker geek smiled. He actually appeared to pity me. 'Ah, *yes*. But Springer never has any *answer*.'

Which was true. All Springer can do is react to extreme situations. He never solves a problem or offers any solution. And they made an opera about him! Overrated.

After a tour of the town, I decided to get out of Tono. The legends were just too much and everyone believed in them. They even tried to tell me there were chameleon foxes in the mountains who were as big as ponies when seen from the front, and as small as a human baby from behind. Besides, the clock was ticking – my deadline loomed like a horse about to make love to a farm girl.

I took the bullet train further north. This time I sat next to a scientist from Niigata who claimed he had invented a·revolutionary new pizza base – made from baby squid. I made my excuses and went in search of empty seats, leaving him to his reverie.

'Squid, baby squid. Plentiful. Cheap. Fullest flavour, superior texture...'

Alone at last, I marvelled at the miracle of engineering that is the Japanese bullet train. You can't tell how fast these things move from the inside, so smooth and integrated is the ride. There are no bumps. The carriages barely make a sound. At 300km/h you may as well be time-travelling into the future: one minute you're here, the next second you're there. I watched Japanese boys break-dancing in the aisle, businessmen asleep with drool on their chins. Tea ladies sold eel and sushi and I drank beer and we were all floating on air. The Japanese bullet train is a mystical experience.

Then suddenly there was change, the air-locked stasis broken by a robot voice announcing the next stop: Morioka. I sprang into action and leapt off the train. For I knew what Morioka signified: *wanko-soba*. I'd heard so much about this ritual, which derives from the feudal era when the peasantry's crops were decimated and there was only *soba* noodle for dinner. Because that's all they had, the peasants felt compelled to make it the best *soba* ever and they were mortally offended if guests said 'no more', even if they were stuffed to the gills.

I dumped my bags in a coin locker and headed directly for Azumaya restaurant, near the station – best *wanko-soba* in town, said the guidebook. I must have been an obvious mark because the second I stepped inside, five waitresses raced over. One pulled up really close.

She placed a 'special *wanko-soba* smock' over my head and explained the rules. 'I bring you 15 bowls filled with *wanko-soba*. You must eat them.'

Once I was on the last bowl, she would bring out 15 more, filling up that last bowl one by one with this new round of 15, even if I pleaded with her to stop. Once I got through that, she would bring out 15 more, then 15 more, and on and on. I could only get out of it by placing a lid over the bowl, but if she beat me and refilled it, I had to eat it.

'It's only plain noodle,' she urged, 'so eat some side dish. But leave room for *wanko-soba*!'

No problem, I thought: the bowls were more like oversized cups and 15 equalled a standard noodle box. Everyone in the packed restaurant stared as I easily devoured the first round. There was even some light applause.

My waitress bellowed, slamming another tray down. 'Eat!'

I got through the second lot of 15, scared of her wrath, but when I flagged on the third round she changed tactics, trying sweet-talk instead.

'One more bowl', she cooed. 'Do it...for *me*.'

After the 32nd bowl I wanted to throw up. I went for the lid, but she was quicker on the draw and refilled the bowl. I had to eat it. That was the rule. After five more bowls I again went for the lid but I was as punchy as Rocky Balboa. Again, she beat me. Some guy next to me snorted derisively and she turned to share a conspiratorial smile with him. Seizing my chance, I slammed the lid home, slumping backwards, exhausted.

'You're very brave man', she said. 'But not good enough for *wanko-soba*. Record is 500 bowls. Not even close!'

I left, dejected, and checked into a capsule hotel. The following evening, I caught the night bus back to Tokyo. My work was not finished, but I already needed a break from Tohoku. I'd be back but I needed to rest and see my friends.

Beside me on the bus was a young Japanese man who kept staring at his reflection in the window, zigzagging his head from side to side and up and down like an electrocuted bird. It was as if he was trying to catch himself out, trying to trick his reflection somehow.

We arrived in Tokyo at 6.30am. Bird-boy was greeted by his girlfriend, who was wearing a costume that made her look like Edward Scissorhands, complete with some kind of mechanical claw attachment and what appeared to be frosting on the outfit's shiny black shoulders. She looked like she'd just stepped out of a meat locker.

I, on the other hand, had no immediate place to go and no-one to see. I was due to meet Nancy and Clare at 5pm, but desperately needed sleep in the meantime.

Two girls walked past, both dressed as Little Bo Peep, one in a flowing blue dress, one in red. Both wore bonnets, extravagant wigs of golden curls and outlandishly large fake eyelashes. I caught their eyes, remembering that in the best Japanese fashion, all the kids go to internet cafés for a nap after a big night out.

'*Sumimasen*', I stammered. '*Internetto?*'

Incredibly, they were brandishing sheep-herding staffs, which they used to point me in the right direction. I thanked my little shepherds and took off.

At the internet café I slumped into a comfy leather seat. Sweet sleep, at last – until a loud American voice woke me.

'Hey dude!' A stocky man in a suit with a bowl haircut leant over from the adjacent cubicle. 'You American? English?' he bellowed. 'Just cruising round?'

'Australian. Just back from Tohoku.'

'Tohoku! Say, what's that island there? Monkey Island?'

'Never heard of it.'

He was fit to burst. 'Oh man. They're breeding superbionic monkeys there! Some kinda crazy research facility. Hey. And I'll tell you this: Tohoku is fulla ghosts. You like Japanese castles?'

'Yeah. Aizu's.'

He looked distant, melancholy. 'Man, I saw a ghost in a castle. Little samurai dude.' He held his down-turned palm just above the floor. 'Only this big! Jesus! He ran straight at me, waving this huge freakin' sword. But I hurdled him...and...and he disappeared.' He let it sink in. 'So, you like Tohoku?'

'Look, I love Tohoku but I feel a little strange right now. I haven't had any sleep, I've been on too many trains and buses, and I need to catch more to go back and finish my work. And I just saw two girls dressed like Little Bo Peep.'

He grabbed my shoulders, fixed me with a level stare. 'Hey, don't sweat it. You don't need trains to travel around Tohoku. You just need *this*', he said, tapping his temple.

'Just remember', he droned. 'It's only a dream...'

The next time I opened my eyes I was back home, work finished, madly writing up my assignment and emailing it to Jackie.

And I'm telling you the American was wrong: this is a true story.

SIMON SELLARS

Simon Sellars is a freelance writer based in Melbourne, Australia. In 2004 he travelled to Tohoku on assignment for Lonely Planet. Or did he? As his bio no longer appears in Lonely Planet's latest *Japan* guide, it's becoming increasingly hard to tell. Maybe the American was right, after all...

DERVISHES

Rory Stewart

A traveler is mistaken for a wandering Dervish in Pakistan and finds out why some people believe the Dervish has 'nothing to do with Islam.'

'Dervish are an abomination,' said Navaid.

'What do you mean by a Dervish?' I asked.

'Dervish? Don't you know? It's a very old concept. Fakir? Pir-Baba? Sufi? Silsilah Malang – that beggar doing magic tricks…?' Navaid was staring at a man who was sitting cross-legged in the street with a ten-foot black python wrapped round his neck. 'That beggar – medieval mystics like Shahbaz Qalander – the people who live and dance at his tomb. They are all Dervish.'

When I first met Navaid at the tomb of Datta Ganj Baksh a week earlier, he had been examining the same snake man. Now Navaid was standing very still, stroking his white beard. The python was asleep and so was its owner and no-one except Navaid seemed to notice them. For the last 10 years he had spent his days at the mosques of the old city of Lahore. He had neither a family nor a job. His voice was quick, anxious, slightly high-pitched, as though he were worried I would leave before he had finished his sentence.

'You foreigners love the idea of Dervish – whirling Dervish, wandering Dervish, howling Dervish – exotic, like belly dancers and dancing camels,' he insisted. 'Surely you understand what I mean?'

'But what's that beggar there got in common with a medieval Sufi poet?'

'One thing anyway – they are both irrelevant,' replied Navaid. 'They both have nothing to do with Islam or Pakistan. They barely exist any more, and, if they do, they don't matter. Forget about Dervish.'

Two weeks later I was walking alone along a canal in the Southern Punjab. It had been five months since I started walking across Asia but I had only been in the Punjab for a few days. The arid mountains of Iran had been replaced by a flat, fertile land and I was struggling to turn my limited Persian into Urdu. I was also getting used to new clothes. I was trying to dress in a way that did not attract attention. I was, like everyone else, wearing a loose, thin Pakistani *salwar kameez* suit and, because of the 120°F heat, a turban. I had swapped my backpack for a small, cheap shoulder bag and I carried a traditional iron-shod staff. In Iran I was frequently accused of being a smuggler, a resistance fighter or a grave robber. In the Punjab, because of my clothes, black hair and fair skin, I was often mistaken for one of the millions of Afghani refugees now living in Pakistan. Afghanis have a reputation as danger-ous men and this may partly have explained why I had not (so far) felt threatened, walking alone along the Punjab canals.

A snake was swimming down the canal, its head held high over its own reflection, shedding bars of water thick with sunlight in its wake. In a hollow between the towpath and the wheat field was a stunted peepul tree draped with green cloth and beneath it the earth grave of a 'Dervish.' A thin bare-chested man dragged a bucket through the canal, staggered to the edge of the path and threw water on the dry track. I watched him weaving up and down the grass bank towards me. The history of his labor was laid across the path in thick bars of color. In front of him, where I was walking, was pale sand; at his feet was a band of black mud. Behind him, stripe after stripe, each slightly paler than its successor, faded through orange clay until, where he had worked an hour before, nothing remained but pale sand. This was his job in the Canal Department.

'*Salaam alaikum.*'

'*Wa alaikum as-salaam,*' he replied. 'Where are you going?'

'To the canal rest house.'

'Respected one,' he smiled and his voice was nervous, 'most kind one. Give me a sacred charm.'

'I'm sorry, I don't have one.'

'Look at me. This work. This sun.' He was still smiling.

'I'm very sorry. *Hoda hafez.* God be with you.'

I turned away and he grabbed my by the arm. I hit him with my stick. He backed off and we looked at each other. I hadn't hurt him but I was embarrassed.

Navaid had warned me I would be attacked walking across Pakistan. 'Violent? Pakistan is a very violent country – the Baluch caught a young Frenchman who was trying to walk here last year and killed him. Or look at today's newspaper – you can be killed by your father for sleeping around, you can be killed by other Muslims for being a Shi'a, you can be killed for being a policeman, you can be killed for being a tourist.'

But I could see the man I'd hit wasn't dangerous.

He was now smiling apologetically, 'Please, sir, at least let me have some of your water.'

I poured some water from my bottle into his hands. He bowed to me, passed it in front of his lips and then brushed it through his hair.

'And now a charm: a short one will be enough…'

'No, I'm sorry. I can't.'

I couldn't. I wouldn't play the role of a holy man. '*Hoda hafez.*' A hundred yards further on I looked back through the midday glare and saw him still staring at me. He had, it seemed, perhaps because I was walking in Pakistani clothes, mistaken me for what Navaid would call a wandering Dervish.

An hour later, I turned off the towpath down a tree-lined avenue. There was a peepul, with its pointed leaves, trembling 40ft above. This one had outgrown its pink bark but its trunk was thin, its canopy small. It looked as though it had been planted when the canal was completed in 1913, and it would probably outlast the canal, since part of the peepul under which the Buddha achieved enlightenment, 2500 years ago, is still alive in Sri Lanka. Further on, among the banyans, the ruby flowers of the *dak* trees and the yellow of the laburnum, was the electric blue spray of a Brazilian jacaranda imported, I assume, by some extravagant engineer. Two men and two boys were sitting on the lawn.

'*Salaam alaikum.*'

'*Wa alaikum as-salaam.* We had been told to expect someone. Please sit down.'

I sat on the charpoy string bed and we looked at each other. They knew nothing about me and I knew nothing about them. They were looking at a 28-year-old Briton, seated on a colonial lawn, in a turban and sweat-soaked salwaar kameez. I was looking at a man, also in salwaar kameez, but with a ballpoint pen in his breast pocket – an important symbol in an area where less than half the men can write their own name. The other man, standing on the balls of his bare feet, staring at me with his hands forward like a wrestler, looked about 60. He had shoulder-length, grey, curly hair and a short beard. He was wearing an emerald-green kameez shirt and a dark-green sarong, a silver anklet, four long bead necklaces and an earring in his left ear. I asked whether I could boil some water.

'*Acha, acha*, boil water,' said the old man with the earring and immediately loped off in a half-run, with his hands still held in front of him, to the peepul tree. I watched him build a fire and shout to a boy to bring a bucket of water from the canal. He and the column of smoke seemed small beneath the Buddha's tree. The man in green returned with the handleless pot of boiling water in his hands. When I took it from him, I burned my fingers and nearly dropped the pot. He asked if I'd like some honey and I said I would very much.

Ten minutes later, he returned breathless and sweating with part of a cone of dark wild honey in his hands.

'Where did you get it from?'

'From there,' he pointed to the peepul, 'I just climbed up there to get it.' I thought I could see where the cone must be – it was on a branch, some way out, about 40ft above the ground. It was a difficult climb for a 60-year-old, even without the bees.

'What do you do?'

'Me?' He laughed and looked at the others, who laughed also. 'Why, I'm a *malang* – a Dervish, a follower of Shahbaz Qalander of Sehwan Sharif.'

'And what does it mean to be a Dervish follower of Shahbaz

118

Qalander of Sehwan Sharif?'

'Why, to dance and sing.' And he began to hop from foot to foot, clicking his fingers in the air, and singing in a high-pitched voice: '*Shudam Badnam Dar Ishq / Biya Paarsa Ikanoon / The Tarsam Za Ruswaee / Bi Har Bazaar Me Raqsam.*' (Come, behold how I am slandered for my love of God / But slander means nothing to me / That's why I'll dance in the crowd, my friend / And prance throughout the bazaar.)

'Who wrote that?'

'My sheikh, my master, Shahbaz Qalander, when he lived in the street of the whores.'

'And where are you from?'

'Me? Well my family is originally from Iran not Pakistan – we came like Shahbaz Qalander.'

Laal Shahbaz Qalander was a 12th-century mystic, what Navaid would call a Dervish. He belonged to a monastic order, wandered from Iran to Pakistan preaching Islam, performed miracles, wrote poems like the one above, and was buried in a magnificent medieval tomb in Sehwan Sharif, a city founded by Alexander the Great. They say his name, Laal Shahbaz, records his brilliant red clothes and his spirit, free as the Shahbaz falcon. He is one of the most famous of a group of mystics who arrived in Pakistan between the 11th and 14th centuries. Their poetry and teachings often celebrate an intoxication with an almost erotic love of God that appears at times to transcend all details of religious doctrine. Their mystical ideas seem to have passed, like the use of rosary beads and the repetition of a single phrase for meditation, from the subcontinent through the Islamic world, and from the Crusaders into Christianity. It is they, not the Arab conquerors of the earlier centuries, who are credited with peacefully converting the Hindus of Pakistan to Islam. Indeed, if the shirt of the man in front of me was like Shahbaz's red, not green, he would look, with his long hair and jewelry, exactly like a Hindu sadhu. And he is one of half a million Pakistanis who gather at Shahbaz's tomb once a year to celebrate with dancing and singing.

'Do you not have land?' I asked, 'Work as a farmer?'

'I used to but I gave it all away – I have nothing now.'

'Nothing?'

'I need nothing else. As the prophet says, "Poverty is my pride",' he replied, smiling so broadly that I wasn't sure whether I believed him.

When it was time to go, the Dervish accompanied me to the gate hobbling slightly on his bare feet.

'Have you always been a Dervish?' I asked.

'No, I was a civil servant in the Customs Department. I worked in the baggage inspection hall of Lahore airport for 15 years.'

At the canal bank, I took out some money to thank him for the cooking and the honey. But he was horrified.

'Please,' I said, employing a Persian euphemism, 'take it for the children.'

'There are no children here,' the Dervish said firmly. 'Good luck and goodbye.' He shook my hand and, bringing his palm up to his chest, added in a friendlier voice, 'God be with you – walking is a kind of dancing too.'

<hr />

When I walked back into Lahore, I met a very different kind of Muslim civil servant. 'Umar is a most influential person,' said Navaid. 'He knows everyone in Lahore, parties all night – meets Imran Khan all the time. And you must see his library. He will explain to you about Islam.'

I was invited to Umar's house at 10 at night because he had three parties to attend earlier in the evening. As I arrived, I saw a heavily built, bearded man in his mid-30s stepping down from a battered transit van. He was talking on his mobile and holding up his arms so his driver could wrap a baggy, brown pinstriped jacket round him but he managed to hold out a hand to greet me. Still clutching my hand, he led me into a government bungalow of a very similar age and style to the canal rest house. We removed our shoes and entered a small room, with no chairs and shelves of English-language books covering all the walls. Umar put down the phone, sat on the floor and invited me to sit beside him.

'*Salaam alaikum*, good evening. Please make yourself comfortable. I will tell the servant to get a blanket for you. This is my son, Salman,' he added. The eight-year-old was playing a video game. He waved vaguely but his focus was on trying to persuade a miniature David Beckham to kick with his left foot.

Umar's eyes were bloodshot and he looked tired and anxious. He never smiled, but instead produced rhetorical questions and suggestions at a speed that was difficult to follow.

'Multan, but of course,' he said, 'you must meet the Gilanis, the Qureshis, the Gardezis – perhaps as you move up the Punjab – Shah Jeevna. I know them all. I can do it for you.' All these people were descendants of the famous medieval saints who had converted Pakistan – Navaid's Dervish or Pirs. It was said that they had inherited a great deal of their ancestors' spiritual charisma – villagers still touched them to be cured of illnesses or drank water they blessed to ensure the birth of a son. They had certainly inherited a great deal of land and wealth from donations to their ancestors' shrines. But Umar, it seemed, was not interested in their Dervish connections. He was concerned with the fact that they were currently leading politicians. Thus the female descendant of a medieval mystic, who once stood in a Punjabi river for 12 years reciting the Qur'an, had just served as Pakistan's ambassador to Washington. Another Dervish, who, it is said, entered Multan riding on a lion and whipping it with live snakes and 600 years later is still supposed to stick his hand out of the tomb to greet pious pilgrims, has descendants who have served as ministers in both the federal and provincial governments. Umar knew them all and, perhaps because he was rising fast in the interior ministry, he was able to help them occasionally.

Umar's mobile rang again. He applauded one of his son's virtual goals, dragged off his shiny silver tie, dark brown shirt and brown pinstriped trousers for a servant to take away, pulled a copy of VS Naipaul's *Beyond Belief* off the shelves and pointed me to a chapter, which I slowly realized was about himself – all the while still talking on the phone.

I had seen Umar earlier in the evening at the large marble-floored house of a wealthy landowner and Dervish descendant. A group of clean-shaven young Pakistani men in casual Gucci shirts had been standing besides Umar drinking illegal whisky, smoking joints and talking about Manhattan. And there he had been, in his brown suit and brown shirt, bearded and with a glass of fruit juice in his hand, not only because he was not educated abroad but also, it seemed, because he had very different views about religion.

'My son,' said Umar proudly, putting down the phone, 'is studying at an Islamic school. His basic syllabus is that he must memorize the whole book of the Qur'an – more than 150,000 words by heart; I chose this school for him.' The boy concerned was trying to decide which members of the Swedish squad to include in his dream team. 'You know, our relationship with our families is one of the strengths of Islamic culture. I am sorry it will not be possible for you to meet my wife – but she and my parents and children form such a close unit. When you think of the collapse of families in the West, the fact that there is (I am sorry to say it but I know because I have been to the West) no respect for parents; almost everyone is getting divorced; there is rape on the streets, suicide; you put your people in "Old People Homes", while we look after them in the family. In America and perhaps Britain as well, I think, there is rape and free sex, divorce and drugs. Have you had a girlfriend? Are you a virgin?'

'No, I'm not.'

'My friend,' he said, leaning forward, 'I was in a car with a friend the other day, we stopped at the traffic lights and there was a beautiful girl in the car next to us. We wanted to gaze at her but I said, and my friend agreed, 'do not glance at her,' for if you do not stare now you will be able to have that woman in heaven.' He paused for effect. 'That is what religion gives to me. It is very late, my friend. I suggest you sleep here tonight and I will drive you back in the morning.'

'Thank you very much.'

'No problem.' He shouted something. The servant entered, laid down two mattresses and some sheets on the floor and led Umar's son out. Umar lay on his mattress, propping himself up on one arm, looked at me with half-closed eyes and asked, yawning, 'What do you think of American policy in Iraq?'

His phone rang again and he switched on the TV.

I reopened Naipaul's *Beyond Belief.* Naipaul portrays Umar as a junior civil servant from a rural background with naïve and narrow views about religion, living in a squalid house. He does not mention Umar's social ambitions, his library, his political connections, his 'close friends' in the Lahore elite. He implies that Umar's father had tracked down and murdered a female in his family for eloping without consent.

When Umar had finished on the phone, I asked whether he was happy with this portrait.

'Yes, of course I am. I have great respect for Naipaul – he is a true gentleman, did so much research into my family. You know most people's perspectives are so limited on Pakistan. But I try to help many journalists. All of them say the same thing about Pakistan. They only write about terrorism, about extremism, the Taliban, about feudalism, illiteracy, about Bin Laden, corruption and bearbaiting, and about our military dictatorship. They have nothing positive to say about our future or our culture. Why, I want to know?'

He pointed to the television news which showed a Palestinian body being carried by an angry crowd.

'Three killed today by Israel – why is America supporting that? Why did they intervene so late in Bosnia and not in Chechnya? Can you defend the British giving Kashmir to the Hindus while the majority of the population is Muslim? Is it a coincidence that all these problems concern Muslims?'

I tried to say that the West had supported Muslims in Kosovo but he interrupted again.

'Let me tell you what it means to be a Muslim,' he said, lying on his back and looking at the ceiling. 'Look at me, I am a normal man, I have all your tastes, I like to go to parties. Two months ago, a friend of mine said to me, "Umar, you are a man who likes designer clothes: Ralph Lauren suits, Pierre Cardin ties, Burberry socks – why don't you do something for Allah? He has done everything for you – why don't you do something for him? Just one symbol – grow a beard."' He fingered his beard. 'This is why it is here – just a little something for Allah.'

He was now lying on his mattress in a white vest and Y-fronts. I didn't really remember his designer clothes. Perhaps he had been wearing Burberry socks. The new facial hair was, however, clearly an issue for him. I wondered whether, as an ambitious civil servant, he thought a beard might be useful in a more Islamic Pakistan. But I asked him instead about Dervish tombs. He immediately recommended five which I had not seen.

'What do you think of the Dervish tradition in Pakistan?' I asked him.

'What do you mean?'

I repeated Navaid's definition.

'Oh, I see – this kind of thing does not exist so much any more except in illiterate areas. But I could introduce you to a historian who could tell you more about it.'

'But what about their kind of Islam?'

'What do you mean? Islam is one faith with one God. There are no different types. You must have seen the common themes that bind Muslims together when you walked from Iran to Pakistan. For example the generosity of Muslims – our attitude to guests.'

'But my experience hasn't been the same everywhere. Iranians, for example, are happy to let me sleep in their mosques but I am never allowed to sleep in a mosque in Pakistan.'

'They let you sleep in mosques in Iran? That is very strange. The mosque is a very clean place and if you sleep in a mosque you might have impure thoughts during the night…'

'Anyway, basically,' I continued, 'villagers have been very relaxed and hospitable in Pakistan. Every night they take me in without question, give me food and a bed and never ask for payment. It's much easier walking here than in Iran. Iranians could be very suspicious and hostile, partly because they are all afraid of the government there. In some Iranian villages they even refused to sell me bread and water.'

'Really, I don't believe this – this is propaganda. I think the Iranian people are very happy with their government and are very generous people. I cannot believe they would refuse you bread and water.'

'Listen to me – they did.'

'Well, this may be because of the Iran-Iraq war, which you and the Americans started and financed. Do you know how many were killed in that war? That is why Iranians are a little wary of foreigners. But look how the Iranians behaved…'

The phone rang again and he talked for perhaps 10 minutes this time. I examined the bookcase while I waited. Many of the books were parts of boxed sets with new leather bindings and had names like *Masterpieces of the West*, volumes 1–11.

When he turned back to me again, Umar seemed much more animated. He sat cross-legged on the mattress and leaned towards me. 'My friend,' he said, 'there is one thing you will never understand. We Muslims, all of us, including me, are prepared to die for our faith – we know we will go immediately to heaven. That is why we are not afraid of you. We want to be martyrs. In Iran, 12-year-old boys cleared minefields by stepping on the mines in front of the troops – tens of thousands died in this way. Such faith and courage does not exist in Britain. That is why you must pray there will never be a "Clash of Civilizations" because you cannot defeat a Muslim: one of us can defeat ten of your soldiers.'

'This is nonsense,' I interrupted uselessly. What was this overweight man in his Y-fronts, who boasted of his social life and foreign friends, doing presenting Islam in this way and posing as a holy warrior? It sounded as though he was reciting from some boxed set of leather books called *Diatribes against Your Foreign Guest*. And I think he sensed this too because his tone changed.

'We are educated, loving people,' he concluded. 'I am very active with a charity here; we educate the poor, help them, teach them about religion. If only we could both work together to destroy prejudice –

that is why people like you and me are so important. All I ask is that the West recognize that it too has its faults – that it lectures us on religious freedom and then the French prohibit Muslim girls from wearing headscarves in school.'

'Do you think Pakistan will become an Islamic state on the Iranian model?' I asked.

'My friend, things must change. There is so much corruption here. The state has almost collapsed. This is partly the fault of what you British did here. But it is also because of our politicians. That is why people like me want more Islam in our state. Islam is our only chance to root out corruption so we can finally have a chance to develop.'

I fell asleep wondering whether this is what he really believed and whether he said such things to his wealthy political friends.

When he dropped me off the next morning, Umar's phone rang again and, as I walked away, I heard him saying in English: 'Two months ago, a friend of mine said to me, "Umar, you are a man who likes designer clothes: Ralph Lauren suits, Pierre Cardin ties, Burberry socks – why don't you do something for Allah…"'

'A beard?' said Navaid, stroking his own, when I went to meet him again that afternoon at the tomb of Datta Ganj Baksh. 'When people like Umar start growing beards, something is changing. But he must have enjoyed meeting you. His closest friends are foreigners.'

I told Navaid what Umar had said about a clash of civilizations and Navaid shook his head. 'Forget it – don't pay any attention. He was only trying to impress you. He doesn't mean it. People should spend less time worrying about non-Muslims and more time making Muslims into real Muslims. Look at this tomb for example. It is a scandal. They should dynamite this tomb. That would be more useful than fighting Americans.'

Behind us were the tomb gates, which Navaid swore were solid gold and had been erected in the saint's honor by the secular leftist prime minister Zulfiqar Ali Bhutto, Benazir's father. He gave gold gates to the tomb of Shahbaz Qalander in Sehwan Sharif as well. 'That beautiful glass and marble mosque in front of us,' continued Navaid, 'was built by General Zia after he executed Bhutto and took power. Then the CIA killed Zia by making his airplane crash. So the marble courtyard we are standing on was built by our last elected prime minister, Nawaz Sharif. It hasn't been finished because of the military coup.'

'But,' he reflected, 'this Dervish of Shahbaz Qalander is all nonsense.

This tomb of Datta Ganj Baksh is all nonsense. It has nothing to do with Islam, nothing at all. There is nothing in Islam about it. Islam is a very simple religion, the simplest in the world.'

Beside us a man was forcing his goat to perform a full prostration to the tomb of the saint, before dragging it off to be sacrificed.

'But what do people want from these saints' tombs?' I asked.

'Babies, money – but the Prophet, peace be upon him, teaches that we should not build tombs. They tempt us to worship men not God.'

'And the Dervish?'

'They are cheaters, beggars and tricksters, who sit at the tombs becoming rich by selling stupid medicines.' He led me to the balustrade. 'Look at him, for example.' There was a half-naked man in the dust below the courtyard, where the snake charmer usually sat. His upper body was tattooed with the 99 names of Allah. 'He's probably got a snake in that box, and,' Navaid dropped his voice prudishly, 'has intercourse with his clients.'

'And the history of these saints, their local traditions?'

'I think looking too much at history is like worshipping a man's tomb. Allah exists outside time. And we should not look at local things too much because Allah does not have a nationality.'

'People say there are 74 forms of Islam in Pakistan. What do they mean?'

'Nonsense.' Navaid was being very patient with me. 'Islam is one – one God, one book, one faith.'

'But what do they mean? Are they referring to Qadianis?'

'Of course not… Qadianis are heretics, they are not Muslims. General Zia has confirmed this in law.'

'Or are they talking about differences between Naqshbandiyah, Wahhibis, Shi'as…?'

'Pakistani Shi'as are not true Muslims. They are terrorists and extremists – worshipping tombs – they are responsible for these Dervish. But in fact there is only one Islam. We are all the same.' He turned away from the beggar. 'There are no real differences because our God is one.'

The politicians had spent millions on this tomb to win the support of the saint's followers. But it was only superficially a tribute to the older Pakistan of wandering holy men. Ten years ago, the courtyard of this tomb was the meeting place for all the diverse groups which Navaid calls Dervish. There was Datta Ganj Baksh, the medieval

Sufi himself, in his grave, and around him were pilgrims, beggars, mystics, sellers of pious artifacts, drummers, tattooists, dancers, snake charmers, fortune-tellers, men in trances. But most of these figures were now hidden in the narrow streets below the marble balustrade. The politician's gift both asserted the significance of the saint's tomb and obliterated the cultural environment which surrounded it. Their new architecture seemed to be echoing Navaid's vision of a single, simple global Islam – a plain white empty courtyard and a marble and glass mosque, bland, clean, expensive – the 'Islamic' architecture of a Middle Eastern airport.

But I still could not understand why Navaid wanted to link these modern Dervishes, one of whom was now shouting drunkenly at us from the street, to the medieval saints. 'Navaid, what do you mean by a Dervish? Are you complaining only about mystics, who belong to a monastic order?'

'Of course not.' Navaid gestured at the man who was now cursing our descendants. 'You think he is a mystic in a monastic order?'

'Then what's he got in common with a Sufi poet or a medieval saint?' I was confused by the way he put medieval intellectuals, mystics and poets in the same group as magicians on the fringes of modern society.

'They're all Dervish – you know where that word comes from – from the Old Persian word *derew*, to beg? What they have in common is that they are all rich, idle beggars.'

I presumed that explained why he didn't call them 'fakir,' which means 'poor,' or 'Sufi', which refers to their clothes.

'But why have you got such a problem with them?' I asked.

'What do you think? Those people down there,' he said pointing at the varied activities in the street, 'wear jewelry, take drugs, believe in miracles, con pilgrims, worship tombs – they are illiterate blasphemers.'

'All right. But why do you reduce the Sufi saints to the same level?'

'Partly because people like you like them so much. Western hippies love Sufis. You think they are beautiful little bits of a medieval culture. You're much happier with them than with modern Islam. And you like the kind of things they say. What is it the Delhi Dervish Amir Khosrow says?' Navaid recites it: '"I am a pagan worshipper of love / Islam I do not need / My every vein is taut as a wire / And I reject the pagan's girdle." That's why I don't like them. Medieval Islamic mystics have no relevance to Islam in Pakistan.'

'Then why do you keep attacking them? Or comparing them to these men in the street?'

Navaid just smiled and wandered off down the courtyard.

Medieval mystics were, I was convinced, not irrelevant. It was they (not Arab invaders) who had converted the bulk of the Hindus to Islam in the first place, while their clothes, practices, poetry and prayers showed strong Indian influences. They were thus both the cause of Pakistani Islam and a reminder of its Hindu past. Furthermore, by drawing the link to the present, Navaid was conceding that the medieval 'Dervish' remained a live tradition in rural Pakistan.

Umar, by contrast, had not felt the need to recognize this. His modern Islam flourished among migrants into Pakistan's cities. He could thus ignore the half a million people who still danced at the tomb of Shahbaz Qalander, and the fact that his friends the politicians were credited with inheriting miraculous spiritual powers from men six centuries dead. His Islam, he felt, was the future. He could safely leave the Dervish behind in a marginalized, illiterate, impoverished world – leave them, in other words, in the rural communities where 70% of Pakistanis still lived.

At last Navaid turned back towards me. 'When I said that Dervish were irrelevant, I meant that Islam is simple, anyone can understand it, it is public, it helps in politics, it does practical things for people. But for a Dervish, religion is all about some direct mystical experience of God – very personal, difficult to explain. Islam is not like that at all – it's there to be found easily in the Qur'an – we don't need some special path, some spiritual master, complicated fasting, dancing, whirling, and meditating to see God.'

I could not imagine Navaid dancing. He was a reserved man, basically a puritan by temperament. When he admitted to being anything other than 'a Muslim pure and simple,' he said he was a Wahhibi. His Islam, like Umar's, was in a modern Saudi tradition, the tradition of the plain white mosque. It rested on a close attention to the words of the Qur'an, it refused to be tied to any particular place or historical period, it was concerned with 'family life,' the creation of Islamic states – an approach that was underwritten by extensive global funding networks. I could guess, therefore, why Navaid was troubled by an otherworldly medieval tradition with strong local roots, personal and apolitical, celebrating poverty, mystical joy, tolerance and a direct experience of God. I could also guess why he wanted to reduce this tradition to a roadside magic trick.

But I might have been wrong. Although Navaid was 50, he was, unusually for a Pakistani man, not married. He claimed never to have had a girlfriend. He was very poor but he did not get a job. Instead he spent his days discussing religion in the courtyards of the ancient mosques in the old city. He could recite a great deal of Persian poetry as well as most of the Qur'an. He was a wanderer and had lived 11 years in Iran, arriving just after the revolution. He was a very calm and peaceful man, he had few criticisms of the West and he rejected most of the religious leaders in Pakistan. Although he attacked Dervishes, he knew the name of every obscure Dervish grave in Lahore. I left him by the outdoor mosque of Shah Jehan. He had seated himself under a large peepul tree, to recite a *dhikr*, a repetitive mantra for meditation favored by the Sufis. As I walked off, I heard him repeating, 'There is no God but God…' with a half-smile on his face, entirely absorbed in the words and I was no longer certain who was the Dervish.

RORY STEWART

Rory Stewart served briefly in the British army and then as a diplomat in Jakarta and Montenegro. From 2000 to 2002 he walked 6000 miles across Iran, Afghanistan, Pakistan, India and Nepal. His book, *The Places In Between*, tells the story of his walk across Afghanistan. He is also the author of *The Prince of the Marshes*, an account of his year as appointed governor-general of two provinces in southern Iraq shortly after the 2003 invasion.

OLD TOAD ON A BIKE

Simon Gandolfi

I am in El Bolsón, a small mountain town in Argentine Patagonia. I am 74 years old and overweight. I should be back home in Herefordshire, England, dead-heading roses, concocting an acceptable excuse for not mowing the lawn or collecting a teenage son from the train station. I am riding a small motorbike for the length of the Americas. How small? A Honda 125 – the original pizza-delivery bike. It's the maximum weight my legs would support, and I didn't want a big bike anyway: they erect a wealth barrier and colour people's perception of who you are. I am here for the people: how they live, their beliefs, their thoughts, their hopes of a better future.

'It's something you need to do', my wife said. 'It's what you've always wanted to do. Go and get young again and write me a good book.'

I bought the bike new in Veracruz, Mexico: my starting point is the first house Cortez built and from which he set out to conquer Mexico. My goal is grander. I have been riding south for the past six months. Central America was easy. Distances were manageable; so was the climate. In the south you freeze on the Altiplano and ride 150 kilometres for a cup of coffee. For altitude, 4700 metres is my record – that was in Bolivia – and I've put 22,000 kilometres on the clock.

Pine forest and snow-capped mountains surround El Bolsón. It is a tourist town. Restaurants, hotels and hostels abound. The buildings are mostly wood – or pretending to be wood. Switzerland and Austria do it better. I have stayed two nights gathering strength for the ride south through Patagonia to Ushuaia in Tierra del Fuego. Distances are vast, so I leave at first light. I am dressed in two pairs of long johns, two pairs of pyjama trousers, cargo pants, three undervests, two long-sleeved shirts, three jerseys, a leather bomber jacket, three pairs of socks and brown leather Church's shoes. I have stuffed two newspapers down my front, wrapped a scarf round my face and wear two pairs of gloves and a blue rain-suit. Imagine a large blue balloon.

The road from El Bolsón climbs out of a wooded valley to open moors, where a few sheep cringe among sparse tufts of coarse grass. The clouds are black and I ride through thin flurries of snow. Two cops wrapped in frost-retardant suits and balaclavas shelter beside a pick-up. I ask what happened to the central heating. One cop says, 'The Government forgot to pay the gas bill.'

Esquel was a hippie haven in the '70s. Now it is a fashionable resort – intelligent hippies tracked the change, became entrepreneurs and now shop with platinum-grade credit cards. The less intelligent continue to roll herbal cigarettes, throw the I Ching or ponder tarot cards. I top up with petrol and head for Tecka.

The road follows a wide, flat river valley of huge sheep paddocks. Skinny trees grow along the river. I startle a flight of green parrots. What are parrots doing up here on the Altiplano? And why haven't the farmers planted shelter strips? Shelter would improve the pasture.

Tecka doesn't look much on the Auto Club map. So much for maps: Tecka holds a treasure. I turn off the highway onto a dirt street. Tin-roofed bungalows are sealed tight against wind and swirling dust. Half a dozen pick-ups are parked outside a petrol station. The petrol station has been out of use for years: the drivers are here for Sunday lunch at the petrol station café.

A true restaurateur is a miracle you happen upon in the strangest places. Evidence starts with the greeting. Tecka, the owner has been waiting all his life for my arrival. Will the plat du jour suffice? A simple gnocchi?

Simple? The gnocchi are al dente. The sauce is a combination of tomato, spring onion, garlic, herbs, country ham and Italian sausage. The quantity is as vast as Argentina. It is served in a dish cradled in a basket. It is divine. So are the fresh-baked bread rolls. The sugar on a crème catalane is caramelised to perfection. The owner is the chef. A fringe of grey hair surrounds his bald pate. He wears a striped apron and beams as he insists I drink a small grappa for the road. Bikers, forget your schedules. Stop here and eat.

I ride out of Tecka into a full gale. A moment's inattention and I would be slammed off the road. I consider turning back. It was a great restaurant – maybe there is a great bed. However Patagonia is famous for its winds. What I consider a gale is probably the standard Patagonian breeze. Hills on the eastern horizon glow topaz blue. Fifteen guanacos stand on a ridge. I passed a stunted tree 10 kilometres back.

Gobernador Costa is a further 60 kilometres southeast on Route 40. The streets are empty. Those out for a Sunday stroll have been blown away. I stop for petrol and a coffee. A pretty young woman operates both the petrol pump and the espresso machine. She asks where I am going.

'Sarmiento', I say.

'That's 260 kilometres', she says.

I agree.

'There's a gale blowing', she says.

I've noticed.

'You should stay the night here', she says.

'Patagonia is famous for wind', I say. 'Will there be less wind tomorrow?'

'Of course there will be less', she says. 'This is a storm. We don't always have storms.'

She fails to convince me. There could be a storm tomorrow. It could bring a more intense wind. If I weaken, I could be stuck here for weeks. I don't have weeks. I want to be home for my eldest son's birthday.

I wrap the scarf round my face, and pull on my two pairs of gloves. The road runs straight as a ruler over undulating moorland. A black dot in the distance becomes a truck. I crouch low over the petrol tank. Wind buffets as we pass. I recognise a face watching me over a fence. He is a young chap, not fully grown, not too shy. I park and dismount – no easy manoeuvre for an overweight balloon.

'Where are you from?' he asks.

'Colwall', I reply.

'In Herefordshire? That's close to Ledbury.'

'Ten kilometres', I say.

'I believe that's where my great-great-grandfather came from', he tells me.

'Very probably', I say and take his photograph.

He is embarrassed at having spent so much time with an old fogey. Off he trots to join his friends.

I hunt through layers of clothes and manage a piss downwind. I tell myself that fatigue is merely a state of mind. I have no grounds for complaint. By profession I am a novelist. For years I have lived in other people's heads. I longed to live my own life for a while, live my own adventure. I swing my leg over the saddle at the third attempt. The motor starts first kick. It's 150 kilometres to Sarmiento. Brmmm-brmmm...

The road dips through hills reminiscent of the Scottish borders. Wind and weather have rounded every crest. The lee side of a hill has collapsed. A curved pink cliff rises above the fallen waves of grassed earth. Wild geese face west into the wind. The nearest pollution must be hundreds of kilometres to the north. I am struck by the clarity of light and the extraordinary depth of blue in the sky. The blue is reflected in the lake on the approach to Sarmiento. The lake at Villa del Chocon was the same amazing blue. So was Lake Titicaca. I have seen parrots today. I have seen flamingos graze in ponds alongside sheep and Hereford cattle. My awareness that flamingos breed in the Andes fails to make their presence any less surprising. Those long thin legs should freeze and snap.

Now, in the evening, I pass cars parked by a bridge on the outskirts of Sarmiento. Sunday fisherman stroll with fly rods along a sheltered riverbank. I turn off the road at a sign offering bed and breakfast. Dogs greet me kindly. A woman shows me a bunkroom with six beds and use of a kitchen that she rents out for $20. I don't have use for six bunks; nor can I use the kitchen. My logic confronts her prices. My logic fails. I take a room in town at the Hotel Ismir for $15. The room is miserable, so am I. I have ridden 600 kilometres. I am exhausted and have hay fever or a streaming head cold.

I shower and walk a couple of blocks in search of a restaurant. Joy deserts Sarmiento in a gale. Bungalows shrink within themselves.

People huddle and watch TV. The Hotel Colon is a rarity. I spy six men at the bar. I guess that they missed out on Sunday church service and have been at the bar much of the day. How will they view an intruder, a Brit? I pass half a dozen times before gaining courage to enter. A set of aluminium doors leads into a porch, from where more doors open to the bar. The doors grate and squeak and clatter. An army tank would make less noise. Conversation ends. The six men at the bar turn on their stools and inspect me. So does the owner. So does his wife. I hold my hands above my head in surrender.

'I am a Brit', I say. 'Am I allowed?'

'They allow horses', says a man in a flat leather gaucho hat.

The Hotel Colon in Sarmiento is the type of dump any respectable biker hankers after. The bar is the right length: six people and it doesn't feel empty; 12 and it doesn't feel overcrowded. Sarmiento is a small town. I doubt there are more than 12 serious bar-stool occupiers. The six in possession have been on the same conversation for a while. Maybe it began yesterday, or last week or last year. It is one of those conversations that expand over time and develop threads that go nowhere and are put to death. Mostly what is said now alludes to what has been said earlier; you would need to have been in on the conversation from the beginning to understand its direction – if it has a direction.

I sit at the far end of the bar, order a small beer and watch the last few minutes of a football match on TV. The conversationalists seem content with my presence. The pool table to the left of the bar hasn't been used in months. It is there because this type of bar requires a pool table. The girlie beer advertisements exist for the same reason. They are expected, as are the three tables, each with four folding chairs, arranged along the wall. The bar-stool residents would be uncomfortable were they absent.

A young couple occupies the table closest to the door. I guess that they are students. She wears spectacles and is perhaps the more confident – or the more pressing – one in their relationship. The obligatory guitar case protrudes from among the bags and backpacks heaped on the floor. I wonder if they are waiting for a bus – or for a parent. I imagine my teenage sons calling home. 'Dad, can you pick us up?' I wonder if my sons are aware of the happiness it gives me to be asked. To be of use is a joy, no matter the time of day or night. I will bitch, of course. Bitching is expected. I don't ask how many 'us' is. I don't ask if the girl is a friend or a girlfriend. Asking would be an infringement. Of course I want to know – not to judge, but because this is part of who they are. However, I do wish that they would sit a while in the kitchen once we get home, let me cook them something, talk to me, let me share a little of their lives. They tend to hurry straight upstairs to their room. I guess it's my age. I'm sort of odd, an embarrassment. You know? Teenagers with a dad in his seventies. And, yes, I am odd. Riding a pizza-delivery bike through the length of the Americas is odd. And I've dragged them off to live in strange places: they attended state primary school in Cuba for a few years. Nor is writing novels a proper job.

I ask Mrs Hotel Colon if there is a restaurant open nearby. She asks whether a steak and fries would satisfy. A steak and fries would be just dandy. I drink a second beer and nod intelligently to asides from my bar-stool neighbours. The asides refer to the general conversation. A mystic would find them obtuse. Mrs Hotel Colon summons me to a small dining room. She says, 'I put a couple of eggs on your steak.' I thank her and ask for a third beer. I take my place back at the bar. One of the stools nods to the owner. The owner places a small glass of clear liquid fire in front of me. I raise my glass in gratitude. The conversation continues. I am blissfully content.

Three beers and dinner cost $7. The room rate for a single with bath is $15. Should you ever pass through Sarmiento, you know where to stay. Take a right at the park, ride three blocks and turn left. The Colon is on your right. Don't bother with the conversation. It won't be comprehensible. You are a year or two late…

SIMON GANDOLFI

Englishman Simon Gandolfi lives in the Herefordshire countryside with his wife and two sons. He has fictionalised his travels for some 40 years in a dozen novels published in as many languages. He has turned finally to travel writing in his midseventies with a planned trilogy covering three motorcycle journeys. Completed in 2008, the first two, on a Honda 125, took him from Veracruz, Mexico, to Tierra del Fuego and back north to New York. The third will recount a ride across China.

EXPEDITION 360:
THE FIRST HUMAN-POWERED
CIRCUMNAVIGATION
OF THE WORLD

Jason Lewis

Flightless Propulsion
Begins in the Mind

There is no glamorous surprise ending to the tale, which is exactly how it should be. If your head is on proper, the difficulties and details of any decent adventure are always outweighed by the final goal. For myself and every brave soul who risked their necks to complete this first human-powered circumnavigation of our globe, Expedition 360 was a tool to reach out to others, and into ourselves. In our luckiest moments, we even learned a little about this giant planet, which is made so deceptively small by the hasty wonders of modern air travel.

Intent primarily on finding answers to the big questions that we all have to address at some point in our lives, I found myself biking tens of thousands of miles across Europe, Central America, Australia, Southeast Asia, the Tibetan highlands, Africa and the Middle East. Friends and I kayaked through the Baja in Mexico and the ancient island cultures of Indonesia. Rollerblading across the US, I was attacked by fire ants, harassed and helped by rednecks and run down from behind by a drunk and nearly blind octogenarian, breaking both my legs at the shins. I hiked across Hawai'i and spent hundreds of days in the open Atlantic, Pacific and Indian Oceans pedalling a claustrophobic, sweetheart sea-maiden of a pedal boat called *Moksha*, Sanskrit for 'liberation'. Now, nearly 14 years since her christening, she is at rest, and I am finally finding my own liberation from boyhood fantasies of exploring the untamed world.

If Your Mind Can Imagine It, Legs Can Get You There

In August 1994, my friend Steve Smith and I were on our way to Lagos, Spain, many weeks and 3500 miles into the most daunting journey of our lives. A month earlier, we had lost our way leaving Greenwich without a map, but eventually found the bustling English Channel and crossed it successfully, narrowly averting arrest by French authorities, who alleged that *Moksha* was little short of a modified bathtub.

After two years of planning, we were still humorously naïve about the scope of our quest, wearing shirts that brazenly predicted the expedition would be completed in only two years. We had begun getting used to the strain a bike can inflict on unconditioned legs and bums, eventually clocking up more than 90 miles a day. We camped every night and took time to delight in the bounties of roadside fruits and the sight of verdant French and Spanish hills, especially the stunning Portuguese border country. Our lungs opened and drank in the humidity of the nearing coast as the wheels spun, humming, on the easiest roads the expedition would encounter for years.

From then on, bikes became my preferred means of land locomotion throughout the expedition. They're fast if you need to meet a deadline, and they can cruise at a leisurely speed when you need to soak in your travels. Bikes have incredible terrain flexibility on and off the road, making impromptu camping and sightseeing much easier. They expose you just enough, connecting you with the local ambiance and exposing your senses to myriad subtle climate changes and microcosms of sounds and smells.

Basic bike repair and maintenance are relatively easy and, although specialty parts can be tough to find in remote places like Tibet, bikes are embraced throughout many dozens of cultures across the continents. If you can't fix your bike on the roadside, chances are that somebody in the next village or town can do it for you, even if they have to cobble together parts from bits of scrap metal.

Don't get me wrong: bikes can be lousy. Southeast Asian monsoon rains forced me into local cockroach-infested hostels for days, or trapped in my tent out in the wild, waiting out ceaseless downpours. Pedalling just about anywhere in Asia is an exercise in blind faith as bikers share the road with animals, pedestrians and blazingly fast trucks on daringly twisting roads. If you survive the roads and the weather, you still have to conquer yourself: in Malaysia, nearing Kuala Lumpur, I almost blinded myself strapping a bungee cord to my bike trailer. The cord whipped out of my hand and zapped me square in the right eye, leaving me with a busted face and a white fog clouding my sight for days. Biking through northeast African countries like Sudan in severely arid conditions can require almost more water than it is possible to carry. The only safe routine is the one I used throughout the Central American leg in 1997: hide from the sun in flood tunnels under the road from noon until midafternoon then cycle until it's too dark to be safe; sleep in another tunnel until sunrise then pack up and ride until noon, by which time the temperature is so scorching you have to wear gloves just to touch the bike frame without getting burnt.

Our March 2007 departure from Djibouti town was quite unceremonious, with several groups of children using me as a slow-moving target to fine-tune their stone-throwing skills. At one point I made the mistake of yelling at a Somali kid who had jumped onto my bike trailer for a free ride. In Asia a sharp retort would quickly nip such behaviour in the bud but in Africa it seemed a different protocol was required; within seconds we were beating a hasty retreat under a barrage of large rocks flung by at least a dozen of the feisty little brutes. If any had hit us in the head, we'd have been knocked off our bikes for sure. In Africa a lot of people seemed to have short tempers and were ready to fight at the drop of a hat, a testament to their ruggedness in such hostile environs.

The Water,
and a Lady Named Moksha

When, what seems like eons ago, on 26 August 1994 I felt I couldn't pedal any further, it was the sage advice of Robert Louis Stevenson that inspired me to write the expedition's first online journal:

> For my part I travel not to go anywhere, but to go. I
> travel for travel's sake. The great affair is to move; to feel
> the needs and hitches of our life more nearly; to come
> down off this feather-bed of civilisation, and find the
> globe granite underfoot and strewn with cutting flints.
>
> *Travels With A Donkey in the Cévennes*, 1879

In October 1994 Steve and I stepped off the solidity of the European continent and crammed our lives into the pedal boat *Moksha* for 4500 nautical miles of liquid existence on the Atlantic. Our destination: Miami, Florida. We had no serious open-ocean training under our belts, and absolutely no clue that four years later we would go through the same mental roller coaster crossing the Pacific.

Life on a 26ft pedal boat is a singularly trying experience, and is definitely not for everyone. Hell, it's hardly for anyone. Sometimes we'd pedal for days and go nowhere, staring at the GPS in disbelief at the power of a half-knot counter current. We simply had to keep pedalling, sleeping and pedalling and pumping drinking water and pedalling in shifts. It was hot and exhausting and, after a month at sea, the constant exposure of our skin to salty air and salt water, combined with the inability to wash properly, led to the formation of lesions, salt sores, which eventually became infected (a major source of discomfort).

In *Moksha*'s stripped confines, Steve and I together bobbed on the Atlantic for 111 days, and on the Pacific for 53, before Steve left the expedition on the Big Island of Hawai'i in 1999. Averaging about two nautical miles per hour, it was much harder than we anticipated. No matter how much Zen a person can muster, too much of anything will drive you mad if you don't develop strict routines. The monotony of a slow-going ocean crossing can bring about mental clarity like any repetitive mantra or meditative state, but the enemy of debilitating long-term fatigue is never far away.

When equipment failed and on-the-fly repairs had to be made, I wanted to smash anything to vent my frustration – but couldn't, because we simply needed *everything*. There is very little room for your body in a pedal boat, much less for luxuries, and that alone makes the simplest of comforts all the more important.

Moksha's other human motors took the form of various friends: April Abril across the Coral Sea; *Moksha*'s builder, Chris Tipper, in the Solomons; Lourdes Arango from Darwin to Dili; and Sher Dhillon over the Arabian Sea. Relationships between the varied crew were often strained, broken down to primitive savagery, requiring nourishment from the most basic of morsels, like the succulence and resiliency of a simple cabbage.

Instead of narrowing our eyes to the next landmass, we offered our minds constant streams of 'psychological carrots'. We pedalled toward energising cups of tea, a nip of Scotch whisky at the next 5° line of longitude on the chart, or a chance to catch up on much needed rest in the tiny, coffin-shaped sleeping compartment known as the 'rat hole'. Sometimes the best thing available to a sea-tired mind was just a refreshing leap into the big blue swimming pool oscillating beneath us. When graced by rain, we jumped onto the deck to soak it up like desiccated human sponges, frantically filling up any random water containers within reach.

The sometimes grey day-to-day was brightened by the escorting schools of big, shimmering turquoise dorados. We encountered elegant finback whales, unsettling sharks and the peculiar birds known as boobies, which would try to land on deck. Occasionally a flying fish would land in our laps, no doubt more surprised than we were. Graceful pods of dolphins followed us, playing and twisting like underwater comets chasing each other's phosphorescent tails.

In addition to the violent side-to-side motion, constant waves of fatigue, nausea and dehydration, human-powered ocean travel can get a little dangerous. An itchy whale used the centreboard as a scratching post and nearly capsized us mid-Atlantic. We were blown off course near Cuba and received an unsolicited visit from an unmarked gunboat carrying armed militia. We finished that leg with a badly timed pedal-system jam very near a reef, followed by a scantly missed catastrophe when a container ship came within a few hundred feet of running *Moksha* down in the Gulf Stream off the Florida Keys. The notorious Coral Sea nearly killed April and me: for 1450 miles, our wills and legs battled nearly constant 20-to-25-knot southeasterlies. Leaving the Solomon Islands, we barely avoided being blown onto a massive reef system east of Papua New Guinea. Sea sickness dogged April for all but the first morning of the 32-day crossing, but she never missed a shift. Unable to make it far enough south to reach Cairns, *Moksha* was plucked at the last minute from the Great Barrier Reef north of Cooktown, in Queensland's far north, by a rescue boat chartered by the expedition's documentary film-maker, Kenny Brown.

Upon our first attempted departure from Mumbai, India, in February 2007, *Moksha* collided with an unmarked wreck submerged by high tide. The entire 46-day voyage was plagued with devastating water-desalinator and equipment failures. After managing to avoid pirates off the Horn of Africa (the world's worst area for maritime piracy, according to the International Maritime Bureau), we closed in on the crossing's completion in a near collision with a container ship outside the Port of Aden.

Leg-powered ocean travel will break you down and alter your mindset. The salt scrubs away all your excess, and you reconsider your needs, your *real* needs. It clarifies you. Often after crossing the Big Wet Bits it would take me days, isolated in a small hotel room, to readjust my sea mind to the 'sanity' required to operate effectively in society.

Moksha helped me to learn to let in the danger, let go of my safety net, slow down and throw myself into the world to accept my fate. She helped me to explore my limits, and how perception, if given room to float and breathe, can bend those limits. As these things have an uncanny way of doing, sometimes the experiences would only reveal their real life lessons later on down the road.

If Your Legs Can't Do It,
Your Arms Can

For 88 days in mid-2001 I mountain-biked 3500 miles to Darwin, Australia, starting from the mouth of the Starcke River near Cooktown, North Queensland. I and many welcome companions swilled down local billy tea, relished the delicious earth-baked damper bread and sweated our way through the flies and the bizarre, sandy, craggy and timeless wasteland that is the cloudless outback. On arrival in Darwin I reunited with *Moksha*, and Lourdes and I safely powered ourselves 450 nautical miles from Darwin to Dili, East Timor. We joined up again with Chris and April, and began kayaking thousands of miles through the vast Indonesian archipelago.

When we left Dili, many people told us we were crazy to attempt such a journey in kayaks. At this point I had 11 years invested in the expedition, and this pattern of local doubt had appeared before each of the legs; self-proclaimed 'experts' came crawling out of the woodwork to tell us a hundred reasons why we shouldn't do it. It seems that some people can't stand others stepping out of line and doing something different. You simply have to research your plan thoroughly, study the maps and sea charts, absorb all the local information you can translate, and do it anyway.

The four of us found sea kayaking much more arduous than we anticipated, in part due to the amount of weight in each boat (two weeks' supply of food and water, and communications and electronic equipment). By the time we hit the beach at the end of each day's paddle, exhaustion was the norm. The usual chores of setting up camp are made quite challenging in this part of the world by the audience of curious locals who will turn up in droves to goggle at anyone visiting their island. Not surprisingly, there is no word in the Bahasa Indonesian language for 'privacy'. A cup of tea was usually high on the priorities list, followed by firewood collection, setting up tents and pulling kayaks above the high-water mark. The last task of any evening was activating an infrared alarm system surrounding the tents and boats, guarding us from both human and animal thievery while we slept.

However, the various difficulties we encountered and an itinerary greatly pressured by visa renewals didn't prevent kayaks becoming my favourite water-travel craft. Provided you don't have to get anywhere in much of a hurry, sea kayaks offer enormous freedom. They allow you to closely explore the intricate detail of each island's coastline, to marvel at the constant unravelling of shallow, crystal-clear waters that are home to throngs of Picasso-coloured fish, which dart in and around the coral and sponges. But at times the kayaks also felt like a millstone around our necks when we were completely knackered, labouring to set up camp or trying to find a hostel in one of the intermittent towns at which we stopped for supplies every 10 to 14 days. And even though we had some of the best kayaks on the market (provided by Current Designs), they were somewhat compromised by the sheer remoteness of the archipelago. The sandpapering effect of hauling the boats up and down the coral sand beaches, day in, day out, eventually rubbed away the gel coat and started to affect the underlying fibreglass. We ran out of paintbrushes early on and Chris resorted to making local equivalents from the fibres of dried coconut husks to apply our meagre supply of epoxy resin. Ironically, had we opted for indigenous-style dugouts made from local materials, we would have had no problems making any necessary repairs along the way.

For six months we hopped through the region's 14,000-plus islands, touching ground on a mere handful, including Alor, Lembata, Flores,

Adonara, Sumbawa, Lombok, Bali and Singapore, as well as the Southeast Asian mainland of Malaysia.

Our typical day began around 4.30am, when we'd make a beeline for the kettle to boil water for tea and coffee. As I discovered when biking across Australia, the Baja and eastern Africa, it's wise to make an early start before the heat of the day increases. After an hour or so of breaking camp and loading kayaks, we'd paddle for around four hours, then stop for a breakfast of noodles or oatmeal whipped up over a fire. By this time we would have nailed around half of our daily quota of 20-odd miles, provided our wills and aching arms didn't have to struggle through any vigorous tidal currents, which can flow at up to 10 knots through the selats, the narrow passages between islands. We found patience to be a virtue when negotiating these: by waiting for up to five hours between tides for a safe window for our crossing, we'd find that a body of water that would have overturned our kayaks just an hour earlier would now be near-flat calm.

We'd continue paddling until around 3pm, then start looking for a decent campsite. It was important to allow enough time to find a quality sandy beach without rocks as, if the low tide has already ebbed, breaking waves can make landing precarious. (Landing at high tide also makes it easier to pull heavy boats up beyond the high-water mark.) Then, in *déjà-vu* fashion, we'd beach the boats, set up camp and meet with the local chief, sharing cigarettes or some small gift to ensure our safety for the night. After we had cranked out an update for the weblog and cooked up a typical meal of fish or veggies and rice, our fatigue would soon have us slumbering under the stars.

The Indonesian odyssey ended in near disaster after a hectic crossing of the supertanker-ridden Straits of Singapore. Indonesian immigration exit procedures delayed us by three hours, meaning that we missed slack water between tides and our 22ft double kayak overturned in a raging 8-knot current, in the middle of the shipping lanes. After spending the night illegally on one of the outlying islands, the next morning we made a successful second attempt to cross to Singapore.

Life in Slow Motion:
Don't Be Afraid

The expedition visited over 870 schools, orphanages and facilities for people living with HIV and AIDS in 37 countries. We created numerous online educational programs and used the adventure as a classroom learning tool to connect students with both the adventure and their peers around the planet.

One day in the middle of the Pacific I received an email from a youngster participating in our Classroom Expedition program. His simple question was an important one, 'Are you ever afraid to die?' That was a decade ago but my answer now would be the same as it was then, 'Yes!' Our first-aid kit always contained a range of pharmaceuticals, like a medicine cabinet for a hypochondriac. (Despite this, I still managed to contract malaria twice in six months.) But for me, more scary than sickness or death is being sucked into leading a life without meaning or purpose – a Living Death: a mediocre state characterised by absence of passion or conviction. It's an invisible plague that creeps up on you; before you know it you are asleep under its spell. My conclusion from travelling the world these past 13 years is that the people who live closest to the earth, and take the time to appreciate it and be intimately involved with it, are the least infected by this disease.

The expedition team and I met many thousands of people who said they could never do what we were doing, even if they didn't have other commitments. We always told them the same thing: you simply needn't be afraid and you don't have to be an expert. All you need to do is begin your journey and keep faith in yourself; the rest will be taken care of. For better or worse, you will learn a *lot* about yourself, and I can think of no better reason to travel than that.

JASON LEWIS

Jason Lewis was born in 1967 in Yorkshire, England. In July 1994 he set off from Greenwich in East London to attempt the first circum-navigation of the globe using only human power. After travelling for 4833 days and 46,505 miles across five continents, two oceans and two seas – by various means of human-powered propulsion – he re-crossed the prime meridian in 2007.

TUK-TUK TO THE ROAD

Antonia Bolingbroke-Kent
with Jo Huxster

Under the watchful eyes of the British Ambassador and a pack of Thai press, Jo and I turned out of the driveway of the British embassy in Bangkok and set off for England. Our mission was to drive Ting Tong, our beloved pink tuk-tuk, from Bangkok to Brighton and, in doing so, raise £50,000 for the mental-health charity Mind. Jo had concocted the madcap scheme on a trip to Bangkok four years earlier, but I never imagined the idea would become reality or that, if it did, I would be riding pillion. But as we've been best friends since we met at school at the age of 12, I also knew how determined Jo is and that, if anyone could do it, she could.

Having been a straight-A student and athlete *par excellence*, Jo suddenly fell into the devastating clutches of mental illness in her late teens. For the next four years she was in and out of psychiatric hospitals. So severe was her illness and her self-harming that there were times when I wondered whether she would ever recover. It is a testament to her strength of character that she did; her recovery should be an inspiration to all mental-illness sufferers.

One evening in September 2005 the phone rang. It was Jo.

'Ants, I'm going to do the tuk-tuk trip and I want you to do it with me.'

I was working as an assistant producer with ITV at the time and, after agonising for a few weeks, decided it wasn't the right time for me to be gallivanting off round the world on three wheels. But after a close friend of mine committed suicide that November, I changed my mind. Losing my friend made me realise that you only live once and never again would such an opportunity come my way. I handed in my notice at ITV and the next five months were spent furiously planning our expedition. The transition from assistant producer to expedition planner wasn't an easy one and the frenetic months leading up to our departure produced my first grey hairs and a lot of sleepless nights.

As novices in the game of overlanding, these few months of preparation were a vertical learning curve for us, which at times felt like being stuck in some warped version of *Challenge Anneka*. First things first: we had to find a tuk-tuk. Thanks to the wonders of the internet, we tracked down Anuwat Yuteeraprapa, Bangkok's king of three-wheelers, who agreed to custom-build us a supersonic model with roll bars, raised suspension and, most importantly, hot-pink paintwork. Multiple visas and documentation had to be arranged, routes researched, equipment ordered, money raised for Mind and corporate sponsors found to help fund the trip. Then there were the more unexpected delights, like skinning rabbits on a survival course in Devon, learning wilderness medical skills and getting our tongues round the Cyrillic alphabet in preparation for the six weeks we would spend in Russian-speaking countries. Oh, and there was also the small matter of passing the motorbike driving test. I'd never sat on a moped before, let alone attempted hill starts, U-turns or straddling a throbbing 500cc bike dressed in full leathers. But, because tuk-tuks are classified as motorbikes on the International Driving Permit, this was an essential prerequisite for the journey. As I sat dejectedly on my bike one afternoon, glowering at the shards of yet another broken indicator lying on the rain-soaked tarmac beneath me, I wondered if we would even make it out of England, let alone back again.

Launching off from the embassy in Bangkok, our first major hurdle was crossing the border into Laos. Thai-registered vehicles driven by foreigners had recently been banned from crossing the main border across the Friendship Bridge and moreover, if we did make it, we were in danger of falling prey to the multiple perils of Route 13, our road to China. But the power of driving a pink tuk-tuk soon became apparent: after a nail-biting two hours at the border we were given special permission and waved through. As we left, one official gleefully told us that there was no way our tuk-tuk would make it to China, so steep and manifold were Route 13's hills and switchbacks. Without heeding his damning prediction, Ting Tong, Jo and I breathed a collective sigh of relief and sped over the Mekong into Laos. One country down, 11 to go.

The customs official was not the first to warn us of the dangers of driving through Laos in the rainy season. Route 13, the main artery linking Thailand, Laos and China, was the haunt of gun-toting Hmong rebels who had attacked several buses in the preceding few years. Floods and lethal landslides were a common curse at this time of year and cars and buses frequently careered off the sides of these steep mountain roads. But as Ting Tong wound her way north through the mountains I was struck not by fear but by the fact that this was Laos' main road – the superhighway linking Laos, Thailand and China – yet it was flanked by tiny hill-tribe villages populated by scruffy children, piglets, goats, chickens, wandering water buffalo, cows and bent old women. As we tukked through each settlement, gangs of naked children screeched in delight at the sight of the peculiar pink vision whizzing past; bare-breasted women in tribal garb turned their heads in astonishment and livestock scattered from the road. I felt sure that a hot-pink tuk-tuk hadn't passed this way before, and the old Hmong women sitting on their bamboo steps must have thought they had finally gone senile as we sped past.

We were met at the Chinese border by Sam, our guide from the CSITS (China Sea International Travel Service). Since it is technically illegal for foreigners to drive in China, we had had to jump through a series of complex and expensive bureaucratic hoops to facilitate the Chinese leg of our tukathon, including paying the CSITS $9600 and obtaining special permission from the army, police and government. And, just to make sure we didn't misbehave whilst in the People's Republic of China, we were to be nannied all the way to Kazakhstan by Sam and a second guide.

After the perfect tarmac of the last 10 kilometres to the Chinese border we were confident that we'd left the worst roads of our trip behind us. How wrong we were.

This was Yunnan, one of China's poorest provinces, thousands of kilometres from the eyes and attentions of the government in Beijing. Yunnan's 'roads' were no more than filthy quagmires that made Laos' Route 13 seem like the M25. By lunchtime on our second day Sam, a nonsmoker for the last three years, was cracking into a packet of cigarettes and complaining of a gall-bladder problem. Quite apart from the mud and deep potholes, we had to fight with literally hundreds of vast construction lorries whose erratic drivers seemed hellbent on making a Ting Tong sandwich. I was so frustrated at one point that I wanted to jump out and pummel the potholes with my bare fists in fury, shout, scream and stamp my feet. Not that this would have achieved anything – but it might have made us feel better. As we tukked into Jinghong on the third night, filthy and exhausted, we celebrated in the knowledge that the next day we would reach the spanking new Kunming expressway and be able to say goodbye to this torture for good.

But that was not to be. Our arrival at the shiny new toll gates of the Kunming expressway was met with shaking heads and a flurry of men in uniform. Three-wheelers and the Chinese expressways, we discovered, are mutually exclusive concepts and nothing we could say was going to change that. We were furious. The CSITS had known we were in a three-wheeler yet had set our 28-day itinerary based on being able to cover in excess of 400 kilometres a day on the expressways. Unless Jo and I could devise a plan to give Ting Tong an extra wheel, we had to face the reality of driving the next 6500 kilometres on disused mountain roads, littered with rocks and potholes, used only by goats, water buffalo and the odd tractor: enough to make any tuk-tuk turn a funny shade of green.

At times over the next two weeks we despaired of ever making it through China, let alone all the way back to England. The days were a blur of bad roads and blue Dongfeng construction lorries. As we crawled along at an average speed of 30km/h, cars sped by on the adjacent expressways that taunted us with their perfect black tarmac. Although the roads in Guizhou, the second province we passed through, were marginally better, the driving was still utterly bonkers; buffalo carts doing U-turns onto the carriageway, trucks coming straight at us down the wrong side of the road, roundabouts taken backwards and a constant, ear-splitting cacophony of beeping.

One afternoon after 11 hours on the road, with me at the wheel, Jo launched into singing *ni hao* (hello), in perfect operatic tones, to all lucky passers-by. Whether toiling in the fields, selling watermelons by the side of the road or just strolling to town, they were all treated to Jo's dulcet tones. Sam hid under his map in embarrassment and I tried to drive straight while weak all over from laughing. The zenith came as we drove slowly through a small town. Tens of Dongfeng trucks were pulled up by the roadside and crowds of people milled around. We assumed it was dinner time and everyone had stopped for their rice and noodles. Jo continued her operatic offerings, safe in the knowledge that we would never see these people again. As we rounded a corner we saw the cause of the crowds, a vast landslide blocking a 50 metre section of the road, caused by an earthquake that had also decimated part of the town. There was no escape. It was 8pm, all the hotels were full, everyone had abandoned their houses for fear of an aftershock, and the only other road was a 300 kilometres diversion along dirt tracks. The only option was to wait and we had no idea how long it would take. Luckily the path was cleared the next day. This episode was a perfect example of how China could be hilariously funny or horribly frustrating at the flip of a coin.

As the days passed, Sam had become decidedly grumpy and unpleasant. His mouth had turned further down at the corners and he had left us in no doubt that travelling in a pink tuk-tuk with two slightly batty English girls was a mortifyingly embarrassing experience. 'Preeease, save my face' had become his most uttered phrase, usually prompted by our renditions of 'Ting Tong merrily on high' or Jo's habit of frequently donning the apron she had bought off an old women in Yunnan. At Lanzhou, in northwest China, Sam was replaced by Jack. He greeted his replacement like a long-lost brother, so relieved was he to be finishing his tuk-tuk experience and to have survived it in one piece.

The last Chinese province we passed through was Xinjiang, a cultural and geographical crossroads, bordered by eight countries and home of the Turkic Uigur people. Compared to the nightmare of Yunnan and Guizhou, this was the proverbial walk in the park. The potholes disappeared, Jack was a delight – apart from his penchant for eating chicken's feet – and exhilarating days were spent driving across the Gobi desert, beside the Great Wall and along the old Silk Road. We felt sure that Ting Tong was the first pink tuk-tuk to drive such a historic route, which was more used to facilitating the passage of silk and spices than three-wheeled anomalies.

After 30 days and over 6000 kilometres, our last day under the Dragon's flag was spent at the idyllic Sayram Lake, where nomads herded their flocks and yurts dotted the verdant mountains. Despite all the hardships, Jo and I felt sad to be leaving China. We had fallen in love with its people and scenery and driving through such an alien country in Ting Tong was never without amusement. On the longest, hardest days people's reactions always alleviated our fatigue. Even on a five-minute tea stop, crowds of 40 or 60 people would cluster round, bombard us with questions, rock Ting Tong's suspension, clamber into the driver's seat and laugh in disbelief when we gestured that we were England-bound. The language barrier caused further comic relief, most notably on the several occasions on which Jo had to cluck, moo and bleat to relay that we didn't want meat in our food. In Guizhou, where the locals have a predilection for dog meat, she added a woof to her repertoire.

Next up was Kazakhstan, famous for Borat, oil and corruption. We'd heard horror stories about crossing the border at Khor-gos – heavy fines, imprisonment for no reason, vehicles being confiscated – so it was with jangling nerves that we approached the heavily fortified border compound. Within minutes a group of intimidating-looking guards, all with guns, had gathered round, scrutinising the strange sight before them. Then a very tall official with a large badge and Terminator-style shades appeared, clearly the boss. Less than an hour later we were speeding towards Almaty, having been showered with presents, money and chocolates, ushered to the front of the heaving melee of Kazakh and Uigur families and escorted out of the compound, with soldiers saluting all the way and gates swinging open in haste. Stunned by our luck, we drove on to Almaty whooping with excitement and proclaiming our love for Kazakhstan.

The kindness bestowed on us at the Kazakh border was echoed daily in the six weeks we spent tukking across the ex–Soviet Union. It seemed that the Kazakhs, the Russians and the Ukrainians had never clapped eyes on a tuk-tuk before, let alone a pink one driven by two girls. People asked us to stay, bought us lunch and spent hours fixing Ting Tong then refused to take our money. Sometimes this friendliness was a little overbearing. The Kazakhs had a nerve-wracking habit of pulling up beside us at 95km/h, close enough to tweak their gold teeth, and firing a barrage of questions at us: 'Where are you from? How much was your car? Where are you going? Do you want to come and stay with me?' The more persistent would practically run us off the road for impromptu photo shoots. These encounters ended with the handing out of phone numbers and insistence that we pay them a visit. And at every border we were handed fistfuls of dollars by the 'notoriously corrupt' officials.

Even more surprising was the reaction of the police. In Russia, where police checkpoints appeared every 50 kilometre, we were stopped 35 times. Every stop was the same, the policemen taking a cursory look at our *dokumenti* before quizzing us about our route, our husbands and the cost of our vehicle. In Ukraine they were far more interested in Jo's leopard-print bikini top than our *dokumenti*, demanding to have photos taken before allowing us to proceed further. The only money we handed over in all these stops was a single Chinese yuan, to a policeman who collected Chinese coins. Travelling as two girls through these countries had been the thing we were most worried about before we set off, yet it was this very fact that proved to be our golden ticket. I feel sure that we would have had a very different reaction had we been two men in a Land Rover.

On 30 July, in the pouring rain, we crossed the Europe–Asia border just outside Yekaterinburg in Russia. We parked Ting Tong's front wheels in Europe and her back wheels in Asia and contemplated all we had seen and experienced – and the looming finish line. It was an extraordinary feeling, straddling these two continents, thinking back on the huge distance we had covered and marvelling at the absurdity of having driven all the way across Asia in our funny pink car. As if we had scaled a vast mountain and could suddenly see our destination through the clouds below, after nine weeks of tukking, it seemed that England was finally within our grasp. Yet Ting Tong had other ideas.

Apart from a snapped accelerator cable and an issue with our front suspension in China, our trusty three-wheeled friend had so far excelled herself. But tuk-tuks are tropical beasts and, as the thermometer plummeted and the rain fell, Ting Tong began to pine for her homeland. As we limped westwards across Russia barely a day went by without Jo having to extract the tool box and *Auto Repair for Dummies* and study Ting Tong's backside. In the Crimea our trusty tuk-tuk began to emit alarming, unfathomable hissing noises from the depths of her engine and veer violently to the right whenever we braked. Much to our consternation we discovered that her suspension had given way for a second time. We had already used our spare set in China, so the nearest replacement was in Bangkok, over 16,000 kilometres away.

We now faced a dilemma. We could wait for several weeks while Anuwat couriered the new shocks to us from Thailand, get on a plane and physically go to Bangkok to pick them up ourselves, or find someone here who could somehow fix her. The latter, although improbable in a country with Lada, Kamaz and little else in the way of motorised vehicles, seemed to be our best option. We were directed down a potholed track to the best mechanic in town, Serva – a Crimean Tartar. Serva turned out to be our saviour, fixing Ting Tong's ailing suspension in under an hour. We thanked him profusely, thanked him some more and set off on the last leg of the trip.

Crossing the border between Ukraine and Poland was perhaps the biggest culture shock we encountered on the journey. For six weeks we had been trundling across the former USSR, and its clapped-out Ladas, gold teeth, stale bread and proclivity for vodka had become as familiar to us as the sound of Ting Tong's engine. Yet in an instant it was all gone. Within 20 minutes of entering the EU we had spotted a Tesco and a McDonalds. It felt like our adventure was nearly over and made us both want to turn round and hot-tuk it back to Thailand.

Due to its size and proximity to home, neither of us had given much thought to the Western European leg of the trip. While China had taken a mammoth 32 days to tuk across, Poland, the Czech Republic, Germany, Belgium and France flashed by in a matter of days. Yet these final few days were among the hardest of our mission, psychologically as opposed to physically. We knew how lucky we had been to drive more than 18,000 kilometres without major incident, and couldn't bear the thought of anything going wrong so close to home. Ting Tong wasn't helping matters by throwing daily tantrums and Jo and I kept thinking of that adage, 'It's not over till the fat lady sings'.

With Krakow, Prague, Cologne and Brussels under our belts we finally made it to Calais on 2 September and drove Ting Tong onto the Eurostar, much to the amusement of our fellow passengers. Two hours later we were driving dazedly round the M25 with people waving and beeping at us. It's hard to explain how odd it felt to be back on home soil, but Jo and I both had an overwhelming sense of being strangers in our own country. We had spent 14 weeks inching around the Tibetan Plateau, across the Gobi desert, through the Central Asian steppes, over the Urals, down the Volga, along the autobahn – and here we were in England. I thought about the people we had met, the beautiful and fascinating things we had seen, the smiles and looks of astonishment as we zoomed past. I didn't want it to end.

The next afternoon, as we crossed the finish line in Brighton, a crowd of family, friends, supporters and press surged towards us. It was a fantastic moment, but very surreal. For the rest of the day Jo and I drifted around in a dream, unable to grasp that we had actually done it. But we had, and with 20,215 kilometres on the clock it was officially the longest ever journey by autorickshaw. The wild celebrations continued well into the early hours of the next morning amid a blur of interviews and questions.

Adjusting to normal life after traversing half the globe in a comical car was harder than we had anticipated. We felt we had seen and learnt so much and been away for so long, while everyone else had just been getting on with their ordinary lives. And, however interested people were, it was impossible to relate what we had really been through. I believe that those 14 weeks were the best of my life, and might always remain so. Yes, it was extremely hard at times, exhausting and stressful, but also incredibly exhilarating, mind-blowingly beautiful and hysterically funny. Driving across the world in a pink tuk-tuk is something I would recommend to anyone. It proved to us that humans are essentially kind, that humour is the key to survival and that risks are always worth taking.

ANTONIA BOLINGBROKE-KENT WITH JO HUXSTER

Jo and Ants were both 27 when they set off in Ting Tong, and had been best friends since the age of 12. Jo developed severe depression in her teenage years and it was her recovery that prompted her to want to do something extraordinary, like driving ridiculously far in a tuk-tuk. She is now studying medicine in London and expecting her first baby in August 2008.

Ants, having worked in television production for four years and travelled all over the world on various TV projects, now lives in Bristol and works for The League of Adventurists, organising charity car rallies around the world.

NOT WITHOUT A HITCH

Mark Honan

It was 2.40am and Jack was shaking me awake. A posse of mossies leapt off my skin as I moved my face.

'Let's hit the road', he said.

After looking at my watch, I felt like hitting him instead. 2.40am? Moving on after only two hours' sleep?

But it was his car, so I merely nodded and began the tentative process of engaging with consciousness. Thanks to a prodigious amount of beer consumed the previous night, my head felt as fragile as an autumn leaf. Rousing myself from my roadside sleeping bag, I found I could barely coordinate the complex task of standing up. Slumping in a passenger seat, though, was something I could just about handle.

We set off, and slump I did. The sluggishness of the Datsun, as it towed the swollen lump of the caravan behind, matched my mood.

This relative bliss didn't last long. 'Your go, mate', Jack announced after a mere 20 minutes. 'I need to save my eyes for later.'

Cheers, mate. What about my eyes? But it was his car, and I was just the hitchhiker, so I slid over into the driving seat. I could barely see and my reactions were like comic timing – delayed, pausing for the punchline. At least there was no traffic, and Australian roads in the outback are straight, if nothing else. So I didn't hit anything. Not even Jack.

———————————

Why hitching? Most people said, 'don't do it'. Media stories about highway murders meant solo males didn't stand a chance of getting a lift, I was told. In fact, I would need to be 'thicker than a whale omelette' to give it a go.

I wasn't deterred. I had travelled enough to know that some of the best experiences are the ones you don't plan. I was in no hurry and was happy to let the pace of my travels be dictated by chance encounters. Besides, I wanted to get to know the people as well as the country, and spending hours in the same small space would force me to interact with drivers.

There was the question of money, too. As an impoverished backpacker from England, a long way from my last job in both time and distance, I needed to spend as little as possible on my trip. I wanted to see Ayers Rock (Uluru) and end up in Melbourne. Beyond that, I was happy to go where people took me. My journey was a blank page of possibilities. Relying on others meant I had no idea where I would end up each night. This just added to the sense of adventure.

That's why, when I said goodbye to Cairns, on the Queensland coast, I ignored the interstate bus and hopped on a local bus to the main highway, where I started hitching. Progress was slow. I travelled just 85 kilometres in eight hours via short, intermittent lifts before scoring a late and very welcome ride into Townsville.

The next day, my idea was to target truckers as the most likely source of long-distance lifts. What seemed a good idea early in the morning seemed less so seven hours later, with exactly zero kilometres travelled. That hot, sultry day I grappled with the hitchhiker's greatest dilemma, namely, 'Am I hitching in the best place?' I was torn between three locations: the gates of a busy cement factory, a trailer park and a roadside café. Hefting my backpack periodically between the three places got me nothing except sunburn. I just couldn't decide which location was most promising. I equivocated, I prevaricated, I vacillated, I passed the time looking up synonyms in my dictionary. Finally, a trucker I approached in the café said he could take me a little way. First stop was the trailer park, where he added a second trailer – in his hands, a surprisingly time-consuming process. Shortly after, he stopped in a garage for a leisurely toilet break and returned with two more hitchers. This male-female, Irish-Finnish combo had also started from Townsville that day, but had immediately been picked up by someone who gave them a five-hour tour round his 12,000-hectare farm. They'd seen cattle herding, shared lunch with the ringers and experienced other farm activities that were much more exciting than my day of choking in the smoke of retreating exhaust pipes. I couldn't help feeling envious and even resentful of their good fortune. Some hitchers get all the luck, it seems, and it's usually females or couples. I realised I just had to resign myself to slower progress, as I wasn't going to wear a dress (for a start, it wouldn't go with my beard).

The trucker planned to let us off at Charters Towers on Highway 78. With just 20 kilometres to go, he stopped again. 'Smoko time. I need a shower and a quick tea', he informed us. 'Won't be long.' It was infuriating to be delayed so near the end of the ride. My annoyance grew as the truckie chatted for 15 minutes with the truck-stop owner, returned to repark the truck 10 metres away, then resumed his lengthy chat. One very long shower later, his 'quick tea' proved to be a very slow tea, punctuated by more inconsequential chat. Two hours after we first stopped, we were all back in the truck. It was now dark, and – oh, great: the truck lights didn't work. After 20 minutes of fiddling with fuses, we were at last on our way again.

We all parted company at Charters Towers, a colonial-era town clinging to its gold-mining past. The truckie had taken over five hours to transport us 118 kilometres. I'm guessing his employer gives delivery loads with a short shelf-life to someone else.

I overnighted in my tent at the edge of a truck park, from where voices woke me at 5am. After a swift breakfast I resumed my task, alternatively thumbing by the road to attract passing traffic and approaching drivers who pulled in to the truck stop. At 10am the latter method brought success. I was finally en route to the outback.

George, a talkative character with a nice line in understatement, was travelling faster than the previous day's ride – in fact he was speeding, judging by the pills he was swallowing. 'I've been driving all night,' he said in response to my quizzical look, 'they help me stay awake.'

I was startled to notice the barrel of a shotgun peeping out from the edge of his seat.

'Is that a gun?' I asked, rather reluctant to draw attention to it.

'Sure. For rabbits, maybe 'roos.' A pause. 'Sometimes hitchhikers.' I checked his expression; he was joking. 'Actually, it's mostly for shooting up road signs. Makes a great twanging sound.'

I looked at the signs more closely after that. Either George was a very busy man, or else plenty of other people shared his passion for pinging signposts. Some simply flung their empty beer bottles at them, judging by the necklace of splintered glass round the bases.

Flat, empty plains stretched out either side of the Flinders Highway as far as the eye could see. There were patches of green from scratchy vegetation, precious few trees and the occasional dried-up creek. The parched colours, the intense light, the sheer vastness of scale – the fact that this was all so different to travel in England more than made up for the monotony of the landscape. As the scenery drifted by, I realised I wasn't sure whether I was looking at 'the bush' or the generally more remote 'outback'. Either way, both terms are understated to the extent that they could equally be applied to somebody's back garden.

George was often on the road it seemed. Sometimes literally. He told me how, as a younger man, he liked to drive down the Stuart Highway to the desert, to get away from the lights, and then just lie down in the middle of the road to gaze up at the stars.

Time passed enjoyably, albeit with my occasional nervous glances at the quivering speedometer, until we stopped for a lunchtime beer in the one-street hamlet of Prairie. As George wasn't going much further, I asked around the bar whether anybody was going west. Jack, an elderly, wiry Australian, complete with grey stubble and Tilley hat, was. After a bit of chat, his initial reluctance dissipated, and he agreed to take me as far as Alice Springs.

Jack was on his way to meet his wife to go opal fossicking in Coober Pedy. They make a decent living doing this, digging down four to eight metres to find the opals. Jack had fought in Korea, then spent much of his working life as a machine operator, despite the fact that (he revealed without shame) he could barely read and write. He grumbled that his wife forced him to tow the caravan, which reduced travelling speed to 80km/h or 100km/h. At that rate, Alice would be a long trip!

It proved to be even longer than expected, as Jack opted to stop at every settlement for a refill of fuel and beer. We soon settled into a routine: petrol first then into the nearest bar. We always stayed for one beer each, then bought some carry-outs to consume in the car. I'd heard that some drivers in the outback tend not to take drink-driving laws too seriously; on the contrary, many take pleasure in drinking *while* driving. Jack's technique was to rest his stubby on the edge of the seat, braced between his thighs for easy access. Despite drinking copiously and not eating all day, his driving remained remarkably steady.

The outback is not empty; not quite. Every couple of hours a small town or settlement materialised in the shimmering heat of the horizon. In between these were vast expanses of red plains, dotted with sparse scrub and termite mounds. On the roadside were many roadkill kangaroos, though I failed to see a live one my whole trip. Also on the roadside were numerous discarded beer bottles. We contributed to this environmental vandalism, as Jack insisted that we chuck our empties out of the window. I was reluctant at first, but it did seem an outback tradition, and 'when in Rome…', or so the saying goes.

Cloncurry is renowned as the birthplace of the Royal Flying Doctor Service, and once recorded Australia's highest temperature, a sizzling 53ºC in the shade. To me, though, it was just like any other sweltering settlement with its meagre scattering of stores, bars and banks. We whiled away the evening in the pub, then at closing time drove 10 kilometres out of town for our overnight stop. Jack pulled up into an unused side turning, switched off the car, then phoned his wife. 'Yeah, we did stop for grog', I heard him admit at one point. 'I only had one beer, though.' He gave me a conspiratorial wink as he said it. That would be true only if 'one beer' in Australian really meant one gallon. Meanwhile, I was contemplating how soft the caravan beds were. I never found out. The caravan was full, apparently, so we slept beside the road, under the stars.

When we resumed driving at 4.30am the next day, I was very hung over. Jack must have been too, which is maybe why he cracked open a stubby shortly after taking the wheel. Mount Isa, a mining town with unsightly smokestacks, was left behind, then there was a fairly hilly section to Camooweal. This dusty, rugged, charm-challenged place is Queensland's last town (before the Northern Territory) and probably the last town in Queensland you'd like to end up in. Nevertheless, it's where, at 9.45am, I had a greasy fried breakfast and Jack had his second beer of the day. As we returned to the car, we saw two busloads of tourists pull up. Everyone jumped out with inexplicable enthusiasm to photograph the 'Next fuel NT 270km' road sign.

Lunch, beer and petrol were taken at that 'next fuel' station, the Barkly Highway roadstop. I imagined the busloads of tourists pulling up and photographing the fuel pumps. ('Hey, don't leave yet,' they'd implore their bored friends back home later, 'here's a picture of the "next fuel 270km" sign – and here are the very pumps the sign was referring to!') Jack snacked on chips, the first food I'd seen him eat.

I was still feeling hung over, and was looking forward to lounging in my seat and gazing vacantly out of the window at the passing scenery. But when we returned to the car, Jack sat in the passenger seat and said, 'Your turn to drive.' Just like that. I was taken aback at his casualness and his trust in my abilities. He clearly didn't think it worth asking any precautionary questions such as 'Can you drive? Do you have a licence? Are you sober?' As it happens, the answers would have been 'Yes, yes, not really', but I drove anyway.

'I've never towed a caravan before', I pointed out.

'Ah, she'll be right,' Jack muttered somewhat confusingly, 'I'll take over this arvo.' He promptly closed his eyes and left me to it.

Thankfully, it all passed without incident, though it was nerve-wracking when huge road trains approached on the narrow road. As they weren't going to give ground for me, I had to pull half-over onto the red dust-and-rubble verges to make room.

More beer and food was taken at Three Ways, the three ways being roads to Darwin, Alice Springs and Mt Isa. The sign saying 'No loitering by hitch hikers' made me doubly glad that I had met Jack. We pressed on another 125 kilometres or so, then pulled up at a lively bar. Three-trailer road trains were parked along the road for 500 metres on either side. I would have liked to have made a night of it there (well, the place did stay open all night), but Jack wanted to carry on. He managed to drive on for another 30 minutes before even he had to admit he was swaying too much. Once again, we unfurled our sleeping bags under the stars.

My last day with Jack began with that 2.40am awakening. With me at the wheel, struggling to stave off sleep, we arrived in Alice midmorning. After our farewells, I immediately checked in at a hostel for a much-needed rest in a real bed.

I spent the next day relaxing and exploring Alice, finding it a lethargic place, probably because the fierce sun makes moving with speed unwise. Locals tend to sit around in any available shade conserving energy, including in the bed of the dried-up river. Back at the hostel I came across the Irish-Finnish couple, and tried not to feel smug when I learnt they'd been stranded in Richmond and ended up taking a bus.

The following lunchtime, after unsuccessfully scouring hostel noticeboards for shared rides, I began hitching at the side of the road. Several Aborigines nearby, noticing my 'Ayers Rock' sign, started jeering and laughing at me. 'Give up, man. You'll never get a lift', they called out. I half-believed them, acutely aware that my only lifts since Townsville had been a result of me approaching people, rather than them stopping. Accordingly, I gave myself an unlikely 2pm deadline before resorting to an expensive bus tour.

The clock ticked round. At 1.55pm Gus stopped.

'Ayers Rock?' I said hopefully, hardly believing.

'Yeah, mate. Hop in', he replied. I enjoyed the look on the Aborigines' faces as we drove off.

Gus was a farmer from down south, and had borrowed his brother's car for a minitour of the interior. Four hours driving later, we rounded a bend and there was Ayers Rock, a massive monolith rising from the flat plains, incongruous in its scale and location, as if tossed there accidentally by a giant's hand. The rock seemed to change colour – from red to brown to orange to purple – when viewed from different angles and at different times of the day. We stopped at several vantage points to snap pictures, allowing us to select alternative foregrounds of barren red earth or swathes of pallid spinifex.

Climbing the Rock is discouraged, as it's a sacred place to Aborigines. But it is permitted, and after a night in the Yulara accommodation centre we quelled our misgivings and took the ascent. We found it very hard work in the heat – the steep, 1.6 kilometre, 348 metre-high climb took two hours. The effort expended did at least emphasise the sheer enormity of this 'giant pebble', supposedly the oxymoronic meaning of the Aboriginal name 'Uluru'. It was somewhat surprising to encounter the odd tree growing from the top of the rock. Less surprising was the magnificence of the panorama from the summit, which took in the full expanse of the arid plains, as well as the Olgas, a harmonious jumble of smaller rocks nearby. After descending, we drove off to give these a closer look. The Aboriginal name for the Olgas is Kata Tjuta, 'many heads'. This, I felt, gave a more sensible sense of their size than the description of Uluru as a pebble, though these were definitely on the King Kong end of the cranial scale. In fact the tallest, Mt Olga, is 200 metres higher than Uluru itself.

As we drove the 260 kilometres back to the Stuart Highway, I pondered whether it had been worth travelling so far through an empty interior just to see a few rocks. The answer was a resounding 'yes'. Calling these natural monuments 'a few rocks' was a bit like dismissing the Himalayas as a bunch of hills.

On the main highway, Gus drove north after a farewell beer, leaving me to try my luck heading south. Passing traffic was sparse – just one car in 45 minutes – and I didn't fancy my chances of getting anywhere that night.

Once again I was faced with a night in the open air. Unfortunately, a storm was approaching from the east, and the rain started tipping down the moment I contemplated sleep. The only available shelter was a covered pathway between the café and the garage. I hopped under there, wryly recalling the café owner's two comments some five hours earlier: (1) 'You'll get a lift easily' and, (2) 'It never rains'. Yeah, right. I wouldn't want him to read my fortune.

Waking up the next morning, I heard someone ask the garage cashier, 'How far to Adelaide?' I peered through the window and saw a driver and his male companion buying fuel and cigarettes. I leapt up, and bore down on them wearing my best smile.

'I couldn't help hearing what you said. Could you take me to Adelaide?'

The two looked at me, then at each other. They could hardly claim they weren't going there. A guarded, impenetrable glance passed between them. A brief hesitation, an imperceptible shrug, and they invited me to get in their car.

These two young men, Kelly and Tom, claimed to be fishermen but looked like gangsters. Tom, in particular, seemed to have stepped from the set of *The Godfather*, with his Italianate features, slicked-back hair, mirrored shades and stud earring. This cultural shift gave a sense of dreamlike incongruity as the semidesert slipped by. The two had been driving down from Darwin since midnight Wednesday (30 hours earlier) and were due back on Monday – that's 6000 kilometres in five days.

'Lot of driving,' I remarked. 'Are you on business?'

'We're on a mission', replied Kelly, repeating that inscrutable glance towards his friend.

'Yeah', said Tom, half grinning, half sneering. 'Looking to make money without working.'

They didn't elaborate and their secretive manner made me reluctant to probe further. I was on the horns of another hitchhiker's dilemma: to be or not to be talkative. Some people pick up hitchers because they fancy company, so I usually feel I should to try to repay the ride by providing interesting conversation. Others stop simply out of good-naturedness, and may not want to be burdened by social chitchat. These two hadn't really invited me at all, so I decided not to instigate further dialogue and instead tried to blend as unobtrusively as possible into the back seat. This was probably the right approach. I began to miss the laid-back attitude and easy companionship of my time with Jack.

There was certainly something shady about these two and their journey. Though they were driving a flash car and had an appearance of affluence, they had no cash and tapped me for a petrol contribution. As we sped past ranges of hills they spoke in undertones between themselves. The odd disconcerting phrase drifted back to me, half-asleep on the back seat: 'blocks in Queensland', 'guns buried in the back garden', a contact who feared jail but ought to fear them more 'if he backs out'.

Driving accelerator to the floor, we reached Coober Pedy after just four hours. I strolled briefly round the small but spread-out town, noting the lorries bearing complicated digging devices and the numerous mounds of earth and stones. I half-expected to see Jack there fossicking for opals, spade in one hand and stubby in the other. I wished him luck, as the place looked harsh, inhospitable and almost otherworldly: the buildings were predominantly underground (to absorb whatever coolness there was in the ground). The town, beneath its sheen of dust, was almost empty in the midday sun, probably because residents were sensibly cocooned in their semi-subterranean snugs.

The twosome had expected to pick up a money transfer in town. As this failed to materialise, they drove more slowly to conserve fuel. Continuing south, the desertlike ambience diminished and the landscape gradually took on a more fertile, greener appearance. Towns cropped up with increasing regularity. The only thing that didn't change was the edgy atmosphere in the car.

The lights of Adelaide glimmered into view just after midnight. Not bothering to enquire where I might want to be dropped off, Tom drove up and down the central streets looking for their friend's flat. I began to wonder if they would ever let me out. Alarmingly, they seemed to be discussing whether I should stay with them. Was

I not to be consulted in this decision? I slid forwards in my seat, straining to hear, ready for flight. As I had no wish to be coerced into joining their 'mission', I hurriedly asked them to stop when I spotted a hostel. To my relief, Tom screeched the car to a halt. I hammered on the hostel door, and managed to secure a berth on the sofa, even though the place was full.

Next day I pressed on to Melbourne. The Dukes Highway was busy, built up, and bustling – a startling contrast to the strung out emptiness and sleepy pace of the outback. A series of short lifts got me to a roadhouse at Coonalpyn. I arrived in time to look on enviously as a smart-looking guy zoomed off in an open-top red sports car. In contrast, my next ride was in a rather more humble carriage: a $200 wreck driven by a man on his way to participate in a speedway meeting. We soon caught up with that red sports car, however, parked at the side of the road with steam billowing from its bonnet. The problem was a split water hose, the driver, Peter, said. We gave him some water. It turned out he was going to Melbourne and would take me there – if he made it that far. Wondering if I was making the mistake of backing the hare over the tortoise, I jumped in. Just 30 minutes later Peter stopped the car again. 'Head gasket's about to go, I reckon,' he said, releasing the bonnet. 'You'd better sort yourself another ride.'

I walked on to the next truck stop and approached numerous drivers over the next two hours. No luck. Just as I was thinking I would have to call it a day, Peter pulled up – he'd managed to fix the problem somehow – and away we zoomed.

Peter was originally a New Zealander and owned a chain of fast-food restaurants. 'Australia is a land of opportunity', he announced. 'I've built my franchise from nothing in nine years.' With the wind streaming over the windscreen and whipping through my hair, I received a tutorial in running a fast-food franchise. 'Consistency is what counts,' I learned. 'The public will eat rubbish, no problem. They just need to know that that rubbish will taste the same each time.' Though I was grateful for the ride, I decided to avoid sampling the fare from his restaurant chain.

It was nearly 2am by the time Melbourne made its appearance, heralding the end of my journey. Thinking back, I realised that I had engaged more with Australia and its people in these few days than in my nine previous months in the country. My 5200 kilometre journey had been built on chance meetings, accidents of timing and arbitrary decisions about the best hitching points. A single alteration at any stage could have led to a dramatically different outcome.

As Jack said one morning, midway through his third beer, 'Most things you do are a gamble. You keep digging around, and maybe you get yourself in a few holes. But one day, if you're lucky, you'll score a stack of opals.'

That seemed a bit like my trip. The way it turned out, I was really glad I didn't back out of hitching in the outback.

MARK HONAN

Mark Honan spent 12 years writing guidebooks for Lonely Planet, covering countries as diverse as Switzerland, El Salvador and the Solomon Islands. Nowadays, with a family to support, he is mostly confined to South London working for the local government, but still manages to take on regular travel writing contracts.

A ROAD WELL TRODDEN

Dean Starnes

Even though it wasn't easy, our bus driver had managed to get his foot up and onto the steering wheel. Given the relative size of his stomach and the cramped confines of his seat, this was no small feat: it had taken several attempts and a clear stretch of road for him to accomplish this without compromising the bus's velocity. Once he was satisfactorily positioned, he took to working on his toenails with both hands, a manoeuvre that necessitated him steering the bus with his foot. As his foot became more engrossing, his glances at the road became less and less frequent. The longest period for which I have been driven on a speeding bus by what amounts to a blindfolded driver using only his foot to steer is 47 seconds. I know this because I timed him.

We had been warned that the Silk Road might be dangerous. Every government with a website and a democracy had been issuing warnings about Iran and the 'Axis of Evil' since Iraq failed to deliver the promised weapons of mass destruction. And while the media banged on about the Iranian nuclear program, I became convinced that it is the Iranian driving style that poses the greater threat to world peace.

My friend Steph and I had crossed into Iran from Turkey under the shadow of Mt Ararat, the legendary resting place of Noah's Ark. Ever since then we had been treated to a number of hair-raising trips and near-miss collisions. Over the years I've been stuffed into more buses than I care to remember, often along with mounds of baggage in the aisles, chickens and other livestock under the seats and, in some countries, a sizable contingent of those travelling 'upper class' (ie on the roof). Nonetheless, I was impressed by how lively a journey could become in the hands of an Iranian motorist.

In Turkey buses tended to be frustratingly slow, stopping frequently, often for seemingly no reason and for long periods. Local music like Islamic pop was usually played at maximum volume and would screech on day and night, without end. Requests to turn it down were treated with amusement and complete disbelief. Deluxe buses were no better. In fact they were often worse as they had the added disadvantage of screening and then rescreening martial-art epics at maximum volume and long into the night.

Another defining characteristic of eastern Turkish buses was their proclivity to upholster their seats in vinyl. Since many roads in eastern Turkey are little more than a series of interconnecting potholes, passengers prone to buttock perspiration would often find themselves slipping and sliding from one person's lap to the next. This is the reason, I believe, that in this part of Turkey men sit at the rear of the bus while the women sit at the front. It is hard to maintain a modicum of decorum when little old ladies, dressed from head to toe in burkas, come shooting across the bench seats like Ben Johnson on steroids. This, I should point out, is only my personal theory about why men and women need to be kept apart and is not something prescribed in either the Holy Qur'an or Turkish bus companies' code of conduct.

Travellers, of course, have been leapfrogging from town to town along the Silk Road for thousands of years. Over the centuries, with the rise and fall of nations, parts of the route were abandoned in favour of new trails, only to be reused a millennium later. Some of the world's most charismatic travellers have left their mark (and in some cases their genes) on the people who live here. Alexander the Great plundered his way east to India on this road. Much later, Genghis Khan returned the favour and plundered his way west. By following the caravans of silk, spices and salt that crisscrossed the Middle Eastern desert, a young Marco Polo was able (with his father and uncle) to eventually reach Xi'an, the then Imperial court of China and the start (or, if you have travelled the other way, the end) of the Silk Road.

Steph and I had more modest ambitions. We aimed to travel using only public transport from Europe to Asia following these ancient trade routes. In this day and age, the idea was neither daring nor original. In fact, during the '60s and '70s, before the Taliban effectively closed Afghanistan to travellers, the hippy trail was a popular route between Europe and Nepal for backpackers. Our motivation was twofold. Firstly, we were interested to see what had befallen this legendary route. How could it be that countries that were for so long the centre of the world were now relegated to its fringes? What had become of the caravans of camels? And as for the great oasis cities of Samarkand and Bukhara, the fulcrum of the Silk Road, what had become of them? Secondly, we couldn't afford the airfare.

The Silk Road isn't labelled on any map or signposted as such on any street. It lies as much in the hearts and minds of the people whose destinies it has helped shape as it does in any physical highway between cities or dirt tracks over mountains. And, while the caravans of camels have gone and silk has been replaced by oil, the road is still there, still travelled, still exotic.

When we reached Tehran, the capital of Iran, the traffic congestion was so bad that locals used motorbike taxis to get around. Motorbike taxis are driven by testosterone-fuelled teenagers on personal jihads. Because there is a general dearth of traffic lights in Tehran, the accepted method of crossing a busy intersection is to nose your way forward until the opposing stream of traffic is forced to slow, allowing you to dash through, horn blaring. Iranians think nothing of doing a U-turn in the face of four lanes of oncoming traffic and, on occasion, taking to the footpath. For a pure adrenalin rush, few things this side of the Berlin Wall come close to riding on the back of a Tehran motorcycle taxi. For further excitement, tell the driver you're late and need to hurry.

Iranians as a rule are unfailingly friendly and, upon seeing our white faces flash by, other motorcyclists would race after us yelling questions, welcoming us to their country and enquiring about the whereabouts of our children. I found it difficult to imitate the studied insouciance of my driver and explain the platonic nature of my and Steph's relationship at the same time. Whenever I opened my mouth, it was all I could do to keep myself from screaming.

But Iran hadn't been the start of our trip. The first country we visited on our Silk Road odyssey was Turkey – the self-proclaimed gateway to Europe. For us, however, it was more the back door to China. The Mediterranean coast of Turkey is popular with European tourists and needs no introduction here, but beyond the bizarre rock formation and underground cities of Cappadocia the tourist crowds thin out and only the hard-core overlanders remain. The further east we travelled, the more Islamic the populace became. People were increasingly devout in their observance of Ramadan and more foreign in their dress. The last sizable group of tourists we met before crossing into Iran had been a bunch of backpackers staying in the tree houses at Olympus. It was there that we meet Fadlullâh.

Fadlullâh gave us invaluable advice about Islamic customs and how we ought to behave. He even taught us a PKK (Kurdistan Workers Party) separatist slogan, which worked so well that every time we trotted it out someone brought us tea. Fadlullâh had the unenviable job of getting all the backpackers out of their tree houses and into the minibus before they got too drunk. This wasn't easy because the optimal time to view the Chimera, the eternal fire of Mt Olympus, was at dusk, which coincided with the time that most backpackers were intent on drinking as much as they could before the happy hour ended or their credit card reached its limits.

According to legend the fire that springs from the rocks of the Chimera is the ignited breath of an imprisoned monster trapped here by Bellerophon on his winged horse, Pegasus, thousands of years ago. Ever since then, until the first Thursday of September last year, the flames have been burning; at one time they served as natural lighthouses for ancient sailors.

Last September the fire fizzled out because I squirted it with my water bottle. This sparked the most dangerous incident on my journey through the 'Axis of Evil'. Many people became unreasonably upset with me when the flames died. For a bunch of supposedly laid-back backpackers, they sure got irritated over what was essentially a mistake. Thankfully, Fadlullâh wasn't such a person. He quickly whipped out a lighter and restarted the fire. 'It happens all the time when it rains – don't worry about it.' I believe I owe my life to that man.

Over the centuries it has been the knowledge and ideas in the minds of men, more than the cargo on the backs of camels, that have brought about the most profound changes in the region. It was the Silk Road that acted as a conduit for Buddhism to spread to China. Sericulture and other trade secrets were disseminated throughout the world on the branches of the Silk Road. The Romans once believed that silk grew on trees. Despite being banned by the Roman senate on economic and moral grounds (silk clothes were considered to be revealing and decadent), it became a fashionable commodity during the Roman Empire. The Emperors of China, striving to keep knowledge of sericulture secret and maintain their monopoly, ordered that anyone caught smuggling live larvae of the mulberry silkworm was to be immediately executed.

Today much of the Silk Road is Islamic and, in accordance with Islamic law, women in Iran are required to wear headscarves and clothing that does not reveal the shape of their bodies. Steph also had to abide by Islamic sensibilities and stay covered. Unfortunately, her most shapeless pants were a pair of pyjama bottoms. Even though she maintains they weren't pyjama bottoms, I'm telling you they most definitely were. Not many people have travelled through Iran in their pyjamas, but Steph has. She questioned me several times whether people could see the shape of her legs through the thin material and I always told her they couldn't, although, if the sun was right, they could – like a tent lit from within. I did this because I wanted to see how tolerant people were of this shoddy dress standard and whether the reports so often retold in Western media were accurate. It was a very interesting experiment.

When people see the shape of a woman – say, for example, a person dressed in slightly see-through pyjama bottoms – the men usually ogle for some time, declare their undying love and, to prove it, follow it up with a quick marriage proposal. The women were mostly unfazed by Steph's clothing, although occasionally one would click her tongue at us to signal her disapproval. Iranian culture is one that prides itself on its hospitality, so a tongue click is quite a statement.

Transport along this part of the Silk Road is unbelievably cheap. We hired a taxi to travel 160 kilometres to a village and it cost US$5. Petrol was about 3¢ a litre and a bus fare across the entire country cost little more than US$25. Central Asia, however, is an entirely different story. While we were there, and for reasons that never became clear, Uzbekistan was gripped by a fuel shortage crisis. Turkmenistan and Iran to the south and Kazakhstan to the north were practically floating on oil, while the people of Uzbekistan and Kyrgyzstan were forced to buy their fuel on the black market as petrol stations ran dry.

The principal way to travel around Central Asia is by shared taxi. These congregate around town markets; once you have found a car heading your way, you must then decide to either pay the cost of the whole car or wait until others show up and split the cost with them. Locals almost always wait for others and no taxi driver dreams of departing with one spare seat remaining. There is little co-operation between drivers to fill one car before attempting to fill the next. Invariably a situation arises in which there are three cars, each with three people and all waiting on a fourth. It wasn't long before I found myself hanging out the door with the drivers, screaming our destination, 'Osh, Osh, Oshhhh', like a semiautomatic at passing shoppers. This is, of course, completely futile. No-one in their right mind goes to the market and then suddenly thinks, 'Hell honey, did you hear that? That guy's off to Osh, we'd better go too.'

If the driver gets frustrated enough, he will rev the engine as if to signify an imminent departure. This is a ruse to flush from the crowd any canny travellers holding back to see which car will fill first. Sometimes the driver will even depart, drive around the block and then pull up back at the market in the hope that this demonstration of his commitment to a quick departure will encourage a few more punters to jump on board.

Once you have succeeded in filling the car (this takes about three hours), you spend the next 45 minutes looking for fuel on the black market. This is tricky because local profiteers have taken to diluting their petrol. In Uzbekistan the trusted method of determining the octane quality of the gas is to taste it. A hose is inserted into the fuel tank and a bit is siphoned off the top directly into the mouth of the driver. A particularly violent reaction, in which our driver's eyes would roll back into his head forcing him to stagger about for a while, normally indicated that the fuel would be judged to be an acceptable standard and our fare would then be collected, so that the fuel could be paid for.

Central Asia lies at the heart of the Silk Road experience. The five 'stans' (Turkmenistan, Uzbekistan, Kyrgyzstan, Tajikistan and Kazakhstan) fit together like a complex puzzle as their borders follow knotted mountain ranges and the whim of former Soviet architects. It was here that the world's great civilizations collided – Iran and India to the south, China to the east, Russia to the north and the Turks, Romans and Europeans to the west. It was to here that, in 138 BC, Zhang Qian was dispatched by the Chinese Emperor to search for military allies; and it was here that the stage was inadvertently set for the establishment of a trade route that would last 2000 years.

Tiny oasis towns in vast deserts grew to form mighty khanates that crystallised into regional power bases. The legacy of this is an arsenal of architecture, each city more exotic than the next. First up was Khivia, once a minor trading post that became a powerful khanate, trading in slaves and synonymous with terrible cruelties. Samarkand has a history as richly complex and intertwined as any Persian carpet. When Alexander the Great captured the city in 329 BC, he was moved to utter, 'Everything I have heard about Marakanda is true, except that it's more beautiful than I ever imagined.' By AD 1370 Samarkand had passed into the hands of the Mongolian warlord Timur, who made it his capital and built the Silk Road's most trumpeted architectural achievement – the stunning Registan, a giddy ensemble of azure mosaic-bejewelled *madrassas*.

With so much on offer it's a wonder that the whole place isn't crawling with tourists. Essentially, many of the difficulties in travelling overland through Central Asia boil down to the difficulties in arranging visas. Some require specific entry and departure dates, others require an invitation from a local operator and all require patience. Steph and I spent days before our departure filling out forms and obtaining invitations from local operators who, for a fee, vouched that we had no plans to take over their government.

I blame Steph for the trouble we had with our Kyrgyz visas. With so much to see we failed to leave the country before our visas expired. In hindsight, we should have applied for an extension – this is what Steph advocated from the beginning. If Steph had stuck to her guns like she should have, we wouldn't have been deported back to the capital to answer a series of allegations. Instead, she believed me when I said that we could effectively extend our visas by altering the dates. This was a stupid idea and she should have known better. But it was pretty hard to detect the alterations unless you examined the visas really closely with a magnifying glass.

I was very surprised when the guards at the borders gave our visas a close examination with a magnifying glass. We had arrived by bus at the Kyrgyzstan border and it wasn't until we were pulled aside by the guards and questioned that it became apparent that we were in serious trouble. One guard maintained we were spies and decided that the KGB should be called in. Meanwhile, our bus had passed through the checkpoints and was now in Kazakhstan with our luggage. Fearing that we would never see our backpacks again, I started off after them across no-man's-land without a passport. This was a mistake because it left Steph stranded in one country facing a jail term, our luggage stranded in another country presumably to be sold at the next bazaar and me caught in the 200 metre gap in the middle without a passport or entry papers for either. Thankfully, an English-speaking official back in Bishkek was reached and we were shipped off to him to have our paperwork sorted out. Fortunately, he recognised that the only threat we posed was to ourselves and that his country would do well to be rid of us.

Between Kyrgyzstan and China lies the mighty Tian Shan mountain range, a significant obstacle for modern travellers and an often deadly one for the caravan traders of the past. Early accounts of the Silk Road describe encountering the bodies of travellers left frozen on the side of the road and the gangs of bandits who patrolled the mountains robbing and killing the merchants who travelled here. Only high-value commodities justified the high risks involved, which explained why, despite its fame, the Silk Road was never used to transport everyday goods. Only those items that were light, valuable, exotic and greatly desired merited the undertaking. Even today the mountain passes are often closed during the winter months and even the most painstaking arrangements can be thwarted by logistical gridlock. There are only two passes into China from Kyrgyzstan – the Torugart and the Irkeshtam Pass. Most of the traffic tackling the passes today are trucks hauling scrap metal and animal hides into China and returning with cheap Chinese-made goods.

The Tian Shan is not easily sidestepped. In ancient times the road split like a braided river as different caravans tried different routes to the East. Some opted to travel from Iran through Afghanistan and into Pakistan avoiding the Tian Shan, only to find themselves on the wrong side of equally fearsome Hindu Kush and Karakoram Ranges. Others headed north across the cold, windswept and waterless steppes of Kazakhstan.

Both roads out of Kyrgyzstan into China lead to Kashgar. Kashgar is one of those fabled cities, impossibly remote, surrounded by the Karakoram branch of the Himalayas to the south and the giant wasteland of the Taklamakan desert to the east. This city is the furthest from Beijing you can get and yet still be in China.

By the time Marco Polo gatecrashed Kashgar in 1266 it was already one of the great trading towns on the route; even today it retains its traditional bazaar culture and is home to one of the most exotic and eclectic markets you are ever likely to come across. Every Sunday, before the first call to prayer from the city's minarets, even before the first glimmer of sunlight, hundreds of donkey carts, horses, sheep, goats, camels and pedestrians thunder into town. By 10 in the morning Kashgar has turned into a bargaining bonanza. Submarkets form in different areas, each specialising in a certain style of goods. In the livestock section, two-humped camels are traded and men recklessly gallop horses through crowds as they test-drive various sway-backed beasts. Meanwhile in the vegetable arena, donkeys all but disappear under colossal burdens of carrots and melons. Over in the household goods area, knives, babies' cots and snow-leopard pelts – freshly poached from the Himalayas – are haggled over.

Going east from Kashgar, your travel options increase. We decided to make the journey to Urumqi by sleeper bus. A sleeper bus is one of those things that makes a lot of sense on paper but in reality is just another set of more refined tortures. The attraction was that we believed that a sleeper bus would enable us to stretch out in comfort as we rolled through the Taklamakan desert. We were wrong. What we didn't realise was that these beds were stacked three high and were slightly too short for your average Westerner. They were also frighteningly thin and, with such restricted headroom, lying in one was akin to sleeping in a coffin. Every bump – and there were plenty of these – threatened to bounce us off our bunks and onto the floor.

A Chinese bus driver's skill is judged by his ability to use at any moment the correct horn from the impressive array with which every vehicle is fitted. Law requires that drivers announce their presence to every cyclist encountered. Admittedly, these were few and far between in the desert, but once we reached Urumqi they numbered in the thousands. Our driver used a tweeter for preliminaries, a bugle or bullhorn if he got annoyed and, if the situation demanded it, an eardrum-shattering air horn. Apart from their ability to use these horns, most of the Chinese bus drivers we encountered were, as a rule, atrocious. They were loath to change gear and preferred to come to an almost complete standstill on a slope rather than change from third to second.

Nor did the situation improve when we decided to try the trains. China is undeniably a great nation and responsible for some of the Earth's greatest cultural advancements. Its people, however, are unfamiliar with the fine art of queuing. China's national sport is the 'huddle'. It is played at train stations with thousands on the 'field' at any given time. The rules are simple: every day a large part of China's population of 1.3 billion goes to the Urumqi train station to shout at the government official who works there. They don't queue for their turn to shout but huddle, pushing and shoving (it resembles a riot) towards the front. After four or five hours a couple of lucky backpackers may find themselves at the ticket window, where they too can shout their destination at the staff member who sits behind the counter drinking tea until being replaced by a new but equally unhelpful employee. This goes on for days until, frustrated and hopelessly behind with their travel schedule, they turn to the black market and buy their ticket at an inflated price.

Once on a train in Western China things don't noticeably improve. White-skinned travellers are a source of amusement and their every action will be closely observed and then commented on by everyone else in the carriage. Of course the Chinese aren't being intentionally rude, they are just curious and, once they understood that we had travelled all the way from Turkey, their fascination with us turned to utter incredulity. While some might find this attention discomforting, I found it marginally thrilling and it prompted me to reminisce about how it had begun. 'We'll jump on a bus here,' I had said, stabbing my finger at Istanbul on a map a year earlier, 'and we'll hop off here. It'll be fun.' And while much of what I had said to Steph that day proved to be wrong, in this I was right.

Increasingly, travellers are once again taking the overland route between Europe and Asia, and the four months it took Steph and me to travel the Silk Road is a trip that has already been made by thousands of others. Perhaps that is the legacy of the Silk Road, not as a path less travelled but as a road well trodden, a road that has outlived the empires that created it, a road that has lasted thousands of years and one that I hope will last for thousands more.

DEAN STARNES

Dean is a great advocate of long trips travelled slowly, and over the years he has backpacked his way through 75 countries and five continents. Currently he's on his third lap of the globe, going strong and probably lost. When not travelling or on the road for Lonely Planet, he's at home in New Zealand working on his forthcoming book, *Roam: The Art of Travel*. His website (www.deanstarnes.com) chronicles his progress.

ON THE LEVEL:
REDISCOVERING TRAVEL IN
THE AGE OF CLIMATE CHANGE

Joshua Hart

Transportation has always fascinated me. After all, moving from one place to another is the way we experience the world. Why then, I have always wondered, do we seek to minimize and homogenize the actual experience of travel, as if it's a waste of time? Surely the quality of the trip should be enhanced, rather than the quantity minimized?

After learning about the environmental and social harm caused by automobiles, and the joys of cycling as a mode of transport, at the age of 23 I sold my car, an appendage that was simply no longer needed. Aviation, however, was a harder nut to crack. My father's side of the family lives in London, and I've flown back and forth across the Atlantic from my home in the US about a dozen times to visit them over the years. I've been aware for some time that one seat on a round-trip transatlantic flight is responsible for emitting the same amount of carbon as driving a car all year, but I never really thought there was a viable alternative if I wanted to see my family. Plus, I have to admit that I always felt a bit like a sophisticated world traveler, sitting there in the airport departure lounge bound for distant cities. However, as I learned more about aviation's impact on the environment, I felt not so much sophisticated as selfish and gluttonous.

Globally, aviation is the fastest growing source of carbon dioxide emissions. Every year, 600 million tons of CO_2 (almost as much as the entire African continent produces) are emitted by the world's 17,700 commercial aircraft, whose numbers are expected to more than double by 2030. This largely discretionary activity is undermining efforts to reduce emissions from essentials like lighting, heating and cooking.

I decided I couldn't be part of it any more.

To be honest, this decision was also a relief. I always hated flying – my palms sweated during takeoff and landing and I had hellish visions of helplessly plummeting to earth (especially after 9/11). I loathed airports, and the way they force you to walk through shopping malls on the way to your plane. I hated the queues, the plastic food, the claustrophobia of being trapped in a narrow fuselage, and the disorientating, dehydrating jet lag. Other people seem to hate flying too, but put up with it because it is cheap and quick. Aviation used to be such an exciting way to travel – a once-in-a-lifetime experience to be savored; now it's a huge industry like fast food, all processed and nothing original or pure.

In 2005, I decided to pursue a master's degree in transport planning at the University of the West of England in Bristol, UK. Having committed to giving up flying, I decided to see whether I could get from San Francisco to England without using either automobiles or airplanes. It took me three weeks to reach Bristol (stopping to see friends in Montréal for a week along the way). I rode Amtrak for four days between San Francisco and Montréal, then boarded the MSC *Malaga* – a freighter ship that took me to Antwerp, Belgium – followed by Eurostar high-speed train to London. Not only was I able to experience the wonderful people and places along the way, I managed to avoid Heathrow Airport and its discontents: an added bonus.

I wrote in my blog nearly every day during the trip. Following is an edited version of my entries.

Day before departure:
San Francisco

So I am actually doing it. No more airports, turbulence or airplane food! Goodbye Southwest, EasyJet, and Virgin! Farewell taxiing, takeoff and landing! *Au revoir* jet lag! I am finally giving up flying, and it is liberating.

Freighters aren't exactly the pinnacle of environmental sustainability, but at least traveling by sea will give me a glimpse of the massive network of container shipping that underpins globalization. I've packed two days' worth of food, shipped my bicycle to Montréal, and sold almost all my earthly belongings. Now it's time to go!

Day 1: San Francisco
to Reno, Nevada

I left my apartment in San Francisco this morning by foot, boarded a historic F-Line streetcar to take me down Market St, then an Amtrak shuttle bus across the Bay Bridge. I waved farewell to all my friends and family as the city's skyline disappeared from view.

I boarded the train at the Emeryville station, a little overwhelmed by the prospect of the three-week journey ahead. We passed through the San Francisco Bay Delta, Sacramento, and began to ascend into the Sierra Nevada Mountain Range, with its beautiful wild flowers and a great view of Donner Lake. As we made our way up the mountain range at a leisurely 25km/h (about bicycle speed) I had a cold beer in the observation car, chatting with fellow passengers and enjoying the large panoramas across the mountains.

Train travel can be such a pleasure. There's room to walk around, socialize, get a bite to eat and go about life while on the train. And because railroads share rights-of-way with rivers, roads and trails, there is interaction with other travelers: as we passed, we waved to people rafting on this hot summer's day, or riding their bikes on the American River Trail through Sacramento.

Driving on the interstate, there are seldom friendly interactions between car drivers. On an airplane you travel from one generic airport to another, typically surrounded by freeways, parking lots, car rental agencies, and fast food restaurants. The only exchanges with the places in between are a fleeting glimpse from 30,000ft, a roar in the sky heard from below, and the ugly legacy of an abruptly warming planet. On the train, you can watch people in their own backyards as you pass by. As you stop at towns along the way, new passengers get on board who can tell you about the places the train has passed through and a diverse traveling community is created.

Days 2-3: Reno, Nevada, to Chicago, Illinois

The scenery is gorgeous, the company is fun, but the drawbacks of Amtrak are starting to show. The train is four hours late, which means I'll probably miss my connecting train in Chicago. I hear bad reports about the food in the diner, but I've managed so far with the food I brought on board. And the restrooms could use some maintenance. Overall though, it's been a great trip. At least there's plenty of leg room! Even though Amtrak is not what it could be, it's all we've got in the States, and a lot better than nothing. I've met a couple of blues musicians from Chicago, Sheldon and Maurice, who taught me the 'Dock of the Bay' chords and the blues scale on my guitar. Could come in handy during the long Atlantic crossing. We had a jam session in the luggage compartment, while other passengers gathered around to hear our impromptu performance – music in motion!

Days 4-5: Chicago, Illinois, to New York City

I made it onto the Lakeshore Limited from Chicago to New York, and now I am sitting talking with Kat, a friendly 19-year-old from Chicago, who is studying design in Providence, RI. We are chatting about climate change, bike touring, and how great it is to meet different people while traveling. There are so many stories on the train, people sad to be leaving, happy to be arriving somewhere, or falling in and out of love. Quite romantic really, if it weren't for the smell of rancid butter in the diner.

Day 6: New York City
to Montréal, Canada

I arrived at Penn Station in New York City yesterday, bedraggled and sleep-deprived from the four days on the rails, yet strangely invigorated. I headed straight for a hotel and slept 12 hours straight. Today I met up with a friend who lives in NYC and we enjoyed a clear sunny day in Manhattan. Now I'm on the Amtrak Adirondack on my way to Montréal, thinking more about my decision not to fly to the UK. My friend Sam says that I am not 'saving any dinosaurs' by not flying. The first thing my dad said to me on the phone when I got to New York was, 'Are you regretting your decision yet?' My cousin Jess from London (who is living in Australia at the moment) thinks I'm crazy. It's like everyone is waiting to pounce and say, 'Aha! I told you so: look what a pain you've created for yourself! Don't you wish you had just flown?'

But right now, having just enjoyed a cup of coffee in the diner car, sitting in a comfortable seat and gazing out the window at a beautiful rural scene, listening to one of my favorite bands, Stars (who are, incidentally, from Montréal), and typing in my blog, I have no regrets. I have seen the US from a different perspective, met new friends and enjoyed the time I have to write, read, and stare out the window. Admittedly I am lucky to have the time to do this, between working for non-profits and going to grad school – I realize not everyone has that luxury.

It wasn't too long ago that all long-distance travel simply took a long time, and people just didn't do it that often. It was special, and cultures were less homogeneous than they are now. All the indications are that we are returning to such a time soon. With the peak of world oil production and climate change, it may not be such a bad thing. No guys, I have no regrets. It's been a tremendous adventure so far and right now I'm looking forward to experiencing Montréal, and improving my French! *Au revoir, États-Unis!*

Days 7-11: Montréal,
Canada

I'm spending a week in Montréal, exploring the city on my trusty touring bike and staying with my friend Richard. I met him at a conference in New York last year and he's graciously offered me a place to stay.

While in Montréal I am working with Velogik, a great organization that Richard runs. The program trains disadvantaged youth, aged 16 to 30, to assemble and repair bicycles, and to pass this knowledge on to younger kids in elementary school, as well as teaching kids about climate change and other environmental ills resulting from car dependence. Like the Recycle-a-Bicycle program in NYC, it enables the kids to build a bike for themselves; many of them would be unable to afford one otherwise. While being trained by Richard, the 10 or so young people who are hired by the program assemble and repair bikes that are later sold as bike fleets for Montréal-area companies. What a great formula for job training and environmental education. As Edward Abbey said, 'sentiment without action is the ruin of the soul.'

Day 12: Port of Montréal, Canada

When I arrived at the docks, the port staff insisted that my bicycle and I be driven to the ship for safety reasons – so much for a car-free journey! The freighter that I'm traveling on – the MSC *Malaga* – is 208 meters long, carries 1000 shipping containers and is staffed by 21 crew and officers. There is only one other passenger, a German lady, who loves the maritime life so much she spends her holiday every year at sea. The crossing cost more than a flight, yet is still pretty good value when you consider it includes three meals a day and en-suite cabin accommodation.

I was a bit apprehensive about boarding the ship and meeting the crew for the first time. After all, I was going to spend 10 days out in the middle of the Atlantic Ocean with them. The literature the company sent me when I booked reminded me that the ship was 'a place of work' and that I should be careful not to get in the way. With this in mind, I cautiously ascended the rather rickety gangway with my bicycle and four saddlebags. The first two crew members I met both welcomed me on board with big smiles, though one of them, Joelas, had bad hiccups. I shared with him my friend Gus's folk remedy – that eating a heaped spoonful of peanut butter often does the trick. Joelas said he'd go to the galley and find some.

One of the crew stowed my bike, then I was shown to my cabin and around the ship by Christopher, the German first mate. Huge cranes were continuing to load the containers onto the ship, so I spent the day exploring Montréal. I returned late to the Port by bus and ran into a now hiccup-free Joelas, who thanked me excitedly for the peanut-butter tip, which had immediately done the trick.

Day 13: St Lawrence Seaway
Conditions: calm, no swell

I was shaken awake this morning in my cabin at about 5am as the MSC *Malaga* was helped out of Port de Montréal by a tugboat, pushing its nose against our side. As the *Malaga's* massive engines took over, we moved downriver toward the mouth of the St Lawrence, and out into the Atlantic. Goodbye North America!

All day we proceeded down the St Lawrence, passing small fishing villages and, eventually, Québec city. The Château Frontenac and the ramparts surrounding the old town are beautiful seen from the water.

Exploring the ship for the first time, I walked up to the bow and along the gangways, discovering the control room on the bridge, where multiple printers and faxes spit out the latest weather conditions in the Atlantic and computers plot the course. I also found the exercise room and a small indoor swimming pool, which is filled with seawater when conditions aren't too rough.

We set our clocks forward one hour tonight, and will do so again almost every night until we reach Antwerp – therefore no jetlag! I found out today that we are adjusting our route south to avoid bad weather and big waves in the North Atlantic – though we all have our eye on Hurricane Ernesto to the south, which may be a factor as we head into the open ocean.

Day 14: South of Newfoundland
Conditions: calm, no swell

I woke up to a dreary, grey, rainy day at the mouth of the St Lawrence. The sea was calm, and there was hardly any motion of the ship. This morning I saw a family of dolphins jumping out of the water alongside us. At breakfast I ate with the Filipino crew. A place had been set for me in the officers' mess, but the crew members are less reserved so I feel more comfortable and have more interesting conversations on their side of the mess hall.

After dinner, I joined the crew for a few games of table tennis downstairs in the gym. They're quite competitive but very good natured, and I shared my case of beer with them. We are passing just to the south of Newfoundland, and there are now swells in the ocean. Tomorrow when I wake up, we'll really be out in the Atlantic Ocean.

Day 15: About 100 nautical miles southeast of Newfoundland
Conditions: 5m swells

The ship was really rocking and swaying when I woke up this morning. I was a bit shaky when I went down for breakfast, but felt a lot worse trying to eat the eggs and toast that were set in front of me. I left half of them and returned to my cabin, where I lost the other half. I felt much better after that, though, thank God. I guess I'm going to have to get used to this rocking and rolling. There doesn't seem to be any rhyme or reason to it: sometimes we roll forward, then diagonally, then left and right. It helps to look at the horizon, though this is difficult when in the companionway without any portholes.

Day 16: About 400 nautical miles southeast of Grand Banks
Conditions: 1.5m swells

Right now I'm sitting in the crew's lounge, with a couple of very drunk German officers and Warren, an AB (able-bodied seaman). I saw flying fish earlier: thought they were birds at first, but then realized they had fins. Pretty cool.

Day 17: About 150 nautical miles northwest of the Azores
Conditions: 4m swells

The sea is relatively calm, though the wind is blowing and it has been overcast all day, and has just started to rain. This has been the most challenging day at sea so far, to be honest. I partied with the crew last night, which was great fun – though I probably had one too many Becks – and then before I fell asleep I opened the window in my cabin in order to get some fresh air. I woke up at some point in the morning gasping for breath: my cabin had filled with noxious smoke from the ship's smokestacks. Apparently the wind shifted. I must have been breathing it in for some time because I felt really poisoned when I finally woke up and shut the window. Ugh.

I guess this is the midpoint of the voyage, so we're getting there. Hopefully the remainder of the trip will be more pleasant than today!

Day 18: About 450 nautical miles west of Spain

Conditions: whitecaps, 4–5m swells

I spent the morning out on the bow of the ship with my guitar. The only sounds up there are the waves crashing against the hull and the wind whistling. In fact, it's the only place on the ship where I can tune my guitar, as back in the cabin the vibrations of the engine interfere with my electronic tuner. It's also the only part of the ship where I can't smell gasoline, oil or exhaust. There's never anyone else up there and it's a nice place to reflect. I get a wonderful sense of freedom feeling the salt spray and the wind, leaning over the railing and watching as we glide across the water. It's also a little unnerving to think that, if I fell overboard, most likely no-one would notice and that would be that.

Day 19: 380 nautical miles southwest of Land's End, Cornwall, UK

Conditions: 2m swells, sunny, slight breeze

I went down to the engine room this afternoon to get acquainted with the beast that is powering us, and our 1000-container cargo, to Antwerp. Wow. It truly is a behemoth. I had to wear ear plugs as well as large external ear protectors (affectionately called Mickey Mouse ears by the crew) before entering the engine room, a cavernous expanse of gleaming steel, whirring motors, dials, switches, and the constant smell and sheen of fuel oil coating almost everything, despite the crew's best efforts to keep things clean. Freighters use bunker oil, the cheapest (and dirtiest) fuel available. It's the gunk that's left over after the gasoline is refined from crude oil.

The head engineer told me it takes about 60,000 liters of this bunker oil *per day* to power us from Montréal to Antwerp. That means about 600,000 liters for the whole crossing between North America and Europe. This will emit about 1,380,000 kilograms of carbon dioxide – about the same as driving a Hummer H2 around the entire planet 69 times. Add to this the massive amount of fossil fuel consumed at the ports to get the containers on and off the ship, and to and from their final destination by road or rail, and it's pretty clear that the international shipping industry contributes massively to global climate chaos and our collective dependence on fossil fuel. It is largely hidden from public view, yet the majority of our consumer goods, from toothbrushes to food, electronics and clothing, pass through the container-shipping network, and each item has its own share of the overall massive impact of this power hungry industry. Think about that the next time you want to go shopping. Do you really need it? Could you buy secondhand or locally made or grown goods? Doing so is not just a hip lifestyle; Planet Earth simply cannot take another 50 years of 'free' trade and globalization. Now what we need more than ever is localization.

Day 20: About 14 nautical miles northwest of Cherbourg, France

Conditions: swells of about 0.5m, sunny, breezy

After the fog cleared this morning, a brownish haze replaced it, along with tankers, sailboats and other cargo vessels visible to port and to starboard. A dead seagull floated by and I knew we had entered the English Channel and arrived in European waters! We should dock in Antwerp around 2pm tomorrow. My plan is to make a break for it on my bike and try to catch the train (through the Channel Tunnel) to London.

At the moment I am sitting in the crew's lounge, typing in my blog while crew members riotously watch *The Weakest Link*. Being about 60 kilometers from the English coast, we are receiving BBC TV on board. It is pretty hilarious listening to a roomful of Filipinos trying to imitate an English accent. We just passed the Channel Islands to starboard.

That we have arrived and are watching the BBC is, in some respects, even more amazing than the experience of arriving on a 747. Traveling from America to Europe at bicycle speed (about 21 knots) gives you a new appreciation of the true distance involved.

======

Day 22: Grandmother's house, London, England

Conditions: sunny, warm

I said my goodbyes to the officers and crew, who were heading with their next load of cargo to the west coast of Africa. After cycling to the Antwerp train station, I sped by rail through Belgium at an incredible 300km/h, through the Channel Tunnel, then pulled into London, which was leafier and greener than I remembered. I had the feeling of coming home, and of a journey about to be completed. I claimed my bike, popped on my Ortlieb panniers, hoisted my trusty guitar on my back, and then I was flying on my bike through London traffic with the thousands of other bike commuters – and trying to remember to keep to the left.

Over the Vauxhall Bridge, I passed Victoria Station and Buckingham Palace, then reached familiar ground as I made my way through Hyde Park, waiting with a crowd of about 40 cyclists at a red light. I felt buoyant and invigorated, a bit wild, as I tried to stay in my lane on the pathway through Hyde Park, sometimes unsuccessfully as oncoming cyclists yelled at me – so sorry old chap! Then I was out onto Edgware Road and pulling into my grandma's street. I had arrived!

So, did I achieve my goal of getting from San Francisco to London without the use of a plane or a car? Yes and no. I did avoid airplanes completely, though I rode in a van when required to do so by port staff at Antwerp and Montréal for safety reasons. It wasn't always easy to disentangle myself from the dominant transport modes, but I am really glad that I decided to go overland, meeting some great people en route, and experiencing the geography between San Francisco and London in a way that was so different from my usual journey.

Now I'm starting a different kind of adventure, one that will bring me into contact with some of the best minds in the world working on our biggest transport problems, and I can't wait to get started!

Postscript: London, England, March 2008

Now, a year and a half after arriving in England, I have nearly completed my transport planning master's degree. The course has deepened my belief that climate change requires a massive shift in our attitude toward transportation. Far from being a sacrifice, it will enable us to enjoy a better quality of life if we embrace a 21st-century version of slow travel, exploring our local regions in more depth, while seeing long-distance travel as a special treat to be undertaken only rarely. I feel I am part of a growing movement that is rejecting much of the fast-paced, fuel-intensive lifestyle that we have been told successful people should aspire to. This movement not only has the potential to bring about better lives and communities and deepen understanding of the world and its people, it can also bring us back from the precipice of environmental catastrophe.

JOSHUA HART

Josh Hart grew up in the suburbs south of San Francisco and studied social psychology at UC Santa Cruz. He has been a professional sustainable transport advocate for the last 10 years, working to improve nonmotorized travel and urban livability. Soon he plans to take the train to the Far East and return to San Francisco by boat to complete his overland circumnavigation. As he'd much rather depend on the wind than on bunker oil to get home, if you know someone with a sailboat who needs a pair of extra hands across the Pacific, you can email him at velorution@yahoo.com. You can read his entire blog at http://onthelevelblog.wordpress.com.

SO CLOSE, YET SO FAR

Scott Kennedy

Most trips start with a tangible goal: a mountain to climb, a river to raft or a road to ride. But this journey evolved from quite a different place: the goal and even the means were much less important than the spirit in which they would be attempted.

I'd had my fair share of adventures; I've been a mountaineer all my life and spent plenty of days above the tree line and chilly nights under the stars. It had always been my dream to travel the world, to the far corners of the map, searching out the unknown, the ragged edge of human potential on the portion of the map still undiscovered. But I was no superman, I wasn't sponsored, I'd never been in the Special Forces, hosted a reality TV show or won some endurance race. However much I might want to escape the shadow of mediocrity and experience the epic adventures of the great explorers, my lofty ambitions and dreams outweighed my resumé tenfold. I couldn't avoid the cold, hard fact that I wasn't Shackleton, Hillary or Shipton. I was an average climber and passionate enthusiast who wanted to have an adventure.

Desire, passion and skill are the easy part. Big expeditions cost more than a new car, so my goals had to be far more localised if they were to become a reality. As ideas bounced around in my mind, a plan suddenly emerged. I couldn't afford to go far and wide to have my great adventure – but what if I made my adventure *how far could I go without spending a cent?*

My eureka moment was followed by a flurry of activity, pulling out maps, poring through guidebooks, searching for the seed that would grow into my trip. The criteria were simple: the trip had to cost nothing, except for buying food – which I would have needed anyway; I wanted the trip to start at my front door and return to the same spot; and of course it had to be hard – doable, but hard.

I considered long-distance bike tours and walking for days on end, but they just didn't add up to something greater than the parts. Then it struck me: I'd ride my bike to the local mountains and climb a peak. I had to laugh at the simplicity and the utter silliness of the idea – which made it perfect. It was a Wednesday night and in the spirit of the moment I decided that I would go on my trip on Saturday – no time for backing out or wising up. I also decided that I would go alone. I wasn't antisocial or lacking in companions, but this was to be my mission.

As I studied the maps, the plan of attack slowly began to take shape. I would bike from my home in the foothills of the Southern Alps near Wanaka, New Zealand, to the foot of Mt Tyndall, 80 kilometres or so away, hike the 1000 vertical metres up to the Cascade Saddle and then camp for the night. At dawn I'd ascend the rest of the way to the summit of Mt Tyndall and then descend back into the valley, retrieve my bike and ride home. It was going to be a big trip, 160 kilometres of biking, 30 kilometres of climbing, all door-to-door in a weekend – it was going to be exactly what I had been searching for.

Saturday morning arrived before I knew it. The two previous days had been a mad dash of preparing gear and steeling myself for the trip. The plan had dictated what sort of equipment I could take. There was no way that I could carry a full complement of supplies and still expect to pedal my bike. I amassed a pile of stuff on the living-room floor and dropped my day pack beside it. Starting with the top priorities, I began to pack: climbing boots, ice axe, crampons, sleeping bag, waterproof bivvy, first-aid kit and a Gore-Tex jacket.

The pack was full. There was no room for a stove, insulation pad or a glut of extra clothing. All of a sudden the commitment needed for this trip ratcheted up a notch. But there was no stopping now. It was the summer; I could eat cold food, sleep on my pack and have a chilly night – it wouldn't be comfortable, but that was part of the experience I desired. I wanted to push beyond my comfort zone a bit.

The day my trip began I woke early, had a hot breakfast and shouldered my pack. It was just before daybreak when I walked out the front door and started to ride. The kilometres fell quickly at first, as I was buoyed on by enthusiasm and desire. The road was quiet, it was too early for the sightseeing tourists to be out and the locals were still tucked into bed. First five, then 10 and all of a sudden 20 kilometres were behind me. The sun was shining now and everything was going to plan.

Soon after the 20 kilometres mark the paved road was replaced by a rough gravel track. The change of surface was a welcome distraction for the first few moments. But soon enough the ruts in the road began to take their toll. Like a compacted gravel sine wave, the road rippled into a washboard. All the momentum that I carried melted away as I hit this impossibly rough surface. The potholes and judder bars were so deep that the suspension fork on my mountain bike bottomed out – sending the vibration through my shoulders, which were already strained from carrying my compact yet heavy pack.

Trying to remain upbeat, I reminded myself that this was all part of the experience and to enjoy it for what it was. But the angel and the devil were sitting on my shoulders. The angel was full of encouragement: 'This is what you've always wanted to do; now you're really testing yourself. And hey, the scenery is stunning and the sun's shining.' The devil wasn't quite so supportive. He was rather cutting in his take on the experience: 'What am I doing out here? I'm not a cyclist – going for a casual ride once a month isn't how Lance trains. And now I'm riding 80 kilometres to the start of a climb – what was I thinking? I've got no business attempting something like this. I'm going to fail; I'm going to have to hitchhike back home, tail between my legs, destined to a life of golf and tennis. This is ridiculous, I should have gone for brunch with my girlfriend. Where is the fun in this?' The opposing thoughts swung back and forth in my mind: the road would smooth out for a moment and life would be great, then the ruts would attack me again and I'd be on the stupidest trip of my life.

After a long, long time I finally entered the national park and left the rutted road behind. From here I would pedal along a hiking trail for 10 kilometres to get to Aspiring Hut, where I would ditch my bike and start the hike upwards. Those last 10 kilometres were fun – I could feel the transition was close. Even though my day was barely half over, changing to walking was going to be a massive reward.

Just putting my mountaineering boots on and taking their dead weight off my back felt like Christmas. It was akin to the theory of aleviating the pain of a stubbed toe by stomping on the other one. My excitement returned and I pushed on – at least I wasn't on that bike any more. It was midafternoon and I'd been on the go for eight hours. Climbing steadily, I could feel a change in the weather. What had started out as a warm, sunny day was beginning to deteriorate. Clouds were building on the southern horizon – nothing too ominous, just a higher concentration of white, fluffy cotton balls. The higher I climbed, the more the wind started to pick up. A gentle breeze was evolving into a persistent cold southerly gust. Cresting the tree line, I had a better view of the approaching system. It didn't look too ominous, just high cloud. Trusting my gut feeling, I kept moving upwards.

The trail steepened; there were small bluffs to surmount, only a couple of metres high, but they kept me focused and in the moment. Every step had to be calculated: there was no one there to catch me if I fell. I climbed higher, finally cresting Cascade Saddle and getting the first view of my goal. Mt Tyndall looked great; there was an easy snowfield I could follow right to the summit. It would be no harder than climbing a beginner slope at a ski resort. I'd bitten off just the right amount; everything was going to plan.

Ascending the rocky ridge, I started to look for possible places to camp for the night. I was within striking distance of where I needed to be the next morning if I was going to make the summit and get back – all the way back – in one day. I found a flat spot among the roughly strewn stones that would make an ideal impromptu bivouac. Dropping my gear, I pulled out my sleeping bag and bivvy. The sun was setting and the air was already starting to cool down. I crawled into my sleeping bag, still wearing all the clothes I brought, and tucked into dinner – a can of tuna, some energy bars and a few squares of chocolate. As I finished eating, darkness fell and I heard a drop of rain slap into my tiny shelter.

Sometime in the night I woke to a thousand out-of-synch drummers pounding a tune on my sleeping bag. The sound of the rain was intense – how had those puffy clouds evolved into this? Everything I thought I knew about weather forecasting was tossed out the window as the rain poured down.

Two hours later, after a fitful five hours of sleep, there wasn't a hint of light in the sky when the jackhammer chattering of my teeth rudely shook me awake. Disoriented and confused, I was trying to make sense of the situation, when a wave of cold rain hit me like a bucket of water. My sleeping bag felt like that apron they put on you before taking X-rays of your teeth. Saturated, it was smothering me in an envelope of cold, wet unpleasantness. As I sat up, my back creaked like a rusty gate – the cold had seeped deep inside me, my limbs were stiff and I had a nauseous feeling in the pit of my stomach. I could see my breath condensing in the sheets of rain that fell upon me. The waterproof bivvy that covered my sleeping bag had been overwhelmed by the incessant rain; it had given up protecting me from the elements hours ago. There was now a generous puddle of ice-cold water pooling underneath me.

As my brain started to put all these pieces together, sudden realisation made it snap to attention. I was in trouble, big time. I needed to get warm, and fast. There was no tent to crawl into, I was wearing all of my clothing, I didn't have a stove and there wasn't a stick of wood on the rocky ridgeline to make a fire. Almost instinctively I started doing sit-ups: I had to do something to kick-start the internal heating system. As I counted out the reps, a glimmer of warmth started to form deep down in my core. For a moment I had hope – but then an instant later I fumbled with a zip and realised that my hands had the dexterity of lumber.

Making my way to my feet, I felt like an old man. Rigor mortis had seemingly already started to settle in as I began to slowly jog in place. Looking around through, the rain I could see the faint outline of the alpine ridge I was standing upon. Somewhere up in front of me was a massive snowfield, lost among the clouds. To both my left and right the valley dropped a vertical kilometre before levelling out.

As the situation moved more into focus, my mind wandered between rational thoughts of doing what I needed to do and the overwhelming urge to cry out in panic. I was near hypothermic, 90 kilometres from home, completely underequipped for the conditions and utterly alone. Through the overwhelming cold one emotion raced through my mind like a runaway train. Fear began to fill the crevices of my conscious thought. I was absolutely scared shitless that I was going to die right there.

I needed to get out of there, and now! Any ideas of climbing upwards were abandoned within a second – this wasn't the time for old ambitions. I had a new goal: to get home; if all else fails, get home. I hastily packed my things, wringing out my sleeping bag like a wet towel before shoving it into the bottom of my pack. Everything else was stuffed in on top of it. When I picked up the pack, my heart sank – my waterlogged kit was twice as heavy as it had been yesterday. I pointed the beam of my head-torch down the trail, not even bothering to give Mt Tyndall a passing look.

Warmth began to slowly circulate through my body. My feet sloshed around in my boots, as the water in my socks started to warm up. As I swung my arms to awaken my hands, the capillaries were forced open; the warm blood rushed into my frozen fingers and burned like magma, nearly bringing me to tears. But the pain felt good – the pain meant I was alive. Moving faster now, I could see the tree line. As I entered the trees, the rain showed no sign of stopping. With every step I got a little warmer and a little closer to home. I carefully eased myself down over the bluffs, past the exposed ridge line and downwards onto the zigzags. The steel-grey sky was soon obliterated by the crystalline green of New Zealand rainforest. Silver ferns, beech trees and moss-covered logs surrounded me. The contrast with the bare rock ridge made me feel welcome – like I'd returned home.

After I had stumbled, slipped and charged as hard as my sodden body could go for three hours, Aspiring Hut was a welcome sight. As I burst through the door, the hikers eating breakfast just stared at me. One of them asked where I had come from. I didn't know quite where to start. I sat down, out of the rain for the first time in what felt like years, and ate my cold breakfast bagel. Someone offered me a cup of tea and for the briefest of moments I contemplated refusing on ethical grounds – thinking that it would somehow tarnish my experience. That fleeting thought was quickly overpowered by common sense. The warm liquid made me feel alive again. But before I let my emotions get ahead of myself, I remembered the 90 kilometres of biking that lay between me and home. I finished my tea, thanked the nameless hiker profusely and saddled up onto my bike.

The rain didn't stop, didn't even let up. As I rode, my mind wandered to strange places. At one moment I was thinking about the ridge, the trip and what it all meant; the next moment, nonsensical things would fill my mind. The relentless pounding of the rough road was just as I remembered but as I crested onto the smooth road the clouds started to clear and, for the first time in nearly 20 hours, I could feel the warmth of the sun. Basking in the heat, I sat in the grass beside the road and had a bit of a laugh to myself. I could finally believe that I was going to make it back home.

The last 20 kilometres slid by as the day grew older. I passed through town, down the road and finally to within sight of my house. I had left here only the day before in the dark and now I pulled into my driveway 36 hours later, just as the sun fell behind the hill. As I walked to the door, I saw my neighbour in front of her house. She looked at me and smiled, giving the thumbs-up sign with a quizzical look. I thought about it for a moment and returned the gesture with a smile. The trip had been a success: not the sort of success that I had planned on – but perhaps something even greater.

In the years since then, I've come to realise that those two days in the mountains forever altered me. My whole notion of what was possible suddenly changed. The door had been thrown wide open into a completely new world of adventure. My willingness to push myself had promoted me from the sidelines to the arena. With this act of stepping up and moving away from the security blanket of conformity, excuses and limitations had been swept away: the only thing holding me back was *me*. In the past I believed that grand adventures only took place in faraway lands, untouched by the cartographer. Geography and finances were my crutches of excuse and procrastination. But after this trip I realised that the chance for an adventure is only limited by the obstacles we build in our minds. I knew that there was nothing to prevent me getting out there to explore and discover the world, to find the edge of what I could do. The Pandora's box of possibility had been discovered and all of a sudden the chance for an adventure was *everywhere*.

SCOTT KENNEDY

Not content to sit still for long, Scott Kennedy has gone on to ride his bike across New Zealand, run several off-road marathons and spend his fair share of time in the mountains. When Scott isn't writing guidebooks for Lonely Planet, he calls Queenstown, New Zealand, home. For more about Scott, check out www.adventureskope.com

TEN MILLION STEPS

*Andy Ward &
Paddy Morris*

*Andy: Slow Down Everyone,
You're Moving Too Fast*

London was beginning to take its toll on me. The four-hour daily commute from my parents' house didn't help matters and, despite living there in a vain attempt to save money and pay off my university debts, I was still haemorrhaging cash at an uncontrollable rate. It had been a particularly miserable few months since the death of my grandfather and I was desperate to find a challenge to get me back into the swing of life.

Paddy had long since been considering a big adventure, having spent most of his university career deep in travel novels. Patrick Leigh Fermor's two books *A Time of Gifts* and *Between the Woods and the Water* had particularly caught his eye and soon a plan was hatched to follow in similar footsteps and to attempt one of the purest forms of travel, an epic trek across Europe. I vividly remember sitting round a campfire on a warm May evening in Dorset when Paddy suggested that we walk from London to Istanbul. I pondered the idea for a moment but it took little to convince me. I also suggested that, if we were going to attempt such a challenge, we should also try to raise an equally ambitious amount of money for the British Red Cross. Four days later we stood beneath Horatio Nelson in Trafalgar Square, about to embark on an unknown journey across Europe with nothing but our rucksacks full of the lightest of our possessions, a beef-stroganoff ration pack and a map to get us to Dover. It was only two hours later, when we reached Greenwich, that I started to comprehend the improbable distance that we had ahead of us and that the journey might not be as easy or as fast as the 47-hour drive that the Michelin route finder had suggested.

Andy: Torrential Rain, a Long Goodbye and Quick Walk to Dover

I had to slightly lie to my parents and tell them that I was only going to accompany Paddy as far as Dover, although I think they secretly knew that I would be going a lot further than just the famous white cliffs. As we gave our friends even less notice than my parents of our impending departure, the send-off parade was distinctly lacking in numbers: in fact, it only consisted of my dear mother standing on Waterloo Bridge and waving us off in the torrential rain. (A note to all the budding walking adventurers out there: walking is so incredibly slow that the final wave can last up to 20 minutes as you trudge away down the long straight road into the distance; I recommend starting just below the brow of a hill.)

It took us an entire day to break out beyond the limits of the M25 and find a suitable village for our first night's camping: the tiny Kentish village of Bean. First stop was, of course, the local pub. Exhausted and desperate to numb the pain in our aching feet and shoulders, we nursed our pints of beer and discussed the first of many long days ahead. The landlord, slightly taken aback at the arrival of two sweaty backpackers, was very amused to find out that he was on the intercontinental walking route between London and Asia, although I don't think any of the pub's patrons believed we had even walked from Trafalgar Square, let alone that we would reach our goal some 5000 kilometres away. They were, however, persuaded to phone the local farmer to ask whether we could set up our tents in his field just outside the village. The local farm turned out to be a wide-boy truck haulage firm, and the lovely green field that we had dreamt of was in fact a vast concrete yard where we were expected to string our tents between the lorries. We braved the guard dogs in the morning to thank our host, after a freezing, wet and uncomfortable first night, and he promptly offered us a lift in the back of his lorry, which was about to depart for Germany. We kindly thanked him for the offer and set off down the country lanes; destination Dover, on foot.

On the advice of a spotty 17-year-old in the local camping shop, we had bought a methylated sprit–fuelled cooker. He assured us that this was the most widely available fuel across Europe and we rather foolishly believed him. We managed to run out of our little stockpile of meths by day three and were only saved by the caretaker of a boarding school, who managed to find some in his garden shed. It turns out that Britain is in fact the only country in Europe that sells meths. We burnt fondue fuel in France, floor cleaner in Italy, paint stripper in Slovenia, pure ethanol in Serbia and, most amusingly, used an extremely potent local home brew called *raki* to cook our meals in Bulgaria.

Each day followed a similar pattern, only with a steadily decreasing distance covered due to some very tired and blistered limbs. It took us five days to walk to Dover. We had always regarded the first week as training for the six months of walking ahead. I can't say our bodies felt too healthy but, as for our mental states, I can remember strangely having absolutely no doubt in our minds that we could and would walk every step to Istanbul. Reaching France was the first of our milestones and it didn't take long before we started to open the throttle, simply to see just how far we could walk in a day. The key to our success was in setting a daily routine and a minimum distance that we had to cover each day. Each morning we would rise just before dawn. The reason for this was twofold: firstly, we often needed to break camp undetected before a local farmer could catch us sleeping in his hedge; secondly, if we could walk (or sleepwalk) for two hours before breakfast, the distances that we needed to cover became much more achievable. The map became our ally. Every evening we would take great pride in marking out a 40 kilometre route for the next day.

The days soon merged into each other but the red line we drew on our maps just kept extending across France from Calais towards Geneva. On the horizon soared the Alps, which we knew we would have to climb at some point to reach Italy. Being complete amateurs, plagued with tendonitis, beaten up trainers and a complete lack of any all-weather gear (Paddy had abandoned his coat by this stage!), were we perhaps chancing our luck?

Andy: Defrosted Neanderthals,
Trigger and Some Very Big Hills

We crossed the border into Switzerland at the Col de Coux above the ski resort of Morzine in the French Alps. The mountain scenery was breathtaking in both senses of the word but we strode up the tracks like seasoned mountain goats, only stopping to refresh ourselves in the ice-cold mountain glacial streams. It was such a relief to leave the roads and footpaths behind and to be able to enjoy walking without the constant fear of being run off the road by incompetent drivers.

The other beauty of the Alps was being able to camp wherever we wished. Life becomes simple on the road. You have only two concerns each day: where your next meal is coming from and where you will sleep that night. The Alps cemented our decision never to pay for a campsite, and we indulged in the ritual of *camping sauvage*. This practice has its merits in the beautiful countryside but led to many an unhappy evening spent searching for a suitable wall or hedge to clamber behind, so that we could sleep out of sight from prying eyes. Some evenings we would have idyllic views from a mountain side; others would be spent under a railway bridge, in a cemetery, or wedged in the ruts of ploughed fields, where we could hardly sleep behind the thin 'camouflage' of our bright red tents for fear of footsteps and approaching cars.

On our first day in Switzerland we arrived at the bottom of a near-vertical climb. To regain some strength we took a break for a quick bite to eat. Paddy went off in search of bread from a nearby refuge, leaving me to chop *saucisson* with our trusty kitchen knife. On his return, he found I had acquired a donkey. My mother had advised me that, should my rucksack become too heavy or an injury occur, a donkey might be an effective solution. Paddy seemed surprised at my resourcefulness and immediately expressed concern that we might have to split our food three ways. 'Trigger' followed us for about an hour before the path steepened to a treacherous ascent where only a thin chain delicately affixed to the rock face provided assistance for the 'you fall, you die' climb, and it was with great reluctance that we left our new friend behind. Paddy's rationing concerns were assuaged.

My pack-carrying ones were not.

At the end of the climb we emerged at the base of an enormous glacial trough, surrounded on all sides by snow-covered mountain peaks, where we found ourselves in the midst of *eine kleine Gruppe* of stark-naked Germans. Such a sight in general is not surprising, of course, but 2000 metres up a glacier, with no piles of discarded clothing in evidence, it made us wonder if perhaps they weren't Germans at all, but defrosted Neanderthals celebrating global warming with a pool party. Not seeking an invite, we slunk off through the boulders for a further three-hour climb to the summit. Dressed only in T-shirts, shorts and trainers, we found that the steady flow of professional climbers, hauling ropes and crampons, only brightened our sprits and spurred us on to the top. The descent was as hairy as the Germans. Forbidden by our own rules to use our rucksacks as toboggans, we shinned down cliff faces, slipped over snowfields, traversed gorges and waded through mountain streams for a couple of hours until we reached the shore of the bright blue Lac de Salanfe. Exhausted from a long day with heavy packs, we set up our tents and collapsed with a warm beer that we had carried for the last three days' walk in readiness for this celebration. The worst of the Alps was behind us.

Four long, hot, mosquito-plagued weeks took us across Italy to reach the Balkans. In the heat of the day we would shelter from the sun in the shade, write our diaries and snooze, and I would practice my new hobby of resoling my boots with discarded rubber from the roadside. The countryside changed as we entered the rolling hills of Slovenia, which eventually flattened out into Croatia.

Paddy: Advice on Campsite Selection for Amateur Ramblers

The previous day's walking had seemed to go on forever, as we tried to position ourselves just short of the Serbian border for a nice early crossing in the morning. This meant, however, that night had long since fallen by the time we came to set up camp. We clambered over a hedge and collapsed in the long grass. Soon the stove was lit, beers had been opened and our little tents had somehow erected themselves in the darkness. Our goulash was quickly devoured and we crept into our sleeping bags, more than ready to take the weight off our feet for the night. A two litre bottle of Croatian ale, too much goulash, and a 45 kilometre trek combined to create the world's best sedative, and it seemed that the alarm on my phone was beeping me back out of my happy slumber before my head had hit the pillow.

Getting out of bed has always been anathema to me and flies in the face of everything I believe in, but the thought of our seventh border crossing waiting just 10 kilometres down the road eventually encouraged me out of my sleeping bag and, careful to avoid touching the soaking-as-ever wet canvas of my little tent, I pulled on my clothes and unzipped the door, eager to get a pot of coffee on the stove and stretch my legs. I'll confess that the sight that greeted my eyes wasn't quite what I was expecting. Our perfect little camping site was on the edge of a minefield. Looking back, it all seems to make perfect sense now: the Serbo-Croat border, all those houses covered in bullet holes and shrapnel scars that we'd passed the day before, the man in the café who'd told us, 'Those Serbs will slit your throats like hogs' – what a perfect place for a minefield! But it left us with a bit of a conundrum as to how to extricate ourselves from that there minefield without losing any of the lower limbs that we so desperately needed for the whole walking-to-Asia caper. Andy had also woken by this stage and was similarly concerned about the quandary we found ourselves in. But, more concerned about breakfast and a new passport stamp, we rather gingerly gathered together our bits and bobs and tiptoed to safety through the hedge and back onto the road, where we breakfasted in a lay-by. Not, obviously, before taking a few snaps of our minefield and its attendant warning signs, which were just the sort of thing to put on our charity website to help bring in some more guilt-pennies from our friends and family back in the UK.

With breakfast over, we cantered off along the road, which was bordered on both sides by acres of scrubland that had been divided into small sections by mile upon mile of red wool. We assumed that dividing the landscape up like this was the only practical way of clearing the estimated quarter of a million antipersonnel mines that are spread over nearly 1000 square kilometres of Croatia. It was a relief to finally cross the border and get into the relative safety of the Serbian town of Sid, where we breakfasted for the second time that day, on a mountain of delicious cheese-filled *burek*. And so the morning began.

From Serbia we gradually continued southwards. As the nights drew in and autumn slowly turned wintry, we crossed into Bulgaria. We had by this stage covered perhaps 4000 kilometres and were in reasonable shape. With the cooler afternoons allowing us to walk from dawn till dusk, the kilometres were flying by. We passed from Bulgaria into the northeastern tip of Greece and, a mere two days later, crossed our tenth and final border to arrive in Turkey.

Paddy: Our Last Night
Under the Stars

Nine days and 320 kilometres later, Andy and I were staying up late, wringing the last little bits out of our last proper night on the road. Our first hour or so of walking the next day would bring us to Istanbul, and another day or two of walking would get us into Asia. But that would be all hostels and pavements, so this was to be very much our last night under canvas. And what a place! We camped on the edge of what our map informed us was the Büyükçekmece Lake, a huge 12km-by-12km lake separated from the Sea of Marmaris by an artificial dam. We had made our way out through a series of spits and islands onto a little grassy oasis from where we had the most spectacular panoramic views of various suburbs of Istanbul, brightly illuminated by the floodlights of hundreds of factories. Serried ranks of electricity pylons marched across the horizon, draping their cables over the last glows of a spectacular sunset, which I photographed through the enormous hole in the bottom of my shoe. I was looking forward to swapping those useless old things for a pair of Stamboul slippers – and would have ditched them weeks earlier had I not bet with Andy that a €14 pair of trainers was perfectly sufficient to deal with the 2400 kilometres from Ljubljana to Asia. A bet's a bet.

Here, at the very last stage of our journey across Europe, I was amazed at the clarity with which I could recall almost every step of the way. And the clearest parts weren't those that we would have expected. Walking down the Champs-Élysées was all a bit of a blur, while, on the other hand, I could recall almost every face in the crowded rural bar in Serbia where we were given our first proper Eastern coffee, so strong and bitter that it seemed to stick to our teeth and we could barely get the last drops down our throats. Our first sight of the Mediterranean – effectively our halfway point – was a haze compared to my memory of the solitary poplar tree under which we rested one afternoon in Italy.

How long ago that now seemed! While it had been amazing to see so many European cities over the previous six months, from Paris and Orléans to Belgrade, Zagreb and Ljubljana, none of these places are inaccessible to everyday city-break tourists, whose experiences often belie the true nature of the culture and people of that country. It wasn't until we got into true rural Italy or the old, forlorn and forgotten industrial towns of the Balkans – and picked apples from the garden of a mad old man with a moped near Aosta, or discussed Voltaire with a polyglot tramp on the winding banks of the Loire, or reluctantly accepted an excess of home-brew from good old George in Bulgaria (who wouldn't take no for an answer, even though it was barely time for breakfast on that baking Balkan summer day) – that we felt that we were tasting a little of what the countries we passed through were really about. With the overharmonising effects of our blessed EU, much of Europe seems to have become homogenised and I sometimes found myself struggling to remember quite which city I was in. Now, looking back, the effect was even more pronounced. Meanwhile, walking down country lanes, struggling through woods, or crossing mountain passes, we never failed to feel an enormous sense of place and time. Life both slows down and opens up, and everything becomes a little clearer. And what was clearest to me now was that it was time for bed. I could hear the occasional heron flying overhead and, in the water by my feet, the rhythm of the ripples was occasionally punctuated by a cluck from the snoozing family of strange grey coots that we had spotted earlier. I slept well.

Paddy: Last Leg(s)

It had taken a couple of months to secure permission from the Istanbul authorities to cross the Bosporus Bridge into Asia on foot. This had not been possible since the late 1970s, when the surprisingly high number of suicides committed by jumping from the dizzyingly high bridge led to the walkway being closed to pedestrians indefinitely. Some way short of the bridge, a small white hatchback began to follow us at walking pace. Three burly men were peering out at us through the foggy condensation of the windscreen. It stopped to let one of the suited strangers out, who then started following us, trying to catch up with our now ever-quickening pace. Andy gripped his walking stick, ready to swipe if the chap got much closer. Then we heard a great shout of 'Mr Andy!' Stunned, we both turned to confront him. Mehmet explained that he was one of three police detectives who had been assigned for our personal safety that day, and would be escorting us for the rest of our journey. Apparently the bridge authorities, whose permission we had needed to cross the bridge, had notified the Department of Tourism about our journey. The Department had consequently set up a press conference at the Blue Mosque, from where our final day's walking was due to start. As they had neglected to tell us any of this, we began our day's walk from the front door of our hotel, and now we were reluctant to back-track the couple of kilometres into the centre of town, despite the waiting cameras. Concerned by our no-show, the Office of Tourism had dispatched a small phalanx of police across the city, some of whom, namely Mehmet and his entourage, had finally tracked us down just short of the bridge.

As the suspension towers of the bridge loomed in the incessant rain, we were joined by two motorcycle escorts. The seven of us set off to cross the final 1510 metre span that links Europe to Asia. Six months older and certainly wiser, we looked behind us at the muddy footprints left in our wake. Between us, we must have knocked up over 10 million of these. Some we could recall, some we couldn't, but I knew that these last ones we'd never forget. Eventually, inevitably, we were able to make out our friends and family beyond the eastern end of the bridge and perhaps more importantly, 200 metres in front of them, an enormous yellow sign proclaiming to the oncoming road traffic and two bedraggled pedestrians, 'Welcome to Asia'.

ANDY WARD & PADDY MORRIS

Paddy doesn't have an adventurous bone in his body, but loves a cheap holiday. He lives in the French Alps and divides his time between skiing and checking the weather forecast. He intends to remain there for the foreseeable future, with his slippers and a comfy chair always close at hand.

Andy has always had an adventurous bone in his body and has travelled extensively throughout his life. He is currently working as the expedition manager for two ground-breaking polar expeditions for 2008. He also has a few ideas up his sleeve for his next little adventure.

BAGHDAD TO BASRA, ON THE WRONG SIDE OF THE TRACKS

César G Soriano

I have always had a love affair with train travel. There's something romantic about the railways that you just can't experience in a tin can flying 30,000ft above the ground. I've hopped aboard famous trains – the Marrakesh Express, the London-to-Paris Eurostar, the New York subway – and one infamous train: the Iraqi Republic Railway (IRR).

Iraq's national railroad was once the crown jewel of the Middle East's train system. Built in the early 20th century by competing German and British engineers, it provided a vital link between Europe and Asia. Then came two world wars, the Iraq-Iran War and the Gulf War. During the US invasion of Iraq in 2003, rail lines were bombed to bits. What wasn't bombed was stripped by looters. Decades of war and sanctions had finally destroyed the country's fledgling railroad network. But it wasn't long before things looked up again.

Saddam Hussein's regime fell on April 9, 2003. In the early weeks and months after Saddam, Baghdad was filled with a sense of wonderment as Iraqis discovered what they had been missing. They quickly embraced new technologies like the internet and cell phones, and rediscovered simple pleasures like traveling. For the first time in years, Iraqis had freedom of movement, no longer trapped by invisible ethnic and tribal borders or 'no-fly' zones. Highways reopened. Iraqi Airways returned to the skies. And Iraqi railways were soon rebuilt and back on track.

I was determined to be one of their first paying customers. In the autumn of 2003 I was in Iraq working as a Baghdad correspondent for the newspaper *USA Today*, so first I had to convince my editors that the trip was newsworthy and feasible – and that I wouldn't get blown up in the process. At that time, traveling through Iraq was still relatively safe. The country was not yet mired by insurgency and sectarian warfare; kidnappings and beheadings of Westerners were not yet making headlines. So, on a crisp October morning I headed down to Baghdad Central Station. No bodyguards, no body armor, Kevlar helmet or weapons. Just me, my Iraqi 'fixer' Sabbah and a plastic bag containing our change of clothes and toothbrushes.

Sabbah was a jovial, rotund man in his fifties, a jack of all trades who worked as a translator, driver and contributing journalist. He knew how to grease the wheels of Iraqi bureaucracy to get things done. And like most Iraqi men of his age, he had served in the Iraq-Iran war of the 1980s. But he was less than enthusiastic about riding the rails. Despite living in Baghdad all his life, he had never once been on a train. Iraqi trains had a reputation of being a poor man's mode of transportation. They were slow, filthy, crowded and unreliable. They were also dirt cheap.

Baghdad Central Station was a dilapidated building with something of a Wild West feel to it. It was a chaotic, dodgy mess of people screaming and shouting, carrying their belongings in plastic bags or ratty old luggage, and pushing and shoving their way through the station. The train waiting on platform two looked like it should have been circling around a Christmas tree. A green-and-yellow, Chinese-made diesel locomotive was hooked up to eight vomit-green passenger cars. All the windows on the train were pockmarked with bullet holes, cracks and, curiously, chewing gum. Several bombed-out train carriages and engines were quietly rusting on the adjacent tracks. One look at the train sent Sabbah into a paroxysm of vocal protests. I was beginning to have second thoughts about my romantic nostalgia for train travel.

The trains from Baghdad went in three directions: north to Mosul through the so-called 'Sunni Triangle of Death', northwest to the Syrian border and south to Basra. We chose Basra as it was the safest and most scenic journey, traveling through the Shiite Muslim holy cities of Karbala and Najaf, then onto the Arab marshlands and Ramallah oil fields and to the port town of Basra. A one-way ticket to Basra was 1000 Iraqi dinars, the equivalent of about 50 US cents. The estimated trip time was 10 hours. The same 300-mile journey by taxi would have taken five hours and cost about US$12, an amount that few Iraqis could afford to pay.

'Absolutely, this train is 100% safe,' the ticket agent assured us. So we boarded it and waited. And waited. The sun grew hotter and the temperature in the un-air-conditioned cars became unbearable. At noon we were ordered to disembark because the train had been cancelled – something about the tracks being sabotaged just south of Baghdad. Or maybe it was a mechanical problem. Different employees gave different answers. 'Maybe tomorrow,' a conductor told us, shrugging his shoulders. 'Yes, come back tomorrow.' Sabbah smiled.

The next morning I dragged Sabbah out of bed and back to the station. Surprisingly, at 8:30am the train departed on time. It was the only thing that would go right all day. The train to Basra was practically empty. Most of the passengers were poor Shiite Muslims, heading south to the Shiite-dominated southern provinces of Iraq. We met some of our fellow passengers. Amad Akal was on his way home to Basra to give his family money that he earned as a janitor at a Baghdad restaurant. Jawad Abbas, a 24-year-old plumber, was going home after a three-day pilgrimage to holy Shiite shrines in Najaf, Karbala and Baghdad.

'It's completely inhumane to make us spend all this time on the train without air-conditioning or basic services,' Abbas said. By ignoring the country's railroads and focussing its energy and resources on the aviation industry, Iraqi's Ministry of Tourism was taking from the poor and giving to the rich, he said.

It took us nearly an hour just to get out of Baghdad, a sprawling city of nearly seven million people. Beyond its shantytowns and squalor, we finally reached the countryside, passing village after village of mud huts and long fields of palm trees. About an hour south of Baghdad, the train approached a few dozen people walking alongside the tracks carrying banners. The few dozen became a few hundred, then several thousand. The train slowed to a crawl as we lumbered past a sea of humanity. They were Shiite pilgrims, all heading to Karbala, and all on foot. They were the poorest of the poor, unable to afford even the 50¢ train fare. Most were clad all in black, some wore sandals but many were barefoot. Some carried green flags and black banners with Arabic script of Qur'an verses or names of dead relatives. They clapped and chanted and seemed happier than those of us stuck on the slow-moving train.

Every now and then, a pilgrim would hop aboard. The conductor and two Iraqi policemen patrolling the train seemed oblivious to the fare-jumpers. 'We never throw anybody off,' Wathek Sattar said as he made his rounds to collect tickets. 'If it looks like they can pay, we will make them pay double. If they are poor, we let them stay.'

Traveling on Iraqi Railways was not exactly the Orient Express. The old train had few amenities. There were no lights. Most of the seats were missing armrests. The toilets were simple holes in the floor that dumped directly onto the tracks below. There were no platforms between cars, so passengers had to carefully hop across an empty void, risking ending up on the tracks. There were no couchettes, no café and definitely no bar. I had only brought a small bottle of water and no food with me. Clearly, I had not planned well. Luckily, one of the train attendants was making a few dinars on the side by selling tea to passengers. He carried a teapot and a bucket of filthy water, which he used to wash the three teacups that were shared by all the passengers. He heated his teapot on a rusting kerosene stove and tank, dangerously perched in the aisle of a crowded passenger car. By noon my stomach was growling and I had become increasingly cranky. An old man across from me happily offered half his sandwich, but I felt guilty about accepting food from someone with so little.

When we reached the station in Karbala, a gaggle of young men hopped on board to sell sandwiches, water and cigarettes to thirsty and hot passengers. After a few minutes, the conductor blew his whistle, a signal for the vendors to jump off the train before it began moving out. But a few of the salesmen stayed on for the long haul. One of them was Akmed Shati. He claimed to be 13 years old, but looked much younger. Every Friday on his day off from school, he told me, he rode the train alone from Basra to Karbala and back home to Basra to earn money for his family. He carried a small plastic cooler from which he sold water, Italian ice, beer, juice and soda. On this day, the little entrepreneur said he had made 35,000 dinars (about $18) – a fortune by Iraqi standards.

There was not much to do but stare out the window at one dusty village after another, so Sabbah and I spent most of our time talking to other passengers. 'The Sheik' would not give me his real name but spent an hour ranting on about the evils of the United States – in fluent Spanish. He said he had spent several years working in Latin America for a nongovernmental organization. Then there was Natak Jabar and his cousin Younis Sabah, both 21, both dressed in traditional long white robes, *dishdashas*. We found them sitting in one of the long freight cars, the cargo doors open and their legs dangling over the sides. Next to them was a large pile of what looked like fishing nets. Sure enough, Sabah, Jabar, and Jabar's five brothers were all fishermen, on their way to the Persian Gulf. Their plan, Jabar said, was to spend three days fishing, then return to their home in Suq Ash Shuyukh to sell their catch.

Jabar, Sabah and most of the male passengers passed the time on the long train ride by chain-smoking. It wasn't long before the carriages were thick with smoke. For nonsmokers like me, relief could only be found by sticking our heads out of the cracked windows or putting our noses to one of the many bullet holes. Despite all this, across the aisle from me, Abdul Yaseen, his wife and their four children were ecstatic about their first-ever train adventure. They were returning home to Basra after attending a wedding near Baghdad. 'I like the train because it's more comfortable, slow and lets the kids have a chance to see the countryside,' he said. His wide-eyed children were peering from the windows, wearing their best clothes, reminiscent of a time when traveling was actually an occasion for dressing up. Abdul's nine-year-old daughter, Haba, surprised to see an American on board, latched onto us and peppered me with questions in broken English: 'Mister, where you from? You married? You have children? You like Arabian music? You like Jennifer Lopez? Mister, buy me Pepsi!'

Around 4pm the train pulled into the station in Nasiriyah, one of the largest cities in southern Iraq. But, unlike our stops at other cities, the train did not immediately pull out but sat at the platform. And sat. And sat. There was no announcement or explanation for our delay. The thermometer on the platform read 100°F. Inside, the train was becoming a steel oven, baking us alive. Within minutes, we were drenched in sweat. The stench of body odor, dirty baby diapers and the raw sewage on the tracks became unbearable. An old woman fainted and was carried outside into the shade and doused with water, and many more of us followed her out into the air. Angry passengers took out their rage on the conductor, who explained that the station manager had refused to give clearance for the train to proceed. Apparently there was only one working track between Nasiriyah and Basra, and a northbound cargo train already had dibs. An hour later, without a whistle or warning, the train began pulling out of the station. Of course, most of us were still out on the platform and had to run and jump back onto the moving train.

South of Nasiriyah, we reached the most scenic point of the journey. The endless monochrome images of brown, dusty villages were replaced by lush, green landscape, fields of corn, alfalfa and date palms. This was the Arab Marshland, a fertile region between the Tigris and Euphrates Rivers that is the legendary location of the Garden of Eden. The setting sun blazed into the windows of the right side of the train. There were no curtains or shades to pull down, so passengers took chewing gum from their mouths and used it to stick newspapers onto the windows to shield their heads from the sun. Ah, so that was why there was gum stuck all over the windows.

At dusk, the train pulled into Suq Ash Shuyukh, a town known for its conservative population who were less than thrilled with the American occupation of Iraq. Dozens of young men were loitering on both sides of the tracks. Peering out the window, I noticed several of them were making threatening gestures, as if pointing rifles at us. It was a tense situation and the train did not stop long. The moment we pulled out of the station, there was a loud crash from the next passenger car. Somebody had thrown a brick through the window, raining glass on a 15-year-old bride and her 25-year-old groom. The bride, Akbal Hussein, received a small cut on her left cheek. Iraqi policemen rushed to her assistance and searched for the culprit, but by then the assailant had melted into the crowd. The conductor, Ziyad Khalaf, sheepishly admitted that this was the third attack on the train in as many days, despite the assurances I had received from staff in Baghdad. 'My supervisors never worry about passengers. They only worry about their desks in their air-conditioned office,' he said, expressing rare public contempt for his superiors.

For IRR employees, the US invasion of Iraq was fairly lucrative. Khalaf proudly boasted that he was now making $60 a month, a big increase on the $8 a month he earned under Saddam Hussein's regime. But, despite US President George W Bush's pledge of millions to improve Iraq's railroad system, which his administration described as presenting 'a seriously negative public image', precious little money was being spent to improve and upgrade it. 'There was a time when everything was completely new and the trains were full of passengers. But when Iraq started its wars with its neighbors, everything began to decline,' said Khalaf, who began working with IRR in 1977.

We made our way to the locomotive to meet Hamad Khader, sitting in the driver's seat of this green machine. This 30-year-old recalled boyhood memories of playing with toy trains and his dreams of becoming a locomotive engineer. He began working for IRR as a ticket taker and conductor, working his way up to engineer. 'It used to be such an exciting job,' Khader said. 'But now, I have no interest. It's risky. It's dangerous. It's just a job.'

The interior of the train turned pitch black when the sun went down. The only source of illumination was the occasional flicker of a lighter or burning cigarette. Quietness descended as passengers settled into sleep. But no sooner had I drifted into dreamland than we were awaked by a howling noise: a dust storm. A giant brown cloud enveloped the train and threatened to shake it off its tracks. Every door and window of the train was open, and it didn't take long for the passenger cars to fill with dust. I coughed and hacked my lungs out for the remainder of the trip.

Near the end of our journey, the darkness was replaced by an orange and blue glow as the train passed through the Ramallah oil fields. The desert seemed to be on fire as we looked at the amazing sight of hundreds of pilot flames burning atop oil wells. This was the heart of Iraq's economy, the source of all of its riches – and of all of its miseries.

Just before 8pm the train chugged into Basra Central Station, nearly 12 hours after our departure. 'This is the absolute last time I will ever take the train,' complained Abdul Yaseen, who earlier had shared with us his love of this form of travel. Tired, hungry and filthy, Sabbah and I stumbled off the train and walked to a nearby hotel for the night. The next morning we returned to Baghdad, this time by taxi.

Iraq's post-war railroad never really caught on with passengers. The trains routinely left stations empty and were regularly attacked by insurgents. In 2004 and 2005 rebels began a campaign of blowing up train tracks in an effort to stop the transport of military equipment. Finally, in the spring of 2006, passenger trains were discontinued altogether. But despite the lack of business, the IRR continued to look to the future. It spent millions of US tax dollars to refurbish

Baghdad Central Station and replace train equipment. In December 2007, with security dramatically improving, passenger trains quietly returned to service. As of 2008 passengers had slowly begun returning to the rails. But most are still scared away by violence and, now, high ticket prices. The fare from Baghdad to Basra has skyrocketed from 50¢ to $3.50. That's inflation for you. But it still works out to about 1¢ a mile, making it one of the cheapest train services in the world.

Would I take the Iraq train again? Ask me in another 10 years.

CÉSAR G SORIANO

César G Soriano is a freelance journalist and former *USA Today* Baghdad correspondent who has covered the war in Iraq since 2003. He is the author of the Iraq chapter of the 2009 Lonely Planet guide to the Middle East. César lives in London with his wife, Marsha.

PEDALS & PADDLES

Alastair Humphreys

At times the river was jade green and steady, with strange boils of water rising and slowly swirling the surface; at other times it was a sliding mirror. Sometimes it was shallow and jolly. I could look down and watch pebbles rush past as though they were dashing upstream: colourful time capsules; orange, grey, white and black, each one colossally old. We slipped silently over smooth blue water and silt fizzed the bottom of the canoe. The river was our road, we were content on our own and confident in the wild.

I had been travelling alone for almost three years, but that summer a good friend had come to share my journey for a few weeks. The only sounds were the dipping of our paddles and the river. Moose swam in the river ahead of us, goofy and striving with huge ears pinned back. They scrambled up the slick bank and disappeared into the undergrowth. Shaggy bears trotted the hillsides. Bald eagles surveyed their domain and watched us from the treetops with utter indifference. From time to time we heard them screech their haunting cry into the silent sky, then soar and plummet downwards with an audible whoosh of air. Above the water, colourful dragonflies hovered and whirred at the surface, and vanished. Beneath us the muscular salmon were racing, resisting all temptations on our trailing hooks. Away from the road, away from the crowd, there was no need for a clock, no need to chat. The silence stood sentinel to time, a tangible presence over the endless river that ridiculed my thoughts of distance or days. The river and the silent emptiness are wed together for ever and each smooth, worn, coloured pebble will outlast us all.

When we tired of paddling, we could simply sit back and drift, gliding along without effort, relying only on gravity and nature's energy. We were moving slowly and unstoppably towards our destination. The movement was out of our hands, in the same way that shuttling along the conveyor belt of airport queues and check-ins and boarding and take-off and foil-wrapped food also shuttles you towards your destination. But there are few other similarities between the two types of journey.

Quiet traders and trappers had lived along the banks of the Yukon River for year upon year, until gold was found and the river flowed with men and dreams of wealth. After scores of years and shattered dreams, and a handful of winners, now I was here, following on. There were still hints of the past. We occasionally passed deserted log cabins, relics of the fur trappers and gold prospectors. The history still breathes, the stories still live, but the river runs on and on and on. I felt optimistic for the world in a place that made man's impact feel so small. It must have been a lonely life back then, requiring real competence and self-confidence in every skill necessary for survival. Walking through an old abandoned settlement, peering into log cabins, I tried to imagine a life so remote that the river and its surroundings equated to the entire world, and the river was the only connection to anything beyond.

We were canoeing without a map. We wore no watches. We did not know what day it was, how far we had come, how far we had to go. As we pitched camp on the riverbank, lit a fire, swam, cooked, ate, and slept beneath a silent sky, we had no idea what the next day would hold. But, although I was new to canoeing, a first-timer in the Yukon, and unfamiliar with worrying about grizzly bears disturbing my sleep, I was well used to a life of motion. It was almost three years since I had closed my front door behind me and begun my journey.

I knew that it would be least one more year before I arrived back at that front door.

―――――――――

There is something primeval and very pure about the human urge to move. We spread across our planet many millennia ago in the greatest journey ever known, a slow, stuttering, almost subconscious expansion of humankind out of Africa, across Asia, over the Bering Straits and on as far as could be gone, down to Cape Horn. Perhaps it is a relic of those days in motion that urges so many people today to keep moving. I had decided to try to cycle round the world in an attempt to scratch my own itch. Uncertain travel held an appeal for me, a luring magic, an intoxicating release from conventional bonds, a chance for self-testing and self-discovery, and the rushing joy of being alive that I rarely felt at home. I was searching for chance encounters and unexpected detours, the sort of experiences that would lead to deciding suddenly, spontaneously, to get off the bike and instead canoe 500 miles down the Yukon River.

Days are long on the road. Pack up and pedal into the dawn. Ride until sunset. It's easy to kill time but you can kill distance only by riding. Roads roll on forever, linking and connecting and reaching so far ahead that to think about the end is to think of something that feels impossible. So settle for today, for earning the small distance that the day's long hours will allow you. Roads drenched with rain, stinging hail, pulsing heat, slick ice, buffeted by winds on loose gravel, deep sand, tangled rocks, thick snow. Roads of smooth tarmac down mountainsides on sunny days with warm tailwinds and scenes of impossible beauty. Roads furious with traffic through grim slums, bland scrub, concrete jungles, polluted industrial wastelands. Monotony in motion. Roads too hard and too long that break you, expose you, scorn you and would laugh at you if they cared. Roads on which you pick yourself up, then have a word with yourself and make it to an end you once doubted. Roads you have never ridden to places you have never seen and people you have never met. Days end. A different sunset, a different resting point, a different perspective. A little less road waits for you tomorrow. A little more road lies behind you.

I wanted to raise my arms and stare in wonder over waves of hazy blue mountains. I wanted to wake in my sleeping bag in the desert as the sun rose between my toes. To shiver in a frost rimmed tent is to truly appreciate the next warm duvet. A parched desert teaches deep gratitude for running water. These are clarion calls to be alive and to treasure life. On the road you learn to appreciate a simplification of life.

I was only two weeks down that road on my way from Yorkshire to Sydney when the attacks of September 11, 2001, shook America. Suddenly war was declared and my scenic ride through Afghanistan no longer seemed like such a fun idea. So when I reached Istanbul, instead of carrying straight on towards Australia, I turned right for Africa. The freedom to choose my own path, to be my own master, was one of the greatest pleasures of my journey.

One of the many appeals of travelling by bike is that you arrive gradually. There is none of the shock you experience when you roll your luggage trolley out of an air-conditioned airport and into the sudden sweating chaos of the developing world. The heat! The noise! The smell! The crowding clamour of men eager to carry your bags, to find you a taxi, to find you a hotel and to con you while you are soft and naive. On a bike you experience the proximity or the distance between people and places that accounts for the way they interact, or do not interact, and consequently the way that the very history of our planet has unfurled. You appreciate the world as a single, gradually morphing blend rather than the separate, isolated communities that air travel, politics and television suggest. I remember when I noticed this: I was in Damascus, one of the most ancient cities on Earth and yet I kept forgetting the fact. I felt that spice markets and hooting taxis and bushy moustaches and kebab stalls and historic heaving streets and noisy mosque loudspeakers were all quite normal. It showed how ideal my bike was for slipping me gradually into different environments and allowing me to see the world as one single entity.

I made it all the way down Africa, to my great surprise. Weeks in the heat of the Nubian desert in Sudan, hauling my bike through hot, soft sand; sleeping beneath the stars, watching new constellations appearing above me as I crept ever so slowly towards the equator, the southern hemisphere and a new ceiling of stars; through the mountains of Ethiopia, the plains of Kenya, and on and on until the end of the road in Cape Town.

When I left home, I had vaguely assumed that I would fly across any oceans I encountered between cycling across continents. However, the idea of trying to make it round the planet without leaving its surface germinated in my mind as I rode the hot and dry roads of Africa. It sounded a lot more exciting than flying. But how would I find a sailing boat willing to give me a lift across an ocean – especially as I had little money?

I introduced myself at the Yacht Club in Cape Town and sought advice. I set about making myself useful, crewing for people who needed extra hands for races, cleaning boats, networking, phoning people and asking around whether anybody knew anybody who knew anybody who was planning to sail across the Atlantic. After six weeks of dead ends and rejections I struck lucky and secured a berth on a yacht across the Atlantic Ocean.

As our first night at sea approached, the breeze stiffened and the yacht began to heel. As we cut through the waves, I felt a basic thrill to be travelling again, to be on the move for no other reason than for the sheer hell of it. I was totally free, and I was a lucky man for that. I sat on the side of the boat with my legs dangling above the rushing water. I hadn't cut my hair since leaving home and sun-bleached dreadlocks whipped around my face. We were chasing the sunset, bearing west, heaving across the planet by the simple force of the wind in our sails. The hull thumped the waves and spray leapt up to embrace me, glowing with sunlight and bent in a scimitar curve as the wind blew it across the deck. I was soaked, frozen, nauseous and grinning like an idiot.

It took 24 days to cross the Atlantic. Think how many people you talk to, how many miles you drive and how many phone calls you make in 24 days. Weeks in the office, weekends at home. Ever-changing horizons. Hours of television, reams of newspapers. Text messages, emails, changes of pants. But, for us, at sea, the world was reduced to blue water and 58ft of boat. There was nowhere else to go. It was a massive simplification of my life, which had already been magnificently pared down when I pedalled away from my past priorities and cares. I loved the experience of crossing an ocean because it was so different to being a cyclist. On the bike I had grown enormously sensitive, literally, becoming so aware of all that was around me, of the sights and sounds and smells and tastes and the feel of the wind upon my face. Out at sea the changes, and the senses, were more gradual and subtler.

Crossing the Greenwich meridian I thought about how I would feel the next time I crossed it. I would be back in London. We all cheered as the GPS rolled over to 0.00.000. I had only 360° still to travel, so I was on my way home now at last. It was a luxurious feeling to be moving without having to invest a single calorie in the movement. The waves thumped, sluiced and fizzed against the hull. Come on wind, take me homewards.

The days blazed beneath a pale blue sky and above an incredibly clear blue ocean streaked deep with shafts of white light. The world felt a simple and pure place. Sunset brought relief from the heat, leaving the world to darkness, us and the comforting glow of the GPS and compass. When there was no moon, the black sky was crowded with so many stars and shooting stars that they seemed to spill over into the ocean, where showers of phosphorescent sparks streamed in our wake like a bonfire, a wake of churning white water that stretched back to Africa and the end of the thin tyre tracks that started from my home. We had begun the voyage with a fat cream moon in a golden halo. The moon was dead ahead and we placed bets on the precise time of moonset. Silver clouds shone as we cruised down the yellow carpet of moonlight. The helmsman heaved on the wheel as we surfed the heavy, fast black waves. Eternal motion, racing ever onwards towards South America.

'Land ahoy!' At long last South America edged above the horizon and into view. Excitement rippled among us, all craning for a better view on the starboard side of the boat. My first thought was, 'wow, it's hilly!' as I switched seamlessly back into cyclist mentality. I was excited to see folds of rock and vertical lines once again after weeks on a horizontal flat blue disc. After so much blue, green seemed an extraordinary, lurid colour to be the dominant colour on land. I have had the same thought when emerging from monochrome deserts. We saw white buildings in the trees and heard the sounds of traffic. We were not the only human beings left on Earth after all.

After the anchor was dropped and after the handshakes, hugs and congratulations, we sat on deck together to savour the unusual stillness of being stationary. It was so exciting to have arrived on the other side of an ocean under sail. I could not wait to set foot on this new world. Celebratory cigar smoke and laughter wafted in the night air. The gentle rolling motion of the anchored boat felt odd after the nuances of the movement of sailing that we had grown so used to. Amid the joviality I sat alone, perched on the boom and hugging my knees. I was nervous. We had crossed the Atlantic but now I had a new continent to ride. From southern Patagonia I planned to ride north, for about a year and a half, up to the Arctic Ocean in Alaska.

During my attempt to cycle around the planet it became apparent that, in many ways, ours is a very small world. The internet, global music and Western popular culture followed me wherever I went. From the seat of a bicycle, though, the world also seemed massive. The differences in lifestyles and opportunities that people had were immense. Being still less than halfway through my journey was a daunting prospect, yet the further I rode, the more I felt at home. After years of reading glossy travel magazines and watching TV travel shows, I had begun the project with my eyes shut, dreaming of adventure and exotic locations. What I had not considered was the 5000 miles between London and the pyramids, the 7500 miles between Cairo and Cape Town or the 5000 miles from Ushuaia to Machu Picchu. I had not imagined the months of slog and the demoralisingly improbable distance, in both time and space, to the next destination. Since then, I had learned that the real travelling is all the stuff in between. The destinations merely added direction to the journey, acting as the frame upon which I could weave the colourful fabric of my experiences. Slowly the journey had come to be the reward. The thousands of miles among the ordinariness of the thousands of people I encountered, in all the villages and towns I rode through, blended into one giant, rolling memory. Extraordinary sights like the pyramids and Machu Picchu are marvellous, but these wonders do not represent the reality of the normal life of the people I wanted to learn about when travelling. This is perhaps the biggest difference between cycling and other forms of transport. For many people who travel, the destinations are what their experiences are primarily about as they move swiftly, isolated in machines, from one place to another. By bike, travel is so slow that it becomes the dominant aspect of the journey.

I had passed through deserts and mountain ranges, mad Arabian melees, Latin fiestas and African funeral parades. I had witnessed strange and extravagant sights and sounds and unfathomable, animated conversations on street corners and in market stalls. Yet I was always just looking into other people's ordinary days. The reverse effect also applied. I, a normal, middle-of-the-road English guy on a bike, gradually became an exotic, extraordinary spectacle, merely by riding a long way from my own natural habitat. My journey round the world was actually a study of the magic of humankind's normality.

Over the Andes the rutted dirt road became so awful that I chose instead to follow the route of an old railway line cross-country across the dry, spiky grass, cropped short and prickly by llamas and alpacas. Barefoot, I waded through broad, shallow rivers that were phenomenally cold.

I asked one man how far it was to a town that I knew was at least 25 miles away. He assured me that it was only 2 miles. People's lives were so localised that there was no point in telling anyone that I had ridden to Bolivia from Patagonia: mentioning the name of a town a day or two's ride away would provoke sufficient surprise and disbelief. Anywhere much further away than that was beyond their imagination. A little girl I met was excited to hear that I had actually been in an aeroplane. She had only ever seen them, tiny and slow, high in the blue sky above her. She was struggling to visualise them. I explained to her that the planes she saw were actually about as long as five buses put end to end, and that the wings would stretch from where we were standing to those men talking by the liquor store over the street. 'Do the animals still go *arriba*, on top?' she asked, assuming, naturally, that nobody ever goes on a long journey without taking a heavy bag of irate chickens or a trussed and miserable piglet along with them.

Many months later I reached northern Canada. Smoke tickled my nostrils and haze hung in the sky. My onward progress was in jeopardy. Forest fires were raging to the north and west, utterly beyond the power of humans to extinguish. All that the fire services could do was to try to manage the blaze. They had closed the only road towards Dawson City, the very road that I had hoped to ride. But in that part of the world roads were new things, newfangled intruders; long before any road reached the north, the rivers had been the roads. I wondered then whether perhaps it would be possible to take to the water to continue the journey. My friend David agreed that it sounded like a fine adventure. We would canoe past the fires and then get back on the bikes again.

Fortunately the Yukon is an easy place to get hold of things like 16ft canoes. We loaded our bikes into the canoe and set to paddling with gusto. For the next 10 days we would be far from road or rescue with no phone to call for help. It felt very liberating. After the canoeing we got back on the bikes and rode up into the Arctic Circle. From the northern shore of North America I headed alone for Anchorage and an Indian cargo ship bound for Asia.

After a staggeringly brutal and exhausting three months cycling through an ice-clad Siberian winter, with temperatures of -40°C, Japan was an intriguing contrast and a welcome, warm relief. In China I chose to follow the Great Wall for its entire length until it fizzles out in the Taklamakan Desert. I was really heading homewards now, chasing the sunset westwards across Asia, back to Europe and – ultimately – back to England. Not only was I following the Wall, this was also the fabled Silk Road, where, once upon a time, traders, leading long caravans of camels laden with valuables, relied on caravanserais where they could rest and resupply during their long journeys. It was exciting to be tangibly connected with so much history along that road. I slept without a tent and it felt exciting and unreal to be lying there on my own, watching a massive orange moon ease up through the trees – in China, on the Silk Road, where so many others before me must have lain on the earth in the same way, resting on their own journeys. I fell asleep; whenever I woke during the night I could estimate how long I had been sleeping by the position of the moon above me. It would be a full moon all over the world and I thought of the people I missed and wondered whether they too had noticed the splendour of the skies that night.

In Uzbekistan the road signs I passed were a list of awesome-sounding places, each one of which I would have loved to cycle to: Samarkand, Dushanbe, Kabul, Tehran, Aktau and Baku. They were a reminder for me of the powerful magic of the road, of the charms and delights and new places that all roads hold if only you keep riding long enough. I had dreamed for years of visiting Samarkand, which sounded to me like the most remote, exciting place on Earth. It lay between gigantic mountains and inhospitable deserts at the end of civilization, yet for centuries had been wealthy, cultured and powerful, the very centre of the world. To crest a hill and see the town before me was a genuine thrill. The fabled blue domes of the mosques and madrassas were delicious even beyond my imaginings, with a white stripe of sunshine seared down the flanks of each dome like curved scimitars. I'd ridden 40,000 miles to get to Samarkand. I'd earned it and I was here at last.

During hard times on my journey I had often dreamed of cycling in France as being some sort of ideal: to ride from village to village and sit in street cafés drinking coffee and basking in warm sunshine. Within 100 metres of entering France I was sitting in a café making the dream come true, celebrating. I was almost home.

France was a green and pleasant land, and the view from my tent each morning of dew-drenched green fields and hedges and steaming cows was so similar to my England. It was almost over. I didn't want all this to end. I wanted to turn round and ride for ever, sleeping in forests and filling my bottles at village fountains. I wanted to remain free and feel the world moving slowly beneath my tyres, having time to watch the heavens move slowly above me. I hoped that the sadness I felt and my reluctance to end the amazing, precious experience actually stemmed from a lazy desire to take the easy option, rather than because I honestly felt nothing could ever be so good again. Going back home, back to England and to the new beginnings I would have to choose, was actually a far tougher path than continuing with this life I knew so well. My mind raced with memories and I had to try to tell myself that the end of the ride did not mean the end of my life. I relished the road, the speed, my fitness, the wind in my face. I sucked up the memories and I was so happy. I felt, in the true sense of the word, fulfilled: filled full with life.

The final leg of my journey was a long day's ride: up through the Peak District and Sheffield and across Yorkshire towards my home. It was exhilarating to be surrounded by familiar, beautiful scenery once again, to not need a map any more, to know where I was going, to be going home. It was a beautiful final morning, frosty and blue-skied. I loved the green hills, the grazing sheep, the fabulous dry-stone walls. The drivers were safe and courteous, there were occasional bike lanes and the road signs were plentiful and accurate. It was good to be home!

My four-year journey round the world will stay with me all my life: the spectacle of a completely empty horizon at sea, a horizon that has not altered in millions of years; the thrill of cresting a difficult pass and seeing a whole new span of planet open up before me, inviting me onwards; the slow-release satisfaction of reaching a far-off horizon. And the extraordinary experience that ended it all: the realisation that, if you keep curiously and steadfastly and patiently crossing sufficient new horizons, you will – one day – see the very first view with which you began your journey once again appearing in front of your eyes.

ALASTAIR HUMPHREYS

Alastair Humphreys left university in 2001 and began cycling round the world. His journey – of five continents, 60 countries, and 46,000 miles – took over four years to complete on a budget of just £7000. The expedition was used to raise awareness for the charity Hope and Homes for Children. Alastair has written two books about his journey, is now teaching 10-year-old boys, and is busy planning another expedition, though not by bicycle! See www.roundtheworldbybike.com.

TO ZANZIBAR THE HARD WAY

James Morrison

'There is nothing to worry about. I know many people in Kipumbwe', says Mr Iddy, looking at us the way you look at a child who is worried about their first night away from home, 'I will come with you. Everything will be fine, yes?'

After a month in Pangani spent teaching English and slowing down to the rural pace of life, my wife Jane and I feel ready for a change of scene. Pangani is a lazy fishing town on the Tanzanian coast, with a beautiful beach that welcomes the warm waters of the Indian Ocean. On a clear day you can catch a glimpse of Zanzibar, perched on the horizon. Most tourists fly there from the mainland or take the big fast ferry from Dar es Salaam but those options are too expensive for us. Mr Iddy, our Pangani expert on everything, recommends the sailing boat from Kipumbwe, a remote village further down the coast.

'Kipumbwe is actually closer to Zanzibar so it won't take as long to get there', he continues. 'I will come with you to arrange things with the captain.'

We are starting to learn the way things work here. We know that 'arrange things with' really means 'collect my commission from', but we trust his judgement. And so, at two o'clock on a hot and humid Thursday afternoon, we find ourselves at the edge of the Pangani River waiting for the bus to Kipumbwe.

'It's only a short way, right Mr Iddy?'

'Yes, of course. It is only 35 kilometres. This should take maybe 1½ hours.'

The bus is overflowing with people, as every bus in Africa is, and we are lucky to get seats. On this typically hot May afternoon the smell of 60 bodies' worth of sweat fills the bus as quickly as the bodies themselves. While we are in motion, there is the slightest of breezes through the window. This bus, however, is the mechanical equivalent of a game of American football: 10 seconds of action followed by a three-minute break. Or 10 minutes if luggage needs to be hauled off the roof. Or 20 minutes if some part of the wheel falls off and some guys have to bang around randomly underneath until it is fixed. Or 25 minutes if the bus reaches the spot where the sun is shining most brightly into our window and there is no shade, and the driver gets out to have a chat and a joint with his buddy. Actually I don't know if he is smoking a joint but anyone who takes 3½ hours to drive 35km must be under the influence of something.

Darkness settles like a mosquito net over this remote edge of the African mainland. The bus limps into Kipumbwe, the end of the road where, being the day's only traffic, it is greeted by the entire village swarming around it. Amazingly, in a country where staring at foreigners seems to be the national pastime, none of these people are interested in the two sweaty white people who tumble out of the bus, except for our curiosity value. This is probably because they have nothing to sell us – there are no taxis, no onward buses, no safaris, no hotels. The bus stops here for the night, blocking the only road in or out, and heads back early the next morning.

Kipumbwe is a tiny settlement on the beach that happens to be the closest point to Zanzibar on the African mainland. Only the most intrepid or cost-conscious, or foolish *wazungu* – foreigners like us – take their Zanzibar voyage from a place like this. The only accommodation in Kipumbwe is a nameless guesthouse opposite the bus. To call the rooms 'Spartan' would be a disservice to those thrifty Greeks of years gone by. Had our room been offered to the hardy soldiers of ancient Sparta, I think most would have gone AWOL and opted for the resort 20 kilometres up the coast.

The guesthouse is six tiny rooms around a central open-air atrium. The rooms even have traveller-friendly names like 'Paris' and 'American' as well as less romantic sounding ones like 'Pakistan' and 'Iraq'. The atrium is in fact merely a concrete floor with some puddles; puddles that look like water but, on closer inspection, seem to at least partly consist of urine. The shared toilet, to the side of the atrium, is simply a roofless enclave that doesn't even have a hole. Instead, it seems, you just pick a spot on the floor and let fly.

Our room is almost exactly how I imagined Nelson Mandela's prison cell to be, minus the law books. It is a 2m-by-3m concrete cube with a thin mattress laid across a raised concrete ledge. The window, barred and partially covered by a limp, tatty curtain, has mosquito mesh, but this is riddled with so many holes it defeats the purpose. The landlady notices us noticing this and says something in Swahili to Mr Iddy.

'She says they have no mosquitoes here', he translates.

'No mosquitoes? On the coast of equatorial Africa? During rainy season?' I respond doubtfully.

'That's what she says.'

'Then why do they have mosquito mesh on the windows?'

'Aha, you make a good point.'

'We'll take it', I say in mock enthusiasm. The landlady smiles; Jane frowns and mentions how many insects and spiders she has counted in the room so far. At around US$1.50 for the night, the room is probably quite fairly priced.

'Right, that's that sorted', I say positively, 'Now, Mr Iddy, take us to Kipumbwe's finest restaurant.'

After dinner we retire to the Paris Suite to count the cockroaches while Mr Iddy heads to the beach to negotiate the terms of our passage with any boat captains that might be going to Zanzibar. It is a quarter to midnight when he knocks on our door, unsteady on his feet and smelling strongly of beer.

'I found the boat that is leaving tomorrow.'

'Oh good', I say, anticipating a good five or six hours of sleep before an early sailing as the sun rises. 'What time do we leave?'

'The problem, you see, is that they must leave when the wind is best. So the boat will go at two o'clock.'

'We have to wait around here until two in the afternoon?'

'No, no, 2am.'

I go back inside to update Jane on developments while Mr Iddy heads back to the bar.

'Are you all nuts?' Jane asks me, 'Sailing in a little boat on the open sea in complete darkness for four hours?'

'Well, Mr Iddy said it usually takes three hours – and we have a torch... Besides, we don't have much option; this is the only boat leaving today. Hey, how bad can it be?' I really must stop saying that.

At 1.55am, without having had any sleep, we are collected by Mr Iddy and we walk down to the dark beach with our tiny torch. The drizzly rain has stopped and our path is lit by the incredible array of stars covering the sky, like a bowl of sugar spilt on a black tablecloth. Being near the equator, I can't work out whether we see the northern or southern hemisphere stars here. It looks like both, just judging by the sheer number of them. At least once a minute a shooting star appears for a brief moment, zipping across the night sky.

It's too dark to see the vessel moored a little way out from the shore, in deeper waters. We imagine a simple but sturdy engine-powered boat for our voyage. The captain will be experienced and courteous and maybe even speak some English. We have paid US$25 each for this voyage, five times what locals pay, so we expect that there will probably only be a couple of other passengers and we will have our pick of seats.

There are actually about seven or eight other people waiting on the shore. 'Are they on our boat?' I wonder out loud, a little snobbishly but surprised that we are sharing with so many others.

'OK then, have a nice trip', Mr Iddy slurs as we shake hands on the shore. 'I'll see you back in Pangani.'

We are helped into a little dinghy that paddles us out to the main boat. 'It looks a good size', Jane says optimistically as the shadowy dhow starts to emerge in the darkness. Indeed it does, probably 10 metres long by three across, very basic – no fancy electronic navigation gizmos or safety equipment here – but strong-looking. The design of the dhow has changed very little in over a thousand years. It is basically a hollowed-out hull with a mast and a strong canvas sail. Our boat only varies from this ancient design by the addition of a small outboard motor at the back.

The dinghy pulls up and we climb aboard the dhow, calculating the best place to claim a seat. I turn on our torch and slowly pan the length of the boat. That's when we see them. Masses and masses of human bodies, squashed together like sardines in a tin. Every possible inch of this boat is covered by a passenger's body or their typically eclectic luggage. Some people have sacks of rice, some have suitcases, others have baskets full of tiny fish and one is even holding a bed headboard and frame. There must be 50 people on board this vessel. In normal circumstances it would have a capacity of maybe eight or 10. Most of them are asleep, no doubt having boarded when the boat arrived hours before. They cringe and shield their eyes when our torch beam hits them so I switch it off again, leaving us with only the light of the stars.

Someone calls out something that includes the word '*wazungu*'. Passengers groan and reluctantly retract an extended leg or roll onto their side until there is enough room for us to squeeze aboard. We realise that the inflated amount we paid for our passage will buy us no preferential treatment on this boat. The two of us have exactly enough space to sit on our backsides on the deck, knees up to our chests and bags clutched tightly in the darkness. The boat is sitting very low in the water, thanks to all the passengers and cargo. We can reach over and touch the sea from our seats.

The boat floats around for another hour while the dinghy delivers more and more passengers. Somehow they all manage to get on. The outboard motor is finally started up with some vicious yanks of the cord at around 3am and we head out to sea.

We are very uncomfortable. Our pampered Western backsides are not accustomed to long periods sitting on hard wood and our limbs and joints are not flexible enough to be in such positions for any length of time. We concentrate on the beauty of our surroundings – the breathtaking night sky and its reflection on the gentle waves of the Indian Ocean. After all, the journey will only take three hours.

Half an hour out to sea, the motor is cut and the sail hoisted. It's an old-fashioned dhow sail with the distinctive Arabic shape and it puffs up elegantly as the wind catches it. The 50 or so people and their assorted sacks and suitcases and bed frames clearly weigh a lot and the bulwarks of the poor old boat are barely above the water line. Any time we hit a wave on the wrong angle, a good portion of it drenches those of us seated around the sides. After one or two of these, we are soaked through.

I check my watch: 4.15am. The distant lights of the African mainland still seem less distant than the distant lights of Zanzibar.

Perhaps three hours was a bit optimistic. Wouldn't it be funny, I ponder during a shivering moment with my head between my legs, if the sail and the outboard motor both broke? Ha! What would we do? There's no mobile phone coverage out here, we're a million miles from land in any direction and there is no safety equipment whatsoever on board, not even so much as a lifejacket. I guess we could all cling to the wooden bed frame. On the positive side, the sea is very warm.

Shortly after I close this internal conversation and begin a much happier one involving a seafood buffet, a loud ripping sound from above jerks awake the sleeping passengers and causes panicked shouts among the crew. The sail has snapped off the masthead and torn. The crew lowers it to investigate. Even from where we sit in the dark it does not look good. But, serious though a ripped sail is, we still have the outboard motor. All heads turn to the back of the boat. The outboard motor guy pulls the string with a flourish. Nothing. Another tug. Nothing. A nervous smile then five more tugs in quick succession, this time with a little more desperation. Nothing.

The captain impatiently makes his way to the back of the boat and has a try. Tug. Tug. Tug. Still nothing. The frightened cries and uneasy attempts at humour have stopped. There is an eerie silence. We are swaying silently in the vast expanses of the Indian Ocean, an unlit, uncovered, overloaded dhow with no lifeboats or lifejackets. Radio communication is years away from this part of the world – no-one on the shore knows where we are. It is the dead of night. We are past the point of no return but nowhere near the point of nearly there.

No longer propelled forward by anything, the boat is rocked by the heavy ocean waves. Left. Right. Left. Right. Gaining momentum on each tilt like a playground swing. People begin to shout to each other in Swahili. Children start to cry. No-one is asleep now. At one point we lean so far to one side that we dip under the water line and the sea slurps in over the bulwarks, before the boat is hurled back the other way, splashing more water into the already wallowing boat. Two men are steadily bailing out but the ship's only bucket cannot compete with the endless waves. I begin planning our post-capsize strategy and get as far as 'scream for help'. It was only a week or so ago, we recall, that a dhow sunk in almost identical circumstances and all of its passengers drowned.

There is a call from the bow end – the sail has been patched up. Everyone watches anxiously as it is hoisted and attached to the mast. Any extrastrong gust of wind could tear it again beyond repair. I check my watch again – 4.30am. I'm reminded of Einstein explaining his theory of relativity: 'One minute spent talking to a pretty girl seems a very short time but one minute with your hand on a hot stove feels like forever. That's relativity.'

The sail holds out, although every gust of wind causes the mast to creak and everyone on board to hold their breath. The waves are strong out here and we continue to pitch from side to side. The antinausea pills we popped before getting on board are no match for this kind of situation. 'I feel sick', groans Jane, who never feels sick. She twists as far as she can without kicking anyone and aims off the side of the boat. Her lack of gag reflex means she can't produce anything more than some spit. I have more success when my turn comes. I point my head downwards but the ship is so low in the water that I don't need to. Last night's dinner of egg and chips is recognisable even in the dark as it floats out to sea. One portion of vomit doesn't make a clean break from my mouth and ends up blowing into the shirt of the man downwind from me. He doesn't even flinch.

Four hours in, it's six o'clock and we don't seem any closer to the glow of Zanzibar's lights than we did two hours ago. The water continues to soak us and increase the layer of salt on our faces. We can't lick our lips because they are covered in warm salt water and we can't dry them with anything because everything is soaking wet.

At around 7am it begins to get light, just as the drizzle starts. We hardly notice it. The man sitting next to – and I mean right next to – Jane has to pee. Without even standing up, he just slides the leg of his shorts up and relieves himself on the deck, letting out a little sigh of relief.

Still no sign of Zanzibar. The lights from the towns have gone out and the grey sky is blocking any view of land. We are both shivering from the wind on our wet clothes; our teeth are chattering. We have lost all sensation in our backsides and I start to get cramps in my legs.

As we close in on hour six, we wonder what else could possibly go wrong. In our sleep-deprived, broken-spirited state, we think we can see the Pirates of the Caribbean on the horizon but it turns out to be just a lone fisherman beating the morning rush. We are thankful for small mercies. The sun that starts to push its way through the clouds is symbolic, the start of a new day, offering the possibility of survival, warmth and hope of finally arriving somewhere. The faint view of some hills appears on the horizon. Either we have gone in a big circle and are heading back to Kipumbwe or we might, just possibly, be within sight of Zanzibar.

It is only another 1½ hours before we make landfall at the small town of Mkokotoni. The boat drops anchor 30 metres from shore and a series of little metal dinghies race out to pick up passengers, at 100 shillings (about US$0.20) a head. There is a lot of push and shove to get on the first dinghy and we can't blame people for being in a hurry to get off this thing. The man and woman who win the race quickly climb onto the dinghy but their haste causes it to capsize, bags and all. They flail around in the water, not sure which piece of baggage or floating item of clothing to retrieve first. We feel sorry for them, but our sympathies are not shared by the rest of the passengers, who howl with laughter, clutching their stomachs and pointing at the poor couple like schoolyard bullies. We feel sorriest for the dinghy 'captain', who must now haul his upturned boat back to shore with the prolonged guffaws of the passengers ringing in his ears, knowing he won't get any revenue from this boatload.

It's 10 o'clock when we touch dry land: 27 hours since we slept, eight hours of sea-borne agony on a trip that had been described to us as three hours of romantic comfort. There will be time for recriminations later. Wet, cold, stiff and stunned, all we can think about is getting down to Stone Town and finding a hotel with a soft bed.

JAMES MORRISON

James Morrison and his wife Jane had their dhow experience during a year-long trip around the world. James hails from New Zealand but now lives in Toronto, Canada. Apart from a story that somehow made its way into the Slovak newspaper *Pravda*, this is James' first published work.

BABS 2 BRISBANE

Barbara Haddrill

When one eco-aware woman from Wales wanted to be a bridesmaid at her friend's wedding in Australia, she faced a dilemma. The enormous amount of pollution that would be emitted from a return flight was too much for her conscience. Not wanting to miss this important occasion she searched for another way, travelling slowly over land and sea.

'Good appetite!' said Viktor the steward formally, then he left me to tuck into my first lunch on board. Such mealtime pleasantries made me smile, especially as it would be the only communication I had with some of the sailors over the next ten days. Viktor was from the Philippines and had been on this ship for eight months. Except, he told me, for an occasional few hours of shore leave in Sydney or Singapore, when my temporary home, the MV *Theodor Storm*, stopped to reload before continuing its eternal circuit around the sea, ferrying cargo up and down and around, from Australia to Asia and then back again.

No-one on board actually knew what the cargo was, only how much each container weighed so the ship could be balanced: 18,559 tonnes of cargo, nine officers, 16 crew members – all male – and I were now out in the middle of the Java Sea. And I had no way of contacting anyone beyond this surreal world. Viktor told me that he had a seven-month-old son at home. His wife had sent him photos by email, but he had never touched his first-born child.

It was a large lunch. Having already polished off a delicious soup – a watery, meaty but refreshing broth – I now faced a lump of meat, a field of potatoes and a couple of fried green beans: good solid sailor food designed for the 'western' officers, who were predominantly Russian and Ukrainian. There was also one Filipino, Reyes, the third officer. He opted out and was given a healthier meal of rice and fish, a choice I wasn't given. But this only served to exclude him and he remained silent for most meals, eyes downcast, except for the occasional furtive look. Next to come into the mess was Alex, the electrical engineer from St Petersburg. 'Good appetite', he said in his clipped Russian accent to everyone as he bounded in and sat down. He was the only officer I had seen smile. He wore bright orange dungarees and a tight blue vest, which revealed his merchant-sailor muscles. Work clothes weren't allowed in the mess: this was clearly stated in a neatly typed notice displayed on the door, along with the set meal times (7.30am until 9am, noon until 1pm and 5.30pm until 6.30pm). Alex was happy to flout the rules this time. Sitting down, he grabbed a toothpick and said, 'Hello again, Barbara.'

'Hi, how are you?' I replied nervously.

'Good thank you. How do you like our ship then? Was it easy to sleep?' he continued in a friendly manner.

'Yes, great, I could have slept all day', I replied, happy to have caught up on the last few weeks of disrupted and nonexistent nights' sleep.

'Wait until the seas get rough, then we will see how you like it', Alex grinned. Then Viktor appeared with his food and he began eating.

The chief officer arrived next. He had finished his four-hour watch at 8am but had been working in the ship's office since then. This was all I discovered about his day because he didn't speak English very well and, as he looked exhausted when he sat down, I didn't press him further.

He began a loud conversation with Alex in Russian so I stared back at my food, frustrated that I was unable to understand. I continued trying to eat as slowly as possible to prolong the meal, knowing there was nothing particular to do this afternoon until dinner at 5.30pm.

I noticed a bottle of vitamin C tablets nestling among a mass of sauce bottles, and a momentary, irrational panic about scurvy hit me. I surveyed the rest of the table: a plastic red-and-white checked tablecloth was covered with white, textured plastic mats designed to stop the plates and cups rolling onto the floor if the ship lurched. A pile of cold meats sat sweating under cling film and the bread bin was full of stale sliced white bread. 'It is best to toast it', Alex warned me, catching my eye.

I was the only passenger travelling on the Singapore to Melbourne leg of the MV *Theodor Storm*'s scheduled journey: 4140 nautical miles over the next 10 days. This was the most important and unusual leg of my journey. The previous night I was finally boarding the ship and the reality hit me hard. My heart was pumping and my mind was racing as we neared the looming prow in the middle of the enormous and industrial Singapore docks. Working 24 hours a day, 365 days a year, there were no breaks here. The lights were on, giant yellow cranes, cargo and minuscule people were moving constantly around this well-oiled machine. I couldn't help giggling nervously and repeating, 'Oh my goodness!' like some overly polite colonial Brit heading off on a cruise ship.

I was travelling in a car with Michael Kahrs, the German shipping agent who was depositing me on board. He ignored my giggling and firmly told me what to do when we got out of the car. 'We must move quickly', he said, 'Follow me. Climb onto the ship by the gangway. We will be signed on and then we will meet the captain and find your cabin.' Outside, the warm, thick equatorial air and the incessant noise of this industrial port bombarded me as soon as I opened the door.

I was allocated the Owner's Cabin on F deck, just below the bridge. It was vast, with a bedroom and a day room containing a giant desk, a television that didn't work, an uncomfortable-looking sofa and an empty fridge. I hung up the scented flower necklace I had bought the day before in Little India in Singapore to celebrate the Diwali festival. The sweet smells filled the room as I began to unpack my few belongings. These items had been my companions over the last five weeks since leaving everything and everyone I knew at home.

Over the last 35 days I had travelled overland from my home in the tiny town of Machynlleth, mid-Wales, across 13 different countries using only buses, boats and trains. Now it seemed I might complete my challenge, my dream to reach Australia without using planes, although there had been a few moments when things looked very uncertain indeed.

After months of planning I was well under way, having already traversed England, Belgium, Germany, Poland, Belarus, Russia and Mongolia in just 10 days. This journey began as a desire to visit a friend whilst not compromising my environmental beliefs, but had evolved into a slow travel discovery of epic proportions, encountering countries, some of which I had barely heard of before, firsthand, with all my senses. Friends and strangers were following me through my online blog and in the news, waiting to see my fate. And the challenge was addictive. Could I show there was a way, a slower and gentler way, to travel without taking to the skies?

Hundreds of people were scattered around, filling every inch of available floor space outside the imposing concrete buildings of the Beijing West train station. Waiting patiently, many sat on hefty boxes and packages that were well wrapped in strips of brown tape. Other passengers made cushions from their giant red-and-white checked laundry bags or old rice sacks, reused and tied with string. Streams of Chinese washed quickly past, occasionally glancing at me, the tearful foreigner, before continuing on their way. Having resigned myself to the fact that my journey may have just reached its end earlier than I had hoped, I allowed the tears to stripe down my dirty, hot face. The last four hours had drained all my emotional and physical resources and now I realised I was alone, a long way from home and unable to communicate in this huge foreign city.

The Trans-Mongolian Express from Moscow had pulled into Beijing Main train station just after midday. After a mesmerising six-day trip, travelling through seven time zones, we arrived just two minutes behind schedule. The heat and emptiness of the Gobi Desert lingered in my memory and sand was still stuck to my skin. My journey was progressing to schedule but now a new adventure lay ahead: China and Southeast Asia to be traversed and discovered. There wouldn't be enough time to do each country justice but enough to get a flavour of the place and greater perspective on the distance I was travelling for my friend's wedding, over 20,000 kilometres across the earth. I had to go backwards now before going forwards – west again and then south. It was slightly insane but it was the only possible route for me, and I had calculated that the carbon dioxide emissions from my journey would be less than a third of those produced by the equivalent flight.

I had discovered there was a twice-weekly train to Hanoi on Sundays and Thursdays. I arrived in Beijing on Monday so I had three days to explore this immense city, including one of the highlights of my trip, a walk along the Great Wall of China, from Jinshanling to Simatai. Before doing anything else, I needed that train ticket in my hand. Beijing and Hanoi are over 2000 kilometres apart and it was imperative that I catch the Thursday train to keep on schedule. I had to be in Singapore by 2 October, where I had finally found a cargo ship to take me over the sea.

My first day in Beijing was an initiation in some unique Asian ways and the tough, humid climate. Helpfulness and generosity abounded but most people seemed to have an underlying unwillingness to admit they didn't know the answer to my questions, preferring to save face and direct me somewhere as opposed to nowhere. During four hours of carrying my backpack and piano accordion, with sweat rolling down my legs and back, walking and taking buses all around the city, I had been helped by many strangers, all of them keen to assist regardless of our inability to communicate through spoken language. Smiles and hand-pointing had got me so far. Then a cheerful lady in the tourist office, which was hidden away behind the fountains and five-star pomposity of the International Hotel, gave me a piece of paper on which she had written the Chinese characters for the words and phrases necessary to achieve my goal. Beijing West train station, bus 52, East Salon and a train ticket to Hanoi all transformed into a few lines and dashes.

First I waved my paper at a smiling man at the bus stop. He was wearing beige utility clothes and carrying a long cardboard tube. He helped me onto the packed 52 bus. We went through the wide, tree-lined streets past Parkson's Department Store and the Capital Museum. Next we passed Tiananmen Square and the walls of the Forbidden City, but I was unable to appreciate them yet, focused only on the ticket. Failure to travel to Hanoi could stop my whole journey dead. I was becoming desperate. At the station, policemen and passers-by came to my aid. Just standing around aimlessly was enough to make someone stop and help me. I stood out a mile here. Following their directions I was sent inside the station and then back outside again, up the escalators and back down. As I was wading through the throng of people to the right and then the left, paranoia descended on me. Was everyone sending me on a wild goose chase?

Venturing inside the immense Beijing West train station for one last time, I summoned all my energy to walk to the last counter available. There was a queue. The man in front of me asked where I was going.

'I want to travel to Hanoi in Vietnam, I need to buy a ticket here today', I said slowly and clearly. He laughed at me.

'You cannot go Vietnam by train. Get taxi to airport, plane go few times week.'

My face tried to remain calm and smiling as my heart sank and my stomach churned.

'But I have been told there is a train; I need to find the East Salon. Do you know where it is?' I asked meekly, determined not to believe him.

'No, there are no trains', he reiterated and, unaware of how painful this piece of news was, he left me standing helpless and alone.

Thankfully the train to Hanoi did exist and I caught it on Thursday as planned, with a ticket bought at my hostel with a 30% surcharge, but still only costing 1136 yuan (£80). Since then I had been on an adventure through Vietnam, Cambodia, Thailand and Malaysia on buses, boats and trains.

The weird just got more bizarre as I went along. Border controls were often the most confusing aspect of each journey. Long waits and language barriers caused worry and amusement all at once. On the Vietnamese side of the border from China, in Dong Dang, all passengers had to succumb to a 'medical check'. We paid the equivalent of 25p to have a digital thermometer pushed in our ear. Mine read 32°C but I was deemed fit and healthy and on this basis was stamped into the country.

There were many highlights, mostly when sampling local speciality food and meeting an eclectic mix of local characters. Eating the lucky elephant-ear fish had undoubtedly helped me when travelling up the Mekong Delta in an old wooden boat. Sharing a whole chicken, head and all, with some Vietnamese businessmen on a train to Saigon may not have helped so much. The surreal situation was accompanied by an endless supply of 'bird-flu' jokes and bottles of Hanoi vodka. It had been exhausting but my confidence and competence at negotiating the splendid intensity of Asia had improved drastically. I even perfected a few phrases from each country. Every step of the way was an unexpected joy, as not knowing what was going to happen next became a thrill. Waking up on a moving train in a new country was exciting. And looking at new and idyllic tropical views of thick, lush rainforests and white travel-brochure beaches never became boring, as I watched blue skies churning into torrential tropical monsoon rains. The confusion and chaos had subsided enough to allow me to make it to Singapore on time and find the cargo ship that was taking me to Australia.

After seven days on board I had done everything there was to do and eaten so much food I was beginning to worry that my bridesmaid's dress might no longer fit. Alex had taken me on a tour of the engine room – it was huge, noisy and hot – and we had watched the volcanic Indonesian archipelago slide by, barely visible through the thick smoke from the illegal burning of their rainforests. I had spent hours watching the officers on their watches on the Navigation Deck, trying to understand their heavy accents as well as their multimillion-pound equipment. Sadly the days of compasses and sextants were gone, but everyone still seemed happy staring out at the comforting sea and sky, the hundreds of flying fish and occasional other ship. Hours spent with the binoculars finally rewarded me with a pod of porpoises on day six. As the time passed, everyone gradually became more relaxed around each other and tentative, unusual friendships began to form.

In the evenings I watched films and played cards in the Officer's Lounge with Alex: the other officers preferred to stay on their own in their cabins, but he and I had become good friends. With the limited selection, it felt like we had watched every action film ever made. The pirated copies with appallingly bad subtitles were only serving to confuse Alex's otherwise excellent English. But finally the novelty wore off and time really began to drag, seconds and minutes ticked by agonisingly. I was so close to completing my challenge. For the next few days the ship rolled on the churning Southern Ocean as we worked our way east along the coast of Australia. Efforts to time my run up the stairs to match the rhythm of the motion and falling out of bed at night as the ship heaved were giving me a headache. And although I had hoped to be able to spot the coast of Australia by now, all I could see were grey sea and clouds.

On 14 October I started repacking my bag: Australia was finally in view, and two days earlier than expected. The ship was coming into Melbourne's harbour as I carefully folded my shiny turquoise bridesmaid's dress, and wrapped it around my wedding gift for the last time before setting foot on Australia. Throughout the journey these items had been a reminder of the reason for my trip and my life left behind. My dress was handmade from organic cotton by a friend, and the gift of a Welsh love spoon for Helen and her husband-to-be was an ancient custom that I wanted to carry on. Traditionally a man would give a carved wooden spoon to a woman to show he loved her, but now they are often given as wedding presents. The decorative designs represent the dreams you wish for the happy couple: a heart signifies love and a chain indicates that it will be forever.

Wales is a beautiful country filled with wonderful people and has an intriguing history, language and culture and it had been hard to leave my home behind indefinitely. My desire to see my friend was great but my environmental beliefs were too strong to allow me to take the journey quickly in an aeroplane. I didn't know how I was going to get home or when, but I had achieved my aim and travelled to Australia without flying. It took me 45 days and there had been a few times on the way when the whole trip had faltered. But even remembering those moments, it was hard to keep the grin off my face.

BARBARA HADDRILL

Babs is home from her low-carbon travels. By using methods other than flying to reach Australia, she reduced her total carbon footprint for 2006 from 10.6 tonnes to 5.6 tonnes. If we are to prevent damaging global climate change, we all need to reduce our personal carbon footprint to a target of 2.4 tonnes. Not flying is one way to do this and a small step in the right direction. She is writing a book about her adventures: *Babs 2 Brisbane* is being released in 2008 by The Centre for Alternative Technology.

CYCLING THE ICEFIELDS
PARKWAY

Andrew Bain

In Banff National Park, road signs are also a sign of the times. Less than 60 years ago, 'To the Bears' signposts directed visitors into rubbish dumps where black bears and grizzlies foraged. Today, along the Icefields Parkway, notices warn motorists to stay in their vehicles if they see a bear. It's a comforting shift, intended to reassure, though somehow it has the opposite effect as I trundle past on my bicycle, a vehicle that has no inside. What am I to do if I see a bear? Stay on my vehicle? Assume the position? Ring my bell in a threatening manner?

Stretching between Lake Louise and the municipality of Jasper, the 230 kilometre-long Icefields Parkway is promoted as 'the most beautiful road in the world', which seems like hyperbole only until you are enclosed within its pin-sharp peaks, crumbling glaciers and duck-egg-blue lakes. It is scenery so overwhelming, and has been so long in the making, that it seems wasted on motor vehicles, whose speed blurs the sharp mountain lines and windscreens deflect noise, scent and wind (and occasionally wandering wildlife). On a bicycle there are no such degrees of separation. The wind is a nurse or a curse, and nature engulfs you. It is for this reason, and not the presence of any bears, that I am on a bicycle, pedalling north towards Jasper at about 20km/h but acutely conscious that a bear at full steam can reach 50km/h. Is it any wonder that cyclists in this part of the world are alternatively known as 'meals on wheels'?

My journey begins not at Lake Louise but 55 kilometres further south in Banff, Canada's premier mountain playground, so that I can also spend a day riding the Bow Valley Parkway up to Lake Louise. Separated from the busy Trans-Canada Highway by the Bow River, it's reputed to be among the best roads in Canada for spotting wildlife. I haven't even left Banff before I'm hearing stories about bikes and bears. In a café the afternoon before I'm due to cycle out of town, I meet a couple of local cyclists claiming to have seen a grizzly sow and cub beside the Bow Valley Parkway the previous day. They describe the encounter with the same insouciance with which outback Australians talk about brown snakes, though it's enough to curdle the milk in my coffee.

So it's with some anxiety that I pedal out from Banff the next morning, trying vainly to avoid the busy Trans-Canada Highway by detouring on minor tracks past the famously reflective Vermilion Lakes. On a seat at the lake edge sits an old man in his eighties; the bike beside him is little younger. He is here for his daily prayer and the inspiration of the mountains that sprawl out before him. 'I mountain-biked all over these mountains', he says, tracing a finger across their tops, recounting stories of the single-track nirvana that he discovered as a septuagenarian. 'But now they say we can't do it. Such a shame. But you will love where you're going. All the animals...'

Though I begin to wish people would shut up about all the bloody animals, they are indeed plentiful, if a little smaller than feared, as I begin on the Bow Valley Parkway. Across my wheel, as though trying to knock me off my bike, ground squirrels dart hither and thither. In the treetops above the Bow River, a bald eagle awaits an early lunch and, around one bend, a pair of bighorn sheep click-clack like tap-dancers along the road – a Fred-and-Ginger pairing that is typically unmoved by the cars that crawl by, but tears away panicked into the mountains at first sight of a bike. I'm finding these Rocky Mountain critters less likeable by the hour.

In the end it becomes a simple task to spot wildlife: I need only look for the traffic bottlenecks on the parkway. A single elk stops around 30 vehicles, and there are people all but prodding it into position for their photographs, unaware or too stupid to remember that elks account for more injuries than bears around these parts. For me, there's a certain consolation to be found in this roadside circus: if an elk – Bullwinkle without the personality – can stop the world like this, I can relax in the knowledge that helicopters and foghorns will probably alert me if there are bears anywhere near the road. Content in this unreliable bit of self-comfort, I ride on through the crowd.

As the views widen from good to great through Moose Meadows (which might now be more aptly named simply 'Meadows', since moose are rarely sighted), revealing a skyline of peaks shaped like chess pieces, a splash of rain arrives to help relieve the effort of the road's first climb, a short-but-sharp ascent through the Hillsdale Slide. The water cools my head but not my legs, which complain out of all proportion to the size of the hill and are already causing me to contemplate the two 500 metre pass climbs ahead with more than a little trepidation. Perhaps I should have done some training, after all, before deciding to ride through North America's major mountain chain; perhaps my true enemy here will not have teeth, but will be my own legs.

A few more kilometres, a few more bumps in the land, and the Bow Valley Parkway ends in busy Lake Louise village, where there is further comfort in the realisation that my bear obsession is near-universal. Here, the village campground is ringed by an electric fence, turning it into a gated community of sorts, intended to keep out a riffraff of bears. I can sleep soundly in the knowledge that my tent isn't going to be torn open in the night by wild creatures, even if a little concerned that I might be – by electricity.

From Lake Louise village, my journey will join the Icefields Parkway all the way to Jasper, but first I wish to see Lake Louise itself. More famous than any other lake in the Canadian Rockies, it's said to be visited by around 10,000 people a day in summer. For this reason alone, I begin packing my tent at 5am for the ride up into the mountains to its shores, a time when I hope the bus crowds will still be snoring and farting in their beds. To reach the lake I have two options: I can take the direct route up the steep road, or meander along the Tramline hiking and biking trail, which, though it meanders gradually uphill, is also supposed to be a favourite bear corridor. I do what any cyclist would do: ride the flatter track, preferring bears to a steep climb.

It's common in the Rockies to pack a bear arsenal – Mace, bear bangers and bear bells (otherwise known around here as 'dinner bells' because of their ineffectiveness) – but I'm relying on more old-fashioned techniques as I ride through the dawn: luck and natural talent. Figuring I have a voice to scare anything on earth, I sing as I cycle, belting out 'She'll be Coming Round the Mountain' more times than even I can stand. No bear is going to find this monotone mouthwatering.

Lake Louise at dawn is an icy paradise, its water as still as ice (and almost as cold) and bluer than the dawn sky. Peaks and glaciers close around it like a fist in a scene that might be described in hackneyed terms as 'breathtaking' were I not already sucking hard from the climb. I count about five other people along its shores, and for almost an hour people trickle in like the meltwater that feeds the lake. At the first roar of a bus engine, I begin my descent and my second day on the road.

Back through Lake Louise village I hurtle, turning briefly onto the Trans-Canada Highway and veering away onto the Icefields Parkway, where the climb to the first of the passes, Bow Summit, begins immediately, though it's spread gently across 40 kilometres. Lining the road is a chain of lakes like fallen pieces of sky, and a verge thick with berry bushes, making this stretch of the parkway a supposed favourite with bears. This day, the bushes are empty of fruit, meaning the bears have beaten me here. Bless them.

At Hector Lake, 3 kilometres along the parkway, I meet Jules, another cyclist heading towards Jasper. From the French-speaking province of Quebec, Jules is that unusual sort of Canadian who speaks no English but, figuring we can share the language of pass-climbing, we pedal on together. Jules has been touring for weeks, while this is my second day in the saddle, and it's not long until he disappears ahead, leaving me in my own little world of struggle. I advance up the hill about as slowly as an ice age but, in truth, I have no desire to move any faster. The road's shoulder is as wide as its lanes, separating me from the traffic, and anonymous waterfalls tumble down sheer rock walls to the road's edge, which is coloured by wild flowers. If I'm to choose between beauty and speed, beauty will win every time.

Over the final 15 kilometres the climb to Bow Pass steepens, working in cahoots with a strong headwind that slows me even further. I stop at a lay-by looking across to the receding talons of Crowfoot Glacier, sitting, waiting and hoping to see ice calve away into Bow Lake, pretending that I'm not simply delaying the final grunt to the pass.

In the end the pass yields willingly, just a flat spot in the ridge hirsute with conifers. It is the highest point along the road – 2068 metres above sea level – with the descent promising to be as sweet as parts of the climb were sour. For the 17 kilometres to the campground at Waterfowl Lakes, I barely turn a pedal, stopping only to mend a puncture before rolling on into camp, where Jules has already cooked and eaten dinner – I will forever claim that he is fast, not that I am slow. My patch of earth in the campground is right beside the Mistaya River, a name that is said to be a Stoney word for grizzly bear. It's not until I'm happily ensconced in camp that I notice the trunks of the trees around me have been pawed and clawed by bears. With two days of trouble-free riding behind me, it concerns me less than perhaps it should.

Around the Waterfowl Lakes a wet night turns to a day of blue perfection, with sharp-tipped Mt Chepren reflected in the still waters so that it resembles a pair of incisors. My downhill run continues for another 20 kilometres to The Crossing, the meeting of the Mistaya and Saskatchewan Rivers, and the only petrol stop along the Icefields Parkway. As you'd expect with such a monopoly, the glorified roadhouse stops most visitors, at least briefly. Seizing the opportunity, it has amassed what is arguably the world's largest collection of souvenirs (though it modestly claims only to have the world's largest collection of postcards), from pewter First Nations to maple syrup to dried elk poo. 'Do we need this?' one old man asks his wife, holding up a wooden owl. Does anybody need a wooden owl?

From behind the counter of its cafeteria there are also familiar words of advice: 'Watch out for bears, won't you', the attendant insists, 'From here to Jasper you'll see a lot of them.' I'm not sure whether to thank him or kick him, though there's a part of me now that actually doesn't want to get through this journey bear-free, that wants to see something big and brown and furry. So it is with more hope than horror that I scan the meadows as I leave The Crossing, willing movement through them. All I see is more ground squirrels and a black garbage bag, which, for a moment, I almost do mistake for a bear.

Across gravel flats, the parkway advances towards the head of the Saskatchewan Valley, where the Yosemite-like rock walls narrow nearly to a close. Stones dribble down rockslides onto the road and almost every hillside is scarred by avalanches. It is humbling terrain, with the cliffs rising hundreds of metres above the road and waterfalls being carried away in the wind before they hit the ground. It might also be terrain that could defeat me – must I somehow ride through this?

– though I'm feeling stronger today, and I will need to be, since the headwind is also stronger and the climb to Sunwapta Pass is steeper than anything behind me. I must again ascend 500 metres but this time over a distance of 15 kilometres. I can already see the road ploughing into the mountains ahead; the road's toughest climb is about to begin.

As the climb begins, I am out of my saddle for the first time, the panniers over my front and rear wheels trying to unbalance me as I stand to crank the pedals, which turn as though stuck in mud. Momentarily I get a vision of Lance Armstrong in the French Pyrenees, dancing on his pedals, sweat dripping from the end of his nose, though the only likeness I can find is the sweat.

I make it to a lookout point about halfway through the climb, where I'm suddenly being photographed as much as the view. I'm also surprised to find I still have a reserve of energy, though I quickly spend it, my legs turning into invertebrates just a few hundred metres later, my eyes locked onto my speedometer, which ticks over so slowly it is surely broken. If I can just grind out the next 8 kilometres, it's mostly downhill for the final 110 into Jasper – if…

It seems like hours later that I rise onto the wide plateau that constitutes Sunwapta Pass, where mountains and glaciers point away to the sky. An icy wind blows in from the Columbia Icefield, turning the Icefields Parkway into the Ice-Filled Parkway. What I want is to celebrate my climb and have somebody coo about what a superhuman ascent I've made. Instead, I get Jeff and Bree.

Rising onto the pass from the opposite side a few minutes after I arrive, the two cyclists stop to trade road stories. I have been creeping along at around 50 to 60 kilometres a day; Jeff and Bree pedalled out of Jasper only this morning and have already cycled 110 kilometres, most of it uphill. Jeff is towing 40 kilos of gear, and before today Bree hadn't cycled for three years. They are planning to ride on another 40 today; my own planned camp stop is only 4 kilometres away, across from the Athabasca Glacier. I no longer feel like celebrating. I dislike Jeff and Bree.

If I'm expecting a dream downhill run to Jasper, I'm quickly corrected. Past the frigid toe of the Athabasca Glacier – the most visible strand of the Rocky Mountains' largest icefield – the road climbs sharply, cruelly onto Tangle Ridge. Atop the ridge, a trio of bighorn sheep nibbles at a roadside salt lick, drawing traffic to a standstill. How strange it must appear to the animals to be watched by tinned people. A short distance on, I'm cheered to learn that not all wildlife sightings on the Icefields

Parkway are so public. What the cars hurry past I dawdle by, and I watch from the saddle as a white-tailed deer drinks from a tarn below road level. As it bounds away across the meadow with balletic leaps, the traffic beside me whirrs blindly on.

The descent from Tangle Ridge is elevatorlike, threading between waterfalls, past the multilayered Stutfield Glacier and onto the braided gravel flats of the Athabasca Valley. Here the mountains are less spectacular, but a raging tailwind blows. Suddenly, I don't care about scenery because the beauty is in the ease of the riding. Another cyclist approaches from the opposite direction but he's so fatigued by the climb and the wind that he doesn't even return my wave.

It's at Honeymoon Lake, only 50 kilometres from Jasper, that curiosity wins my inner bear battle. Perhaps the lactic acid has leaked from my legs to my brain, but when I see entries in the campground register suggesting that black bears had been sighted twice in camp just the previous day, I decide I'll stay the night, even though I've pulled in only to fill up with water. The expectation of seeing bears has become a desire to see bears, though the register proves to be false advertising. If there were bears enjoying Honeymoon Lake yesterday, there bloody well ain't today.

I plan, then, for a dawn start to my final day, a time when wildlife is at its most visible, when the road will be empty of cars and hopefully full of beasts. I'm woken in darkness by the howl of a wolf, which seems a hopeful beginning, and cruise out into a world that seems to have stopped on its axis. There's no wind, not another person and no large animals: just me, the chirp of birdsong and the murmur of the river. It's a silence that seems to preclude the presence of anything so threatening as a bear, though I stay on my vehicle, just in case.

ANDREW BAIN

Andrew Bain has cycle-toured on four continents. He is the author of *Headwinds*, the story of his 20,000km bicycle journey around Australia, and also of Lonely Planet's *A Year of Adventures*. At the time of publication he was cycling across the European Alps, towing his kids along behind.

ON THE LAM ON THE LONG ROAD TO LHASA: HOW FAR BACK CAN A BACK ROAD GO?

April Orcutt

Deep in Eastern Tibet I looked down from the edge of a 40ft cliff at the mud-brown river roiling over boulders. The raging Yi'ong Zangbo spanned a hundred yards from cliff face to cliff face and the roar of the rushing water echoed through the isolated canyon.

A little way down the river to my left, an exhausted driver rested in a muddy bus stopped near a few battered boards, all that was left of the washed-out bridge. A drenched German traveler on the bank fished his wet clothes, hooked on rocks, out of the river and put them back into his equally wet suitcase. A soaked Swiss couple sat on a boulder nearby, the woman clutching her bleeding ankle and crying.

Across the chasm in front of me stretched a cable about an inch in diameter. On the cable hung a hook and pulley. A loose 'basket' – made of baling wire looped three or four times around a narrow 4ft board – dangled from the hook.

Earlier I had seen a Tibetan man sit in that basket, then three other Tibetans pushed him and the basket over the edge. The man slid slowly downward over the river toward the opposite cliff. Near the end, with his bare hands he pulled himself along the cable and up the bank. The Tibetans on my side pulled another wire to bring the basket back.

I had to decide: which way would I try to cross the river? Stumbling on rolling boulders through a thigh-deep torrent and probably drowning; or flying over racing waters in a loose, flimsy basket and probably falling, smashing onto rocks and breaking all my bones before drowning? Or should I, like the Swiss couple, give up my attempt to travel overland to Lhasa, 300 miles to the west?

'This,' I thought, 'is a really stupid thing to do.' Then, suddenly, the Tibetan men pushed the basket and me off the cliff.

———

Four months earlier, in February 1986, I had read an article in the *San Francisco Examiner/Chronicle* that announced: 'China has opened 137 more cities and regions to foreign travelers, including the exotic capital of Tibet.' Now there was an opportunity: independent travel to long-closed Lhasa, 'the exotic capital of Tibet,' with its huge gleaming-white Potala Place, traditional home of the Dalai Lama, and its mystical Jokhang, the most sacred temple for Tibetan Buddhists and the destination of thousands of pilgrims.

It was an opportunity that didn't last long, either. Just a couple of years later, after Tibetan monks in Lhasa rioted against Chinese suppression of Tibetan culture, China again closed Lhasa to independent travel. Only supervised groups were – and are – allowed. Most of the rest of Tibet remains officially closed as well. And the monks continue to protest the dissolution of Tibetan culture.

At the time I didn't really think I could get to Lhasa, which is the world's second-highest capital at 12,000ft. Flying was the only permitted way to travel there, and I feared altitude sickness from suddenly arriving at an elevation higher than the summits of most countries' mountains. But why let reality stand in the way of travel? I headed to Asia. After traveling solo in southwestern China for a month, I bussed westward to Dali, a pretty town on a strip of land between Erhai Lake and the Diancang Mountains. Dali is one of the areas China now promotes as Shangri-La, the mythical *Lost Horizon* locale where people don't grow old but do reassess their lives.

Although Dali put me closer to Tibet, I despaired of reaching my destination because Lhasa was still at 12,000ft and still accessible only by air and the rest of Tibet was still closed to foreigners. And then I met Steve.

I was ordering dinner in the Coca-Cola Restaurant when he walked in carrying a 1st-edition guidebook to Tibet, published just two weeks before. Steve, a college professor from Florida, said he wanted to travel overland to Lhasa. The road crossed a dozen mountain passes and four of the world's great rivers: the Yangzi, Mekong, Salween and Brahmaputra. The trip would take at least two weeks and would involve extremely rough, bumpy, isolated travel for 1300 miles – mostly on dirt roads, hitchhiking with Tibetan pilgrims in open platform trucks. 'One other thing,' he added, 'is that it's illegal for foreigners to travel those roads.'

Just getting to Dali had been a problem when Steve accidentally got on a bus that wasn't supposed to carry foreigners. 'Before we crossed a police checkpoint,' he said, 'the driver made me get out and walk around a hill. He said he'd meet me on the other side. My backpack was on the bus so I was really nervous about it, but the driver did wait for me.'

I looked at Steve's book. It warned about 'landslides, mudslides, snow, washouts and even glacial blockages,' but it also said, 'The best time to attempt the trip is from April to June.' The date was May 31. 'I'm looking for someone to travel with,' Steve said. 'I don't want to travel overland to Lhasa alone.'

My trips at home were usually off the beaten track – although often with the security of my Volkswagen bus. Steve's slow road trip would solve my acclimatization issues, and I wanted to see the Potala and the Jokhang. Still, I made a worry-list about traveling roads the Chinese decreed off-limits:

1. Would there be any transportation?
2. If trucks went by, would they pick us up?
3. Would we get stuck in tiny towns?
4. Could we even make it to Lhasa?
5. Was this nuts?

Steve had his *Tibet* guidebook, but it focused mainly on other roads and areas around Lhasa. This overland route had hardly been tested. I listed more personal concerns:

6. Becoming sick with no medical care – but I was healthy and hadn't gotten sick yet.

7. Getting injured with no way to get out – but I was a cautious person who didn't do stupid things.

More than delays, illness or injury, I feared serious altitude sickness. And Steve had the book. *Tibet* opened doors. Maybe the Chinese would close them, but the book gave me hope.

'I'll go,' I said.

Within ten minutes of meeting, we were planning to travel illegally overland to Lhasa. Two days later we bused to Lijiang, a village set against Yulong Snow Mountain, where we intended to talk a trucker into carrying us north into Tibet.

First Try: Skedaddling North
from Lijiang

We met a college student who had been selected by the Chinese government for a career as an English teacher and who wanted to practice his English. After talking with him for several hours, we asked for *his* help.

'We're going to try to go overland to Lhasa,' Steve said.

'But you can't do that,' the student said.

'Yes, but we're still going to try.'

'But you can't do that.'

'Yes, well, could you please translate something for us – write it on a piece of paper that we can show a bus driver? Would you please translate: "Please tell us before we come to a checkpoint so we can get out and walk around it and meet you on the other side"?'

He became very nervous. 'You can't do that.'

'Yes, but we want to try.'

'But you can't do that.'

It wasn't that he didn't *want* to help us – but he could not comprehend the idea of doing something forbidden. The conversation upset him.

'I'll say that a friend in Hong Kong wrote the note,' I said.

Finally, reluctantly, he wrote it – although for all we knew, he wrote, 'These foreigners are trying to sneak into Tibet illegally. Stop them!'

We never found a truck heading north. We did find white cotton surgical-type dust masks, which we thought we might need later.

Hatching a New Scheme

We rode buses and trains more than 500 miles east and north to Chengdu to try a different route to Lhasa. In this big blocky city with a 20ft Mao statue, we ran into Susan and Dave, a British couple that Steve and I had met a week earlier in Dali. I liked the idea of traveling in a larger group of co-conspirators and with another woman, so we convinced them that riding in the back of an open truck on dirt mountain roads would be fun. They decided to join us.

Now we colluded on a new plan. The book said, 'Lots of travelers have tried – and failed – to get started from Chengdu.' Steve said, 'We'll have to be inconspicuous.' As the audacity of this on-the-lam journey began to sink in, I added another item to my worry-list:

8.   Being arrested and thrown into a Chinese Gulag.

We would buy tickets for as far as we could: to Kangding, a two-day 230-mile journey to the gateway to Tibet. The bus didn't run often – but it did run the next day. After Kangding, we would hitchhike.

That evening I wrote cheery letters to my parents: 'Three friends and I are traveling by road to Lhasa. There won't be many post offices along the route so you won't hear from me for a month or two. Don't worry – I'll be fine.' To three close friends I wrote: 'Tomorrow I'm heading into Eastern Tibet with an American guy and a British couple. I'm sending you their names and addresses because, in case I disappear, they will have been the last people to see me. Assuming, of course, that they themselves make it through.'

*Days 1 & 2: Hightailing it
West from Chengdu*

The next morning we boarded the bus in Chengdu. It wouldn't get us all the way, but it would get us 230 miles closer. Starting at little more than sea level, we rode all day past green fields and through towns crowded with sober throngs wearing grey or blue Mao jackets and caps. By evening in Ya'an my nose was sniffly.

The following day we left at 5am in the rain. The bus sped up the narrow, winding mountain road. We twisted along cliffs without guardrails and squeezed past trucks barreling toward us. Drop-offs fell thousands of feet. I added number 9 to my worry-list: 'Driving over the edge of a cliff.' I felt sicker.

At one of our rare pit stops – a literal pit, covered with a few boards and surrounded by haphazardly nailed-together wood walls – Susan and I had barely entered the makeshift shelter before our male driver leaned on his horn.

'Doesn't he know women wear layers?' she asked.

'Do you think he'll leave us here?' I said. I added another item to the worry-list:

10. Being abandoned in a rickety and disgusting outhouse.

Late in the afternoon we arrived in Kangding, elevation 8200ft. Through the bus windows we saw lively Tibetan Khampa men playing pool on a dozen tables filling a plaza. Some of these Khampas, fierce warriors who ruled this area for centuries before the Chinese took over, wrapped red yarn around their long black hair. Others wore tan or black flattened bowlers. Women, who stayed far from the pool tables, had braided red yarn in their hair and wore black skirts with woven multicolored-striped aprons. Both men and women wore chunky silver, turquoise, and orange coral jewelry.

Before leaving the station, we learned that in three days a bus would head for Batang, a two-day, 260-mile trip. Batang was 20 miles from the border of present-day Tibet. Luckily, the clerk sold us tickets.

We knew we must remain inconspicuous in Kangding. We discreetly stepped out of the bus station: Steve at 6ft 3in tall, Susan with light-brown wavy hair, Dave with a beard, me with sun-bleached curls, and all of us carrying backpacks. We might as well have carried klieg lights. A crowd of curious Khampas immediately surrounded us. They laughed and followed us until we disappeared into a hotel. We hoped none was a snitch who would sell us down the river to the cops.

*Days 3 & 4: Lying Low
in Kangding*

The next two days it was easy for me to be inconspicuous because I awoke with a cold and stayed in bed. I put a big check mark next to number 6 on my list: 'Becoming sick.'

Susan, Dave and Steve hiked up to the Ngachu Monastery, but a government delegation arrived so they sneaked away and ran down the hill.

Day 5: Up & Down on
the Dust Bus

Our bus to Batang climbed for hours until we crested a hill and entered a huge plateau, which did actually feel like we had climbed up onto 'the Roof of the World.' The great plain of the Tibetan Plateau stretched toward distant mountains. Herds of black yaks looked like buffalo grazing on the light-green grasses. Tibetan men wearing cowboy hats rode horses, and two-story mud-walled dwellings resembled Native American pueblos. Round-faced, brown-skinned, high-cheekboned Tibetans with their silver, turquoise and coral jewelry reminded me of the Diné or Navajo. I felt like I was literally in a time capsule traveling to the back roads of the American West 150 years ago.

After a while, past Xinduqiao, the road split. The northern route was paved. The southern route was dirt. The bus went south. Dust billowed around us. My medical-style dust mask wasn't enough to filter out the grit. I folded a red bandana into a triangle and tied it around my face on top of the mask. I looked like a surgeon preparing to rob a bank. I wanted to keep the windows closed so the dust would stay outside; but, because dust doesn't stay outside, Dave wanted to open the windows so when new dust blew in, old dust would blow out.

For four hours we raced down a long valley. Our driver drove the bus like he would ride a bicycle, saving effort by not using his brakes. Along the way we started seeing Tibetans riding on the broad open unprotected seatbelt-less beds of 'pilgrim trucks' – the kind of trucks we knew we, too, would soon be riding. When we stopped for the night in Yajiang, a town where Tibetans and Chinese lived on opposite sides of the Dri-chu River, we met a bedraggled American who had been riding on one of those open trucks – one that had flipped over. One of his companions broke her collarbone and another badly injured her back. To get to the nearest hospital they were put on the open bed of another truck – and sent back to Chengdu. 'The police locked up my backpack for the accident investigation,' he said, 'so I can't leave town. Could you spare some toilet paper?'

Day 6: Vamoosing on the
Last Bus to Batang

The bus left at 5am. I discovered that, on only our fourth travel day, we would go through Litang, which the book said, at over 15,000ft, was the second highest town in the world. I fretted, breathed deeply and tried to remain calm, but to my list I added:

11. Getting altitude sickness from climbing more than 3000ft higher than Lhasa

and

12. Breaking eardrums from having a head cold at extremely high elevation.

Near noon we crested a pass. I saw a village at least 1000ft below us. I asked the Tibetan woman sitting across the aisle from me, 'Litang?'

She answered, 'Litang.'

Yet my heart beat, my lungs breathed and my ears drummed. On my worry-list I crossed off 'altitude sickness' and 'breaking eardrums.'

At the lunch stop in Litang we met a Swiss couple, a German man and a Buddhist American man. They were on another bus, a bus that only traveled occasionally – a bus that was headed for Lhasa. We had to get on that bus. With the help of a Chinese-herbalist passenger who spoke a dozen words of English, we arranged with the drivers to switch buses in Batang – but for the switch to work, our bus needed to get there first.

After lunch we drove slowly up a very long, steep valley, crested the pass and descended rapidly for hours. Steve said, 'We must be below sea level by now.' At 6pm we approached Batang, which was actually at 8858ft, and gathered our packs. Our bus stopped and we piled out, yelling 'Thank you!' The bus left. The four of us stood at the side of the road, facing east and scanning for the new bus. When we saw it, we waved our arms and jackets like we needed that bus to save our lives. And maybe we did.

This bus carried us three miles to a hotel, but the hotel staff refused to sell us desperados food or rent us a room. In a nearby store, we bought the only cuisine available: canned mandarin oranges and plain cookies. At 9pm the hotel staff finally gave us a room – maybe, I thought, to confine us miscreants until the arrival of the sheriff having ratted us out.

Days 7 to 10: Making Tracks on
the Tibet Roller Coaster

Although we had traveled across historical Tibet since Kangding, we had formally been in Sichuan. When China took over Tibet, it gave big chunks of its land to four other provinces, and the Yangzi formed the current official border between Sichuan and Tibet. The bus now drove south along that iconic river. Clear Tibetan river water coming from the west disappeared amid the muddy waters of the Yangzi.

The bus crossed the bridge and approached a red-and-white striped stanchion-and-arm blocking the road. 'This is it,' Steve said. 'This is the border with Tibet.' We culprits prepared to enter truly forbidden territory – the place the Chinese government *really* didn't want foreigners to go.

'Duck,' said Steve. We, who had been waiting a week – or a lifetime – to see Tibet, hunched down in our seats. As with other petty criminals for whom excitement overwhelms fear of capture, we lifted our heads high enough to snap photos of the gate. The driver opened his window and talked to the guard. Slowly the red-and-white arm began to rise. It seemed to take forever to open the gate to Tibet, but it did finally open. The bus entered.

We had made it to Tibet. But we were still 785 miles from Lhasa. The bus now began a hot, dusty four-day roller-coaster ride through desolate country. We left the Yangzi, crossed the Mekong and Salween, and entered the drainage of the Brahmaputra. In between we crossed five passes, three over 15,000ft. Steve tried to take a photo of the bridge over the Mekong and, from nowhere, a Chinese military guard ran screaming up to him. After a few tense minutes, the incident passed with no arrests.

Dinners throughout the journey continued to be rice, peanuts and salty greens in broth. In all hotels we had one room with four beds, each with a yak-butter-infused bottom sheet, a coverlet, a wood-chip pillow with a small hand towel over its pillowcase and a dusting of dirt. Whenever we opened the doors for ventilation, curious Tibetans crowded around our doorway, each trying to peek in, so four or five smiling faces would be angled and stacked along each side of the doorframe. Watching us fold clothes or pull books out of packs provided endless entertainment. Although these people were always sweet, I realized I never want to be famous. We hoped no-one in our audience would squeal about us perps to the Chinese G-men.

Halfway through the roller-coaster trip, the scenery changed to dense forests and lush semitropical bushes. Jagged peaks with blue glaciers poked above grey clouds. Rivers grew wider and rougher, their waters filled with milky glacial silt. Rain fell.

The guidebook warned about the area: 'If there's flooding from torrential rain, the road will be impassable.' In Tangmai, the bridge had washed out so, while waiting for it to be repaired, we would spend that night there...and the next night...and the next night...

Days 11 to 13: Holing
Up During Storms

Truckloads of Tibetans camped near the hotel during the rain in Tangmai. Three Khampa men bore swords in sheaths at their waists and kept their right arms free from their heavy coats so they could wield the swords more effectively. Anytime one of us brought a camera near them, they drew those swords like they knew darn well what they were doing. Then they would laugh, and we would laugh. These fascinating men had an untamed look about them with a mischievous sparkle in their eyes. To my worry-list I added:

13. Beware of Khampas brandishing swords.

On the third night in Tangmai, a tremendous storm dumped torrents of rain all night long. In the morning I put a big check mark on my list alongside number 3: 'Getting stuck in tiny towns' – although Tangmai, with only a hotel and two tiny restaurants, was only a minuscule truck stop, not so much as a town. Could we even make it to Lhasa? Was this nuts?

Around noon the herbalist came over and pointed excitedly at the bus, so we quickly packed and got on. It headed down the muddy road toward the river crossing, six miles away. In many places rockfalls and mudslides had gushed down the steep cliffs and onto the narrow road. A fallen tree stopped our progress. Steve, Dave and others got out and tugged and pulled it off the road. A little further on, boulders blocked our way. Using their bare hands, passengers cleared the debris so that our vehicle could ease past. The slippery road became so narrow I thought the bus might tumble over the edge. The driver's pained expression made me think he felt the same. In several spots I got off and walked, a luxury not afforded to the driver. When we finally reached the crossing point for the tumultuous Yi'ong Zangbo River, the driver fairly collapsed over his steering wheel. We had traveled 1000 miles, and there was no bridge. 'Now what?' I asked.

The German grabbed his suitcase and waded into the icy river. The Swiss couple waded in. She slipped. The German fell. His suitcase popped open. They all slogged back to the riverbank. I knew I couldn't wade across.

We heard the herbalist yelling excitedly. He waved his arm for us to follow him up the side of the cliff. There we watched the man in the flimsy basket cross the river. 'I can't do that,' I said. 'no way.' But I saw no alternative. I wasn't going back.

After a dozen people crossed safely, with reservations I said OK. The Tibetans adjusted the wire basket around my pack and me and, before I was ready, pushed me over the edge.

I dropped. Air rushed through my hair. Mist hit my face. My heart raced. I grabbed at the tiny wires of my open-air gondola. The roar of the river became all-encompassing as I hurtled towards the rocks. Suddenly the basket bounced as the cable stopped the fall. I started breathing again and smelled the dampness from the rain and river. All I could see past my feet were the raging waters and boulders as the basket slid slowly toward the opposite bank. I should have been more terrified, but I felt exhilarated. When I didn't think too much about what I was doing in this jury-rigged aerial tramway, I actually enjoyed the basket trip: floating gently through the air, looking closely at a show of nature's power, experiencing a Tibetan can-do spirit of camaraderie for solving problems, accomplishing a formidable task without the use of modern conveniences.

More Tibetans helped me get out on the other bank. When we four had crossed, I said again, 'Now what?'

We walked a mile and discovered a big open-platform truck crowded with the other bus passengers. We climbed up, squeezed in and sat on our packs. The truck departed, and rain fell again. Once more the road wound up and, in the open and in the rain, we bounced along over a nearly 15,000ft pass and down many miles to Bayi.

Days 14 & 15: More Miracles

The next morning another bus magically appeared outside the hotel and, for two more days, we rode past green mountains, snowy peaks and ruined monasteries. We crossed another very high pass decorated with prayer flags. The valley flattened and the Kyi Chu River meandered. Yaks, black nomad-tents, pueblo-like houses and groups of prayer flags dotted the landscape. Fields of yellow flowers filled the valley.

Someone took a photo of the four of us covered in 15 days of dirt and 1300 miles of dust, but we all look very happy. In the distance we could see the bright white Potala Palace of Lhasa.

APRIL ORCUTT

April Orcutt is a California writer, college professor and pro-ducer-writer of documentary, public-affairs and science television programs. April continued her 4½-month solo Asia journey by traveling overland west to the border of Nepal, east back to Lhasa, north to Dunhuang and Turpan, west to Kashgar and south over the just-opened Khunjerab Pass into northern Pakistan.

FROM LONDON TO HELSINKI ON TWO LITTLE WHEELS

Agnieszka Flak

I was spitting dust; my face was burning after days in the sun's glare and the dead insects plastered on my windscreen were too many to count. But the satisfaction of crossing 2700 kilometres of Europe from London to Helsinki on a motor scooter was sweet – the best part being able to say: 'I have arrived'.

People told me I was mad and reckless to rush off to my new job in this way: four days on the road in all, averaging 90km/h, and more terrifying moments than I dare count. After all, zipping along the motorway like a mouse in a herd of elephants is not everyone's idea of fun. But the jug of beer at the end of the day – be it German, Polish or Estonian – had never tasted better than after hours and hours staring ahead, manoeuvring in traffic, and anxiously hoping to reach the next petrol station in time.

My trip started in London: I set out in autumn with a duffle bag tied on my back, a small rucksack clamped between my legs and an adventurous friend wedged behind me. She was my personal DJ, changing tracks on the MP3 player we shared, and also the blinker when the lights of my Vespa did little to make trucks and lanes of cars let me pass.

On the ferry in Dover we parked right next to the Harleys and Suzukis, feeling part of the club: not dressed in black biker leathers, perhaps, but we thought we had class. We waved goodbye to the coastal town and the English hills we were leaving behind. This had been home for a year, but now it was time for a change. With our helmets in our hands, we took the obligatory photo on the upper deck to celebrate the start of a trip, with no idea how our journey would end.

After we drove off the ferry in Calais and into the right-hand traffic, France, Belgium and the Netherlands passed in a glance. We were amazed we could traverse four countries in just one day.

At 151cc, my scooter engine was just above the legal minimum for driving on Europe's motorways. Other drivers seemed astonished to see a woman among the speeding traffic driving something that resembled little more than a bicycle. It felt like elbowing our way through a crowd: tall trucks in front, behind and to our left. Occasionally the winds pushed us perilously across the traffic lanes. Motorcyclists honked and shouted the odd 'hurray'; whenever a car overtook us, an amazed and confused look and fingers tapping on foreheads was all we would get.

Once the trucks left our back, we relaxed. Then I focused on not losing my passenger, who was dosing off as trees, fields and highways passed in a flash. Finally, to keep her awake, I told her to count out loud the roundabouts or signs we passed and, fortunately, that helped. Scootering is not the safest way to get around: concentrating for hours can be tiring – that was where the music helped – and with wheels as small as my Vespa's every hole and bump in the road can deal a fatal blow.

It is a bit like sitting on a toilet, someone once told me, and sometimes I couldn't help feeling the truth in that. You cannot move for fear you might lose your balance, yet just sitting there and staring ahead in deep concentration can seem like a big waste of time.

Driving up the North Sea coast was mad, even I admit. No buildings to protect us from the wind racing in off the sea. Whenever

I accelerated, the wind, rain and hail hit my face in intensified rage. Dortmund in the dead of night, 14 hours later, was never a more welcoming sight.

After a family visit and a short break from the road, it was time to resume my journey alone. By now, the clock was ticking: I was in a hurry, due to report for my new Finnish assignment in just three days.

Fields of wind turbines seemed to dance to the bluegrass tunes in my ear, as the mist of the waking day curled around me. 'Tuck-tuck, tuck-tuck' was the rhythm I drove to, watching every hole, every potential skid that might have ended my ride. The German autobahns let me test the scooter's limits – 120km/h, it turned out, far above the official 96km/h the dealers tell you. The bike shook and it felt like all its parts were clinging on for dear life.

I stopped in Berlin for a coffee and a chat with an old high-school friend: the detour added three hours to my trip, but connecting the dots in my life gave me a point of reference during the lonely journey and I phoned a few other friends during the days that followed and in the places I passed through next.

As I headed for Poland, I chose hills and country roads when time allowed – a welcome break from the daunting highways. Where Germany's roads were smooth, the Polish ones were rough. Drivers made me veer off course, gesturing that there was no room for scooters on the country's one-lane roads. The 'highway' ended 100 kilometres before Warsaw. Along with hundreds of trucks, I had to switch to dusty roads where I was blinded by lights coming towards me and from behind. One driver nudged my back number plate and thought it was jolly fun. Not I.

The fact that I was a woman seemed to draw attention at every petrol stop. Motorbikers would come over with a grin, rub their leather shoulders on mine and ask about my destination. At other times men would circle my scooter and inspect it like a piece of porcelain. 'What sort of engine's in that machine of yours?' they'd ask. And 'Are you really travelling on your own?' they added each time. Later they would return to their cars or buses and tell their friends about the mad woman on the other side of the car park. I could not but feel proud.

One of these encounters stands out in my mind. A pilgrim bus stopped next to my scooter and a priest sitting in the front came over and asked me where I was heading. Hearing my plan, he said straight out, 'You're mad!' A minute later he called over all the passengers from his bus. 'Please join me in a prayer for the wellbeing of the girl with the lion heart', he said, 'May she arrive where she is heading, and may she do so in one piece.'

I have always loved two-wheelers, ever since the moment when my mechanic dad put me on the back of my uncle's old BMW when I was only five. I could have easily made this trip from London to Helsinki in a two-hour plane journey, gone by boat via Sweden or even travelled in the protective shell of a car. But the day I moved to Italy and bought my little scooter, a love affair was born and I could not think about starting any new adventure without those two wheels, big headlight and windshield parked under my house. For me, riding one of these 'crotch-rockets' on a fast windy road is a way to clear mind and soul. It requires so much concentration and focus there is little time left to worry about anything else in the world. I come back mentally and spiritually refreshed – no matter how physically draining the ride itself might have been.

Warsaw, capital of my native country, was the next overnight stop. It was already 2am when I pulled in, after hours of searching for the right road to take me into the heart of the capital's web of streets. My map was of little help, especially after temperatures had dropped to near freezing and I could barely hold it with fingers that looked like icicles with veins.

Leaving the city, the trucks followed me like ducks in a march – I hated them for their size, but appreciated the company during the lonely nights. Driving a scooter can be a lonely affair. There's plenty of time to think; I chose to sing at the top of my lungs instead. It made me feel less alone, no matter how off key I was. Passing through Lithuania and Latvia's flat countryside at night was probably the worst of it all: with only one car every 20 minutes, road signs scarce and petrol stations scarcer – unnerving when driving a scooter with a small tank that holds just over eight litres of gas.

A petrol station every 110 kilometres was an absolute must. I thought that, if I took the primary roads, one would show up in the distance every hour or so, but Poland and the Baltic countries proved me wrong every day. The orange warning light blinking on the tachometer regularly added an extra adrenaline kick to my trip.

Somewhere between Lithuania's border town of Marijampol and Latvia's capital, Rīga, the scooter came to a sudden halt, with nothing but fields and a 'Rīga 200km' sign in sight. I waited for half an hour, hoping another vehicle or even a lazy tractor would pass by and share some of their fuel to get me to the next stop. But as the night grew darker and colder, I decided that pushing the 150 kilogram scooter might be the smartest option of all. I sweated like a pig and cursed myself more than I dare remember: a mechanic's daughter should know better than to embark on a road trip without spare petrol and a toolbox tied to her back.

But then again, a road trip is also about doing something silly. It's about testing your limits and reaching the extremes, I guess, be it fighting for space with trucks or trotting next to the bike and pushing it, having never felt so lonely and ridiculous before. But each time you succeed, the satisfaction is vast, whether it's passing a wagon as big as my house or finally seeing the bright yellow Shell sign appear around the bend. For the rest of my route I marked each petrol stop on the map to make sure I reached it in time: I thought better not to chance it twice.

Every border crossing was a test. Most officials would let me pass with a wink; but my Italian licence plate, German passport, greeting in Polish and the cotton mask beneath my helmet were too much for the Latvian border guard.

'Madam, please, off bike...now', he said. He took me to his little booth and asked me to take off my helmet and my bandana, so that he could see whether that passport with its pages falling apart was really mine. An hour-long interrogation followed, covering my life story, and the more I pressed him to hurry up, the more he relaxed in his run-down reclining chair. The white glucose tablets he found in my bag looked suspicious as well, he said with a smile. 'Why would a woman choose to cross a border in the middle of the night, alone, if she had nothing to hide?' he asked.

Finally, at midnight, he let me go and I jetted off towards Rīga, hoping to find a bed and get a few hours of sleep before embarking on the road again.

Once in a hostel in central Rīga, I took a shower and put lots of lotion onto my wind-roughed skin. Exhausted, I quickly fell asleep. The other 11 backpackers partying in the same room seemed more a dream than reality. I slept next to the window, throwing a glance down to the road now and then. 'You're more than welcome to park your bike out here', the receptionist had said. 'I'm just not sure if you will find it there in the morning as well.'

The next day I took it easy and wandered around Latvia's capital, stopping for pierogies at a tiny place called Sievasmates Piradzini where I could choose from dumplings stuffed with meat, mushrooms, fruit or cheese. They were nearly as good as the ones I remembered from home: I crammed my bag with some reserve supplies, just in case, along with the sugar boosts I always had on hand to keep me awake.

Eating healthily on a trip like this is not easy, with autogrills and small food joints along the way determining what you eat for breakfast, lunch, dinner, and then breakfast again. I started ranking the various types of hot-chocolate machines and organising my petrol stops around the places that had the brands I preferred. In my left-hand pocket I kept a bag of sweets, easy to access during times of greatest fatigue: with my right hand on the accelerator, I would reach for one, and then another, until I was sure I wasn't going to fall asleep. Every few hours I would take a long rest, spread out on the grass away from the road or highway and take a nap.

Leaving Rīga, I felt I was almost there. I had less than 300 kilometres to go and my direction seemed clear – yet I spent the next three hours entering and leaving the city as I searched for the right exit road to take me on my way. My sense of direction had not failed me on the journey so far; with five maps and various printouts in my backpack I had more information than I really needed. But in the end I mostly relied on my memory as I couldn't hold the enormous maps while driving and had no co-passenger to keep them from flying away.

But that day the main streets leading into Rīga's centre were transformed into heaps of cement; bridges were closed and street diversions led all around town. I was stuck in narrow queues of traffic for hours, with no space to do a U-turn, even for a vehicle the size of my scooter. People in cars started rolling down their windows, daunted by the midday heat. Those directly to my right gave me a thumbs up, then started asking me something in Latvian, pointing at my windshield and drawing circles in the air. Seeing the confusion on my face, the passenger got out of the car and came over, spat in a tissue and started wiping my insect-covered shield. 'How driving if cannot see?' he said with a grin. At last I saw an opportunity to escape the jam and mounted a narrow strip of pavement between the two opposing lanes of traffic: another chance to put my manoeuvring and balancing skills to the test.

Soon I was on the roads of Estonia. Passing through the Baltic countries in quick succession as I did, one might think about how intrinsically similar they seem to be. But the Lithuanians, Latvians and Estonians I met along the way made me realise that they inhabited three different worlds, the details of which I only began to comprehend.

A road trip is an adventure, more for the sake of the trip itself than the destination one hopes to reach. There is little time or energy to explore places, interact with locals or savour home delicacies: I made a few notes in my journal, planning to return to take a dip in Estonia's crystal-blue sea, stroll through the streets of Rīga, go mushroom picking in Lithuania or dance the night away at one of the local festivals.

I had a few more hours left, with the last ferry departing at 7pm and some 300 kilometres more to go. I saw the huge 'Tallinn' sign at that city's entrance and stopped for a photo of my two wheels posing in front of it. By now I had given up asking others to take a photo of me on the scooter because one of us always ended up outside the frame. With the crucial moment recorded, I hopped on my scooter again and followed the signs for the port. A ticket purchased, a bend negotiated and I became the last one to board the final ferry that day. I waved to the rooftops of the medieval town of Tallinn and promised to come back soon.

With the harbour soon out of sight, I received a message on my mobile phone. 'Are you still alive?' asked my future boss, adding 'Will you be able to report tomorrow at 7am?'

When I boarded the ferry, I had been the only bike, parked between rows of cars. When I got off in Helsinki a few hours later and the frosty wind hit my face, I no longer wondered why. The border guard suggested I should consider winter tyres. 'With the Finnish weather, you know, it's just going to go downhill from here', he said. I paid little heed. I grabbed my passport and drove out of the port into the streets of the frosty Nordic capital.

I had arrived.

A scooter is fine for driving in Helsinki and, with care, on the snow too. I soon learned how to avoid skidding and how to navigate around masses of ice. But even my trusty well-travelled Vespa, which had originally taken me from Italy and over the Alps to London, could not survive the vandals who trashed it just a month later. It's now at the mechanic's, with bruises and scratches covering it from head to tyres. The windshield is in pieces, along with the licence plate, mirrors and lights, but the motor is still intact and that is what I'm counting on for future trips.

Again I turn my plastic globe around and plan the next ride: wherever that 151cc heart will take me, so be it.

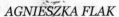

AGNIESZKA FLAK

Agnieszka Flak is a Reuters correspondent in Finland, where she arrived after previous stints for Reuters and other publications in Europe, Africa, Asia and the Americas. This was her second-longest trip aboard her scooter after driving across the Alps from Turin to London a year earlier. A mechanic's daughter, she could not imagine a better way to get into trouble and find a friend in no-man's-land. The original, shorter version of this story was published by Reuters in 2007.